THE AIR BATTLE OF THE RUHR

Dedication

This book is dedicated to the men who flew to the Ruhr and to the many who failed to return. Their efforts, courage and dedication must never be forgotten. The standards they set were of the highest order and worthy of all the acclaim we can bestow upon them.

THE AIR BATTLE OF THE RUHR

RAF Offensive March to July 1943

Alan W Cooper

WRENS PARK

First published in the UK in 1992
by Airlife Publishing Ltd

This edition published 2001
by Wrens Park Publishing, an imprint of W. J. Williams & Sons Ltd.

British Library Cataloguing-in-Publication Data
A catalogue record for this book
is available from the British Library

ISBN 0905 778 62 6

Printed in England by St Edmundsbury Press Ltd, Bury St Edmunds, Suffolk.

Contents

THE BOMBER AIRMAN'S LAMENT

Phantom bombers on the old airfields
where do you fly tonight?
Are you off to visit Berlin, Hamburg, Nuremberg or Mannheim
or somewhere in the Ruhr, east of the Rhine?

Phantom bombers on the old airfields
where do you fly tonight?
Through a moonless or full moonlight sky
giving battle as you fly.
Returning shrouded, but with your spirits aces high.

Ghostly engines, silenced by time
outlined at dispersal by rings of rime.
With ghostly guns of noiseless rattle
patiently waiting the phantom hours of battle.

Phantom bombers on the old airfields
Where do you fly tonight?
If you will only wait for me to join you
in the air battles of long ago
it will be in the company of my old aircrew.

Louis Patrick Wooldridge DFC
ex 51 and 578 Halifax Squadrons

Introduction

To all aircrew who flew in 1943 the one target then, and even still today, that made their stomach muscles tighten, was the Ruhr; 'happy valley' or the 'land of no return', as the aircrew knew it. To someone who did not fly in that period it's best described as the air battle of the Somme or Passchendaele, in which the bombers and their crews went out time and time again similar to the 'tommy' who, in World War I went over the top time after time.

There were targets within Bomber Command that on occasions were recorded as being quiet trips, but this was not so with the Ruhr. As soon as the coast was crossed, it was a case of running the gauntlet to the target and back, through enemy searchlights, heavy and light flak and fighter aircraft, all intent on one thing — to knock you out of the sky. The mental strain of continually having to key themselves up to face this, contrasting with rest days or aborted operations when they would unwind, relax and try and forget the war, was considerable. The effect was rather like a coiled spring continually being wound, run down and then wound up again. There were also times when, having actually got to the perimeter of the airfield and ready to take off, a signal to abort the operation would be received. This often induced a feeling of anticlimax among the aircrew. Until you had got those magic thirty operations or trips recorded in your flying log-book (that little official blue RAF book, which recorded operations in red ink, and non-operations such as training flights, air tests, etc. in blue ink) there would be no respite and no choice but to get on with it and get the trips under your belt. Many of these little blue books have very few pages used, and the last operation recorded in it would have been entered by someone else, probably the adjutant, on behalf of the missing airman. These entries and the ones in the operation record book showing the battle orders, are all that is recorded to say for many: 'I was there'. For those who survived it was a case of carrying on and entering operations in their log-book, including hours flown, the target — just the bare facts. Each month it would be inspected by the flight commander and then, suddenly, you would be told one day, the operation that night was your last or the last for your first tour of operations.

Perhaps the full extent of the contribution by Bomber Command in its offensive against the Ruhr and the German industries will never be evaluated, as much of its efforts were in the dead of night, unseen by most; not like an army which goes into battle viewed and recorded by many observers. But the efforts of the crews who went, whether successful or not, can never be doubted. They were young men with an average age of 21, undertaking tasks and facing dangers that in a peacetime Air Force would be faced by much older men. For an example, had Guy Gibson been in 617 Squadron today, he would be, at the age of 25 (which was his age when he led the famous 'Dambusters' Raid) one of the youngest members of the squadron. The commanding officers themselves, in many cases, were only in their twenties, and not only having to face the same amount of danger but also to lead from the front, and to do so without showing any fear.

For the men who completed their tour of operations, the look of ageing rapidly set in on their faces, changing from a boyish look at the beginning of their tour with, perhaps, a sense of adventure, to later, a look of dazed disbelief similar to shell-shock or being punch drunk. Commanders had to cope with the strain of sending men out time after time and hoping their judgement and planning were right. These commanding officers and flight commanders not only had the responsibility of leading and showing the way in the air but also had to face the same dangers as the rest of the aircrew. Many of these commanders were lost during the Battle of the Ruhr period; men whose experience would be missed. A number of them paid the price of flying far more than they were required to do, being always the first on the 'Battle Order' for difficult operations.

The casualty rate was high. In the period of the Ruhr Battle, over 1000 aircraft and 5000 aircrew went missing, many to become names on memorials or to be buried in far-off lands. Others would spend the rest of the war languishing in a prisoner of war (POW) camp, although some would evade capture or escape and live to fight again. For those who did not return, their last sight of the UK would have been the groundcrew waving them off with Godspeed and good luck. Was it worth it? All those men at the peak of their youth, many too young to vote but old enough to die for their country.

Nearly fifty years later, looking at it on a broad scale and with all the facts available, it's difficult to see how it could have been prevented. All the men who were killed, I am sure, would have said, 'yes, it had to be done', and would have done it again if called upon. All of these men at the time were volunteers. One could be conscripted to join the services or the RAF, but not compelled to fly on operations. The comradeship of these men, flying as crews, and with each depending on the other was memorable. Without doubt now, although costly, the 'Battle of the Ruhr' was a success and played a significant part in the ending of the war in Europe.

1 Bomber Command

It was during 1915, that one first saw the beginning of a tactical bombing programme. This was put into practise by the Royal Flying Corps (RFC) at the Western Front, in France. The plan was to do as much damage as possible to enemy reinforcements and communications. Its basic philosophy was to deprive the enemy of supplies and back-up, and it was as good as any frontal offensive, while minimising one's casualties. The first Victoria Cross awarded to the RFC, was in carrying out this type of attack. Second Lieutenant Rhodes Moorhouse had dropped a 100lb bomb west of Courtrai railway station. To do this, he had to fly alongside the belfry tower of Courtrai church, and it was from this position that the Germans fired upon him with rifles and machine guns, hitting him in the thigh and stomach. He managed to reach his base at Merville, but died the next day of his wounds.

In 1916, the standard bombs carried weighed 230lb, and so attacks became more ambitious and constant. Enemy airfields, billets, and ammunition dumps were attacked. In 1917, eighteen bridges became the main target when German troops were depending on supplies reaching them at the front via these bridges.

In October 1917 a special unit was formed, later known as the 8th Brigade. This unit contained squadrons of DH 4 day bombers, and FE2B's, and Handley Page night bombers. In June 1918, after carrying out 142 raids, the previous squadrons were joined by newly formed ones and this unit was then titled the Independent Force with Major-General Hugh Trenchard as its commander. Its role was to make a sustained offensive against the German industries. In the last months of the war this force dropped 550 tons of bombs, a large proportion at night, causing a noticeable reduction in German production and further strain upon German morale, already stretched to breaking point. In October 1918, Handley Page aircraft were armed with the heaviest bombs, 1650lb, to be used in World War I. The new Super Handley Page bombers were capable of carrying thirty 230lb bombs each. These aircraft were to be used to bomb Berlin, but the armistice in November 1918 stopped the attacks from being carried out.

In October 1917, the then Secretary of State for Air, Winston Churchill, was acutely aware of the need to get to a target, identify it and attack it. On this subject he wrote:

> The dominating and immediate interests of the Army and the Navy have overlaid air warfare and prevented many promising lines of investigation from being pursued with the necessary science and authority. As a result, it remained true even at the end of the war that aerial warfare had never been practised except in miniature; that bombing had never been studied as a science; that the hitting of targets from great heights, by day or night is worthy of as intense a volume of scientific study, as for instance, is brought to bear upon perfecting the gunnery of the fleet; that much of the unfavourable, accumulated data showing the comparative ineffectiveness of bombing, were the results of unscientific action. For instance, dropping bombs without proper sighting apparatus, trained 'Bomb' droppers (the equivalent of 'gun layers'), instead of dropping them in regulated salvos by specially trained men, so as to 'straddle' the targets properly. It is believed by the sanguine school that a very high degree of accuracy, similar to that which had been attained at sea under extraordinarily difficult circumstances, could be achieved if something like the same scientific knowledge and intense determination were brought to bear.

On the 11 November 1918, when World War I came to an end, the RAF had the largest Air Force in the world, with nearly 233,000 officers and men, 23,000 aircraft and 700 airfields. This was soon to change, the number of squadrons being reduced from 300 in 1918 to only 24 in 1921; and of those 24 only a few serving in the UK. The attitude of the two Senior Services, the Navy and the Army, was that the RAF had little or no offensive power. But they did agree that the RAF would be useful for reconnaissance and artillery spotting.

In 1925 a pledge was given that the RAF should be built up once again, the yardstick being that it must be equal to any foreign Air Force within striking distance. But as the nearest foreign Air Force was France which was not an enemy and so not likely to attack the UK, the policy remained only in principle and progressed very slowly. The Air Staff at the time, however, were thinking on the right lines for the future, deciding that an attack and defend situation would be the right policy for any future war. In conjunction with this it was decided that the new Air Force of the UK should have about one-third more bomber than fighter squadrons. However, in the 1930s the disarmament conference of Geneva was in full swing and some of the proposals at this conference included total abolition of all military aircraft, or an upper limit in the weight of bombs they carried. While this was going on and the proposals were being discussed, the Air Force was not allowed to order modern bombers, and all research work into the offensive use of air power almost ceased.

The financial crisis of 1931, and the unhelpful attitude of the Navy and Army meant all expansion and progress in the Air Force came to a halt, and ammunition and spare parts were allowed to be run down and not replaced. In 1933, when Hitler came to power as Chancellor of the Third

Reich, Group Captain AT Harris, later Commander-in-Chief of Bomber Command, was urging that all-night bombers should practise formation flying. In fact, he said as far back as 1926, when he was a squadron leader, that formation bombers would be better able to defend themselves when returning in daylight or twilight from long raids. To some degree he was successful, as on the 15 October 1926, an amendment was made in the Flying Training Manual to permit a limited amount of night training in formation flying but with not more than three aircraft at a time. But it was not until 1933 that a satisfactory formation-keeping flight of aircraft was achieved. On the 17 August 1933, Harris once again urged for formation flying. He went on to say that, 'formations may be necessary to penetrate well-lit defence areas wherein the need for heavy development of defensive fire-power may become as real as in daylight'. The net result was that in 1934, 58 Squadron flying Virginias, and in 1935, 99 Squadron flying Heyfords, were instructed to practise formation flying.

In 1935, Europe had a rude awakening when Hitler re-formed the German Air Force, in direct contravention of the Treaty of Versailles; with this came a strong feeling that Germany would go to war within the next few years. The United Kingdom, limited in resources of manpower, material, and money, was going to have to give priority to the Services in preparation for such a war. The eyes of the Government were opened after Sir John Simon, the Foreign Secretary, had visited Germany, and made a report on the progress of its military air power. He reported that Hitler had said to him that Germany's Air Force was now equal to the RAF, and also that conscription in the German Air Force had been instituted.

Although money was very tight at this time, the Air Staff took such steps as were open to them to prepare for a possible war in the future. The money that was available was spent in keeping the aircraft industry in existence. Design and drawing offices were also kept open. The country owes a lot to those men who struggled on in the belief that the safety of the country would depend on the existence of a substantial and well-equipped aircraft industry.

The Air Staff formed two very important committees under the chairmanship of Sir Henry Tizard, their role being to study offensive and defensive air warfare. The first priority was to keep the sea-lanes open. The RAF were told to assist the Navy in this work, and so Coastal Command was formed. The second priority was the air defence of the United Kingdom against Germany's large bomber force. These first two priorities were defensive, but the third priority took the form of offensive action, which involved Bomber Command forming plans for a suitable type of aircraft to carry out bombing missions against Germany. This would require a powerful four-engine bomber with a range of 1500 to 1800 miles, have a Service Ceiling of 20,000 feet and a speed of 250mph, and be able to carry a 12,000lb maximum bomb load. This was in fact, carrying on from the idea hatched at the end of World War I involving the development of the Super Handley Page bomber. The main objective of Bomber

Command would be to attack and destroy Germany's industrial and economic life, if war broke out.

On the 14 July 1936, Air Chief Marshal John Steel was appointed Air Officer Commanding-in-Chief of Bomber Command. With the re-organisation of the RAF came also the creation of Fighter and Coastal Commands. In 1936 the prototype Vickers Wellington bomber made its first flight. On the 12 November 1936, Mr Winston Churchill stated in the House of Commons that Germany had no less than 1500 first-line aeroplanes, or 130 to 140 squadrons. The Prime Minister, Mr Baldwin replied by saying that in his estimation the figure was too high, although he could not give the exact figure. In comparison, the RAF had 78 squadrons, all based in the UK. In May 1937, Mr Baldwin retired from office, and was replaced by Neville Chamberlain. Although plans were made to expand the RAF, very little developed, certainly nothing in the shape of a four-engine bomber.

In 1937, the defence costs were financed by a Defence Loan and not by the annual Budget, and as a result the progress of the RAF's expansion slowed until it was too late to complete the plans made in 1935. Air Marshal Sir Edgar Ludlow-Hewitt took over the reins of Bomber Command from John Steel, and soon realized that the training of bomber crews left a lot to be desired. It was discovered that only 84 pilots were trained in night flying, and only thirteen above the rank of flying officer. When in 1937, Harris took over No.4 Group, he told the Marshal of the Royal Air Force that he did not have one fully-trained crew, or one modern war aircraft. On the 7 October 1937, he wrote to Sir Edward Ellington, who was then the Inspector General of the RAF, stating:

> The heavy bomber's task, with all the modern implications of long range operations and bad visibility, is indeed in a class by itself, both for difficulty and complication. That the training for fighter pilots cannot be sufficient for war crews of modern heavy bombers goes almost without saying. The difference made by the all-weather flying requirement and the long ranges of the modern bomber must be admitted and legislated for. The analogy is in taking the skipper of a Margate summer pleasure steamer on short excursions in fine weather, and then putting him on the *Queen Mary* and saying, 'there you are, now keep her going for 365 days and nights of the year between here and America'.

On the 9 March 1938, Harris asked for all aircraft on bomber stations to be used for flying practice.

On the 22 March 1938, Bomber Command received a report from the Air Targets Intelligence Committee, which dealt with power, fuel, chemical, engineering, metallurgical, and transportation targets in Germany. It mentioned the possibilities of crippling German war industry by attacking coking plants and power stations in the Ruhr area. This became plan W.A.5 and was sent to the Air Ministry on the 28 July 1938. The plan emphasized the Ruhr's importance as the industrial nerve-centre of

Germany, with 75 per cent of its output of coal and iron coming from the area. The paralysis of the Ruhr region could, so the report maintained, prevent Germany waging war on a large scale in less than three months.

In September 1938, Prime Minister Chamberlain returned from Munich and spoke the now immortal words, 'I believe it is peace for our time'. All that it was in fact, was a breather, and as history now shows there was twelve months to prepare for the war that came. At this time Bomber Command had been given low priority and was not ready for the conflict that lay ahead. Most of its aircraft were the older type (Blenheims and Fairey Battles), which were not up to the task of bombing offensive such as the four-engine bomber would prove to be.

In 1938 an interim bombing programme had been decided upon for use in the event of the outbreak of war. This resulted in the policy of restricted bombing which governed the first phase of the war, up to the German offensive in the West. In the event of Germany refraining from air bombardment in the West, the onus of initiating air warfare would be left to the Allies. It was most important that no action be undertaken which could be interpreted as an attack on civilians or non-military objectives as such action might be used by the Germans as an excuse for indiscriminate bombing, and might also alienate neutral sympathies from the Allied cause. The policy agreed upon by the British and French Governments therefore, was to limit air attacks to objectives of an indisputably military nature.

They were Navy warships, at sea or in harbour, dockyards, barracks, storage units or dumps and other establishments used by naval personnel. Army Units, such as fortifications, and coastal defence works, barracks, billets, dumps and other establishments. Airforce Air Units, Military Aerodromes, depots, bomb stores, and anything to do with the German airforce. Lastly Transportation targets and factories and bulk stores of fuel.

At the end of August 1939, the strategic value of some targets were assessed by the Plans Section of the Air Ministry. It was considered that attacks on the Ruhr area, in the early stages of a war, would be effective. If these attacks could be mounted before the German defences were at full strength, then a crippling blow could be struck. The French however, held the view that targets in the Ruhr should not be attacked until later on. They feared retaliation against their factories, which at that time were defenceless. Other targets considered included attacks on the two Dortmund-Ems canals, and the Mittelland canal at Minden. Another option, which was to be used, was propaganda raids over all parts of Germany by means of leaflet dropping. These raids would familiarize the air crews with the conditions to be encountered in their future bombing missions.

The Air Ministry concluded that heavy bombers were best adapted for a strategical role, and for indirect support in attacks on communications and depots deep into Germany, east of the River Rhine. These attacks would be combined with one of the major plans, such as operations against the Ruhr. The medium bombers, such as the Fairey Battles and Blenheims, would be used for direct support of the land forces. The French, however, wanted the entire bomber force to support the land forces. They did not appreciate that heavy bombers were unsuited for this role. They were strongly opposed to attacking the Ruhr or other targets in Germany east of the River Rhine until the enemy had initiated similar attacks.

In August 1939, President Roosevelt appealed to European nations not to bomb civilian populations or unfortified towns. A reply to Roosevelt's appeal was published on the 1 September 1939, and confirmed that any bombardment would be confined to military objectives, provided this was also observed by Germany. About this time, Canada pledged its support to Britain in any conflict with Germany. At the Reichstag in Berlin on the 1 September 1939, Hitler stated: 'I will not wage war against women and children. I have ordered my Air Force to restrict itself to attacks on military targets.' On the same day his Air Force bombed over sixty towns and villages in Poland.

2 War is Declared

Some minutes before eleven o'clock on the morning of Sunday, 3 September 1939, a number of high officials and civil servants were gathered together in a room at Richmond Terrace, Whitehall. On a table was the government War Book. This book laid down the action to be taken by all three Services in the event of the outbreak of war. The men in the room did not need to look at its contents, as many of them had helped to draw it up. In England precautionary measures had already been taken, and unofficially the country was on a war footing. In the case of Bomber Command, the order to mobilize had come on the 1 September. When eleven o'clock came, the Secretary to the Cabinet entered the room and said: 'Gentlemen the British Empire is at war with Germany'. In the streets outside, men and women saw the barrage balloons rise to their operational heights, and at 11.15a.m. the Prime Minister Neville Chamberlain broadcast the now immortal words from Downing Street: 'This morning the British Ambassador in Berlin, handed the German Government a final note stating, unless we hear from them by eleven o'clock that they were prepared at once to withdraw their troops from Poland, a state of war would exist between us. I have to tell you now, that no such understanding has been received and that consequently this country is at war with Germany.'

The King also made a broadcast on the 3 September, in which he said: 'For the second time in the lives of some of us we are at war. We have been forced into a conflict and are called, without allies, to meet the challenge of a principle which, if it were to prevail, would be fatal to any civilized order in the world. There may be dark days ahead and war can no longer be confined to the battlefield, but we can only do the right as we see the right and reverently commit our cause to God. May he bless us and keep us all.'

Bomber Command began the war with only 33 squadrons and a front-line strength of only 638 aircraft, of which 398 had two engines. In the main, the available aircraft were Fairey Battles, Blenheims and a small number of Hampdens, Whitleys and Wellingtons, which could only be classed as medium, not heavy, bombers. In comparison, the Germans had 1600 long-range bombers, 335 dive bombers and 50,000 aircrew.

In Bomber Command, No.1 Group became the advanced Air Striking Force operating in France with Fairey Battles, their main role being photographic reconnaissance. Number 2 Group, based in East Anglia undertook the same role but operated with Blenheims. The only group allowed to develop the Bomber Offensive in the first year of the war was No.3 Group, operating with Wellingtons from Norfolk and Cambridge. Number 4 Group's role operating with Whitleys, was propaganda raids over Germany. The aircraft were loaded with leaflets and flew in all kinds of weather conditions dropping their leaflets, which were printed in German, over selected cities and towns in Germany. It's not known what effect the propaganda raids had on the war, but the experience the crews gained was invaluable for future bombing operations. Number 5 Group operated with Hampdens from bases in southern Lincolnshire.

At 7p.m. on the day war was declared, 51 and 58 Squadrons were alerted for an operation that night. This was to carry out a reconnaissance of the Ruhr, and to drop leaflets in the following priority areas: Bochum, Krefeld, Duisburg, Mülheim, Dortmund, Barmen, Elberfeld, Düsseldorf, Cologne, Gladbach and Frankfurt. These leaflets, which became known as and were code-named 'Nickels', carried a message from the British people to the German people. From their temporary base at Leconfield, three Whitley bombers of 51 Squadron led by Flying Officer Milne took off at 9.30p.m. and were followed twenty minutes later by seven Whitley bombers of 58 Squadron led by Squadron Leader Sutton. Between them they carried over five million leaflets or 'Nickels'. Each aircraft carried 1800lb of 'Nickels', held in bundles of 5000 by rubber bands. The bundles of leaflets were held together by string until discharged from the aircraft by a specially adapted flare. This had to be carefully timed or one would end up with an aircraft full of leaflets. The rubber bands held together each bundle long enough for it to get clear of the aircraft.

The crews of 51 and 58 Squadrons were told to look for dummy airfields, anti-aircraft guns, enemy airfields, and to note the effect of searchlights. They entered Germany from the north, and also returned the same way. No opposition was encountered from enemy fighters or guns but considerable searchlight activity was observed. At that time, the Germans had some 900,000 men involved in the defence of Germany. All three aircraft of 51 Squadron arrived back safely, Flying Officer Milne being the last to land at 6.15a.m. But for 58 Squadron things were not so smooth. Squadron Leader Sutton landed in France, being short of petrol. Flying officer O'Neill had engine trouble and also landed in France. For a while Flight Sergeant Ford was reported missing, but later at 6a.m. on the 4 September, he also landed in France.

In all, some 5,400,000, leaflets had been released. These leaflet dropping operations were undertaken for the next few weeks, including the first drop over Berlin on the 1-2 October. The leaflets dropped on Berlin contained a message informing the German people of the fortunes hidden abroad by the Nazi leaders. Any Germans on the ground who picked up the leaflets were ordered to hand them in and not to read them, otherwise they would be punished. The German High Command were not too disturbed by these raids, but were surprised the English bombers had been able to cross powerfully protected frontiers.

On the 4 September 1939, the King sent the following message to the RAF:

> The Royal Air Force has behind it a tradition no less inspiring than those of the older Services, and in the campaign which we have now been compelled to undertake, you will have to assume responsibilities far greater than those which your Service had to shoulder in the last war. One of the greatest of them will be safeguarding these islands from the menace of the air. I can assure all ranks of the Air Force of my supreme confidence in their skill and courage and in their ability to meet whatever calls may be made upon them.

On the 6 September, South Africa declared war on Germany, followed by a similar declaration by Canada on the 10 September. On the 27 September, the Air Ministry announced that some 18,000,000 leaflets had been dropped over Germany since the outbreak of war.

3 The Waiting Game

On the 10 May 1940, two very important things happened which would have a great bearing on the outcome of the war. Firstly, Winston Churchill became Prime Minister in place of Neville Chamberlain and secondly, the Ministry of Aircraft Production was formed.

On the previous day, 9 May, the Chief of the Air Staff had to recapitulate all the arguments in favour of an immediate attack into Germany at a meeting of the Chiefs of Staff, because the General Staff had suddenly gone over to the French view of an offensive on Germany. On the 22-23 April 1940, they had at last been persuaded at the Supreme War Council meeting to agree that a main force of heavy bombers should carry out an assault on marshalling yards and oil refineries in the Ruhr in the event of German aggression against Holland and Belguim. The importance of the Ruhr area had already been noted, including the fact that five out of ten lines of communications serving the German army in the West, ran through this area. The targets chosen varied from time to time in priority between blast furnaces, oil installations, factories, power stations, and marshalling yards. The targets chosen in April were oil plants and marshalling yards. The attack would take place if the Germans invaded the Low Countries. The bomber force would fly direct through Holland and Belgium to the Ruhr, as it was felt that this route would be shorter and less well-defended. This would be a day attack, although a night attack was also planned, and its aim was to dislocate German war industry by doing material damage to specific plants, and preventing people from working in the plants by the use of delay-action bombs. Some disruption would also be caused by people seeking cover in air raid shelters. It was also a way of conserving British bombing strength.

On 10 May 1940, the Germans invaded France and the Low Countries. Bomber Command gave all the support possible to the Allied armies, but within a few days Holland and Belgium had fallen, and within a month, France would be asking for an armistice.

On the night of 15-16 May 1940, some 83 aircraft, consisting of Wellingtons, Whitleys and Hampdens, took off for the first attack on the Ruhr of World War II. Fourteen targets in the Ruhr area were bombed. For Bomber Command the gloves were now truly off. On the night of 24-25 May 1940, came the first attack of many on the Krupps factory in Essen. This target was to become a familiar one to the crews, who were heard to say, as they made up their operational flying book or log, 'There's always an "R" in the month'. The war in the Ruhr had started with leaflet dropping, now it was the real thing — bombs. Despite these attacks on the Ruhr, the German defences continued to build up and the smoky haze of the Ruhr Valley also hampered the aircrew when trying to locate their targets. The Germans had surrounded the Ruhr with a number of guns of all types, and also searchlight batteries which the crews remember even today more than the guns and the flak. This was the most heavily defended area in Germany, and to the aircrew it was known as 'Happy Valley' or 'The Land of No Future'.

Between 27 May and 4 June 1940, and in support of the retreating armies Bomber Command put a curtain of bombs around the area of Dunkirk. Today, this period is known as the 'Battle of France', and No.2 Group with its six squadrons of Blenheim aircraft, flew some 1546 sorties, and lost for their efforts, 80 aircraft and 240 aircrew in 38 days. In total for this period, Bomber Command lost 145 aircraft. Most of the aircraft lost by No.2 Group were shot down by flak. All German defence formations were equipped with light flak batteries and their personnel trained to deal with air attacks. The Allied air forces had no intelligence system to collect and distribute local information as to the positions of these flak units. Pilots were ordered to attack targets whose defensive strength was unknown. In the absence of this information, planning the route to and from such targets was not efficient and this seriously reduced the success of operations, and added to the many casualties. An intelligence system was developed later in the war and was used in the 'Battle of Normandy'.

On the 30 May 1940, a new bombing directive was issued by the Air Ministry. Number 2 Group, because of the large number of operations it had performed and the casualties it had suffered, was to be used only on a reduced scale while they re-grouped with aircraft and crews. A heavy bomber force was to be used to attack Germany by night, the objective being to continue to dislocate the German industries, particularly aircraft factories in areas such as Hamburg, Bremen, Frankfurt, and the Ruhr. Oil installations were also a priority target.

On the 20 August 1940, Winston Churchill made a speech in the House of Commons:

> British airmen who, undaunted by odds, unwearied in their constant challenge and mortal danger, are turning the tide of world war by their prowess and by their devotion. Never in the field of human conflict was so much owed by so many to so few. All hearts go out to the fighter pilots, whose brilliant actions we see with our own eyes day after day, but we must never forget that all the time, night after night, month after month, our bomber squadrons travel far into Germany, find their targets in the darkness by the highest navigational skill, aim their attacks, often under the heaviest fire, often with serious loss, with deliberate, careful discrimination, and inflict shattering blows upon the whole of the technical and war-making structure of the Nazi power. On no part of the Royal Air Force does

> the weight of the war fall more heavily than on the daylight bombers who will play an invaluable part in the case of invasion and whose unflinching zeal it has been necessary in the meanwhile on numerous occasions to restrain.

On the 3 September 1940, he made another speech:

> The Navy can lose us the war, but only the Royal Air Force can win it. Therefore our supreme effort must be to gain overwhelming mastery in the air. The fighters are our salvation, but the bombers alone can provide the means of victory. We must therefore develop the power to carry an ever-increasing volume of explosives to Germany, so as to pulverise the entire industry, and scientific structure on which the war effort and economic life of the enemy depends, while holding him at arm's length in our island.

On the 5 October 1940, Air Chief Marshal Sir Richard Peirse, KCB, DSO, AFC, became the Commander-in-Chief (C-in-C) of Bomber Command, taking over from Sir Charles Portal who became the Chief of the Air Staff (CAS). The first operation in which 100 bomber aircraft took part, including 42 aircraft which flew to Berlin, occurred on the 7-8 October 1940. In the same month came a breakthrough, when a radar system known as *GEE* or, to give it its official title, TR (Technical Research) 1335, was offered to Bomber Command. This system was invented by R J Dippy of the Technical Research Establishment. Something was badly needed, as it had been found that only 51 per cent of bombs dropped were anywhere near the target, and on one raid, in 75 per cent of the aircraft flown, the aircrew were unable to decide whether or not they had even found the correct destination, let alone bombed it. One of the drawbacks of the *GEE* system was that it was limited to a range of 350 miles from the ground station. However, the ability to fix a position within 350 miles of the UK and to contact their base on return without difficulty was something beyond the wildest dreams of the air navigators of Bomber Command. In November 1940, Bomber Command recommended the provision of *GEE* as a matter of the greatest urgency in all its aircraft. As a result, *GEE* stations were built at Daventry near Northampton, Stenigot, and Ventnor on the Isle of Wight, to provide a chain directed at the Ruhr.

The *GEE* system involved the reception in an aircraft of pulse transmissions from three transmitters, placed over a base-line of approximately 200 miles, the time difference in the reception of the pulses by the aircraft being indicated on a scale on a cathode-ray tube in the aircraft. One transmission was the 'Master' and the other two transmissions were the 'Slaves'. The *GEE* system enabled the aircraft to fly to any desired point by following a series of accurate 'fixes', or by chosing and flying along the hyperbola or curve which passes through that point. An accurate 'fix' can be made in 90 seconds or less at any desired time without the necessity of transmissions from the aircraft. The ability to fix the position of the aircraft instantaneously, enabled the navigator to find wind speed and direction with considerable accuracy. With *GEE* it was, therefore, possible to find targets within the limit of the range of the system under any conditions of visibility, and to 'home' back again to any airfield within the scope of the pulse transmission.

Aircraft of 115 Squadron were used for the training of this new system, and in June 1941, three navigators from 115 Squadron were sent to the Telecommunications Research Establishment on a special course. This training was completed in August 1941. On the 18 August, the CAS decided that enough tests had been carried out, and 1418 Flight — later the Bomber Development Unit — began to try out the best operational technique for *GEE*. They began to train the navigators of the ten selected squadrons chosen for operations scheduled to occur by the end of Feburary 1942.

The introduction of two call sign publications — CD.014 and CD.0212 in October 1940, was a big step forward in the endeavour to conceal the Order of Battle. They provided separate and variable callsigns for operational and non-operational flights and thereby caused the old system of using one callsign for all flying to be discarded. The intelligent use of these different callsigns did much to increase the difficulties of an intercepter trying to relate to callsigns to particular squadrons and to a large extent covered up the build-up of Bomber Command during the initial stages of its expansion.

On the 22 June 1941, Germany invaded Russia, and that evening Churchill made a speech in which he said: 'Any man or state who fights against Naziism will have our aid. Any man or state who marches with Hitler is our enemy.' He went on to say: 'We shall bomb Germany by day and night in ever-increasing measures, casting on them month by month, a heavier discharge of bombs and making the German people taste and gulp each month a sharper dose of the misery that they have showered upon mankind.' On the 14 July, he declared: 'We have now intensified for a month past our systematic, scientific, methodical bombing on a large scale over the cities, seaports, industries and other military objectives in Germany. But it is only a beginning.'

In February 1942, Air Chief Marshal Arthur Harris was appointed Commander of Bomber Command. He was a man steeped in the knowledge of bombing and how a bomber force should operate. The force he had was not a lot better than it was in 1939, comprising 378 bomber aircraft of which, only 69 were heavy four-engine bombers.

By the 21 February 1942, a new method of bombing was created called the 'Shaker' technique. It could be used in cloudy or foggy weather conditions. To put this technique into operation, the bomber force was split into three sections:

Section 1. Composed mainly of Wellington aircraft fitted with *GEE*. Their role was to drop the flares to illuminate the targets.

Section 2. Fire Raisers consisting mainly of medium or heavy bombers fitted with *GEE* and carrying their maximum load of incendiary bombs.

Section 3. The followers, all non-*GEE* aircraft in the bomber force, and any *GEE* aircraft not included in sections 1 and 2.

It was the basic idea of the later Path Finder Force, with its purpose of locating and marking a target accurately, before the main bombers arrived. However, a lot of research and experimental practice would have to be done before this technique could be perfected. The 'Shaker' idea was tried out in a simulated exercise on the 13 February 1942, the target area being the Isle of Man. This was thought to be ideal because the accuracy of the *GEE* 'chain' in the area was approximately the same as its accuracy would be over the Ruhr. The code-name for this exercise was 'Crackers'. A similar exercise was mounted on the 19-20 February, and this time the target was the railway station at Bryncir, north-east of Pwllheli in North Wales. The exercise was conducted under clear but hazy conditions.

The first operation that the *GEE* system was used was on the 8-9 March 1942, Essen being the main target. The operation was carried out by 211 bombers, of which 74 were fitted with *GEE*. The raid lasted two hours and ten minutes but the results were disappointing when after-raid reconnaissance revealed no damage to the main target area. The main problem was that when the aircraft with the incendiary bombs arrived, the flares had burnt out. As a result, the bombs were spread over a wide area, mostly short of the target, and consequently the following non-*GEE* aircraft's bombs were also dispersed. As a target, Essen was especially difficult to find because of prevalence of thick industrial haze, and also to the way it was situated in the Ruhr Valley. The 'Shaker' idea depended on visual identification, but Essen did not have clear, recognizable land marks and was near other towns of a similar size.

The situation came to a head in August 1942, when the Germans started to jam the *GEE* system, which reduced its range to 250 miles. It was not considered to be of use any more as an aid to target identification, and so the Path Finder Force (PFF) was formed. The first operation undertaken by this new force was on the 18-19 August 1942, against the town of Flensburg. It was not a success, Flensburg not being hit at all in the attack. But on the 28-29 August, in an attack on Nuremberg, the 'marking' by the PFF was successful. Between August and November some 31 operations were undertaken by the PFF of which thirteen were successful and seven partially successful, on targets in Germany and Italy. The method used was similar to the 'Shaker' one, the crews in the PFF were to be the best in Bomber Command, the basic idea was the German system of 'Illuminators' and 'Fire Raisers', their role to bring all the following aircraft of the main force in which would have inexperienced crews, and allow them to drop their bombs with the minimum loss of time.

Up to the end of 1942, the PFF had no radar aids to assist them in locating their targets, and no spare marker-bombs to enable them to mark these targets satisfactorily. But the introduction of a new aid called *OBOE*, enabled a pilot to fly his aircraft along a directional radio beam emitted from a ground station monitoring the aircraft's progress and keeping it on the correct track. This had been reached along the beam where the bombs were to be released, the second ground station gave the signal to do so. Illuminators would mark the target with flares having made a positive identification that it was the correct target and the Main Force Fire Raisers, with the inexperienced crews would be able to drop their bombs with a minimum loss of time. A very simple system to light up the area for the people behind to see it. However, as with *GEE*, the *OBOE* system's range was limited to about 250 miles or 402 kilometers. *OBOE* was used for the first time on the 20-21 December 1942, in an attack on the Lutterade power station near Sittard, Holland near the German border north-west of Aachen. The force of six Mosquitos was led by Squadron Leader Harry Bufton, AFC, Commanding Officer of 109 Squadron. The raid was only a partial success, but it was a start and some teething problems would be ironed out. On the 31 December, a raid by the PFF consisting of six Lancasters and two Mosquitos, was made against Düsseldorf. Some damage was done to the town but only one of the two Mosquitos' *OBOE* systems functioned on this occasion.

The year of 1943 would see the real beginning of a major bomber offensive against Germany take place. Despite the gallant and devoted efforts of many crews since the war started, little effect had been achieved so far, but from small beginnings, much was learnt and put into practice in the coming year.

At one minute passed midnight on the 1 January 1943, No.6 Canadian Group finally became operational after being formed back in October 1942. They had been formed under the British Commonwealth Air Training Plan agreement of 1942. The delay had been due to the need to form enough RCAF squadrons that would make an all-Canadian Group an economic formation.

The Allies' Casablanca Conference, between the 12 and 24 January 1943, resulted in a policy of a heavy air offensive against the German war effort and the morale of its people. A directive was sent to Air Chief Marshal Harris on the 4 February 1943, that detailed a bombing policy which in principle, was to last to the end of the war. The Chief of the Air Staff, Charles Portal told Harris that what this policy was basically saying was to obliterate Hamburg, Bremen, and Kiel, and when the weather did not permit attacks on these targets, then raids should also be mounted on the most potent German industries, and that Berlin and the Biscay Bases were to be regarded as subsidiary targets.

On the 8 January, the PFF became No.8 Group of Bomber Command. Its Air Officer Commanding Don Bennett, was promoted to Air Commodore and shortly after that was promoted further to Air Vice-Marshal, so bringing him in line with the other Group Commanders. This came about after Harris had written to Portal requesting that Bennett be given the proper rank for the job he was doing. So in a matter of twelve months

Bennett had risen from Wing Commander to Air Vice-Marshal. Never more so, has such a rapid promotion been deserved.

On the 16-17 January 1943, target indicators were first used by a force of four-engine Lancasters on a raid to Berlin. On the 30-31 January, H2S was first used on a raid to Hamburg. Both of these operations were only partially successful, but as with the *OBOE* raids, it was a start and a taste of things to come.

Just four of the 1,000 German flak guns that were protecting the cities, and towns in Germany from air attacks by the Royal Air Force. (Imperial War Museum)

Sir Arthur Harris, Lady Harris and daughter Jackie walking in the ground of Springfield, Great Kings Hill, High Wycombe the residence of the AOC Bomber Command and still the residence of the AOC of RAF Strike Command. (Author's collection)

A dangerous place on any bomber airfield, the bomb dump which in this case is RAF Binbrook. These were always sited well away from the rest of the station. (Ted Loveridge)

Wg Cdr Clive Sinton shows that a Commanding Officer's day is never over: when not flying there is always the endless paperwork to catch up on. (Clive Sinton)

4 The Ruhr and Rhineland

The area known as the Ruhr or, as the Air Ministry called it, 'Weapon-smithy of the Reich', consisted of the Ruhr and Wupper Valleys. The region covered some 40 miles from east to west and 25 miles from north to south, a total area of 1000 squares miles. The two valleys, separated by a belt of open country, were almost entirely built-up and contained fourteen prinicpal towns. Of these towns, Essen could be compared in size and population with Manchester; Duisburg with Leeds; Dortmund with Edinburgh; and Düsseldorf with Sheffield. The built-up area of the fourteen towns covered about 26 square miles, and had a pre-war population of approximately 4,115,000. The Ruhr was by far the most industrialized area of Germany, producing 71 per cent of Germany's coking coal and, at the peak of its war-time effort, 61.5 per cent of Germany's pig-iron and steel production. The Ruhr's production of the special steels most urgently needed in the war, accounted for two-thirds of Germany's total supplies.

The Ruhr has been mined since the thirteenth century, and when Prussia annexed Essen in 1802, there were no fewer then 127 coal mines, most of them in the Ruhr Valley and within a few miles of Essen. It was the discovery in the UK of steam power and puddling (the method of converting cast iron into wrought iron by smelting with coal) that enabled the iron industry to be developed, away from the hills and forests, to the valleys and plains in the north, where the coal mines lay. Essen was fortunate in having an abundance of coal and iron ore close by.

It was in August 1819, that the Krupps family began what was to be a long history of involvement in armaments, but it was not until World War I that this family became world famous for the manufacture of armaments and barbed wire. Barbed wire had its biggest boom in World War I, being an important factor in the defences of both armies and was also used extensively in World War II. The Krupps factories were the largest manufacturers of weapons of war that the world had ever known. When World War I started in 1914 it had a work-force of 83,000 people which, by 1918, had increased to 165,000, and at the height of the war were producing nine million shells and 3000 field-guns a month. One of its most famous guns was 'Big Bertha', which could fire a projectile weighing almost a ton, a distance of nine miles. Another famous gun was 'Long Max' which was used to shell Paris, in the Spring and Summer of 1918, from a distance of 75 miles away; its barrel was 112 feet long and the gun was enclosed in a concrete bunker in the middle of a dense wood.

As soon as possible after 1918, Gustav Krupps bought his way into the Swedish armaments firm, Bofors and sold them many of his blueprints, patents, and secret manufacturing processes. A major loophole in the treaty of Versailles, was that although the making of weapons inside Germany was forbidden, it did not say anything about German firms producing weapons outside the country. Another point was that although all machinery in Germany that was capable of making weapons of war, were destroyed, the blueprints Bofors received from Krupps, were not. Bofors also got help from Krupps' technicians to develop and build Krupps weapons of the future. As early as 1926 they began producing tanks but because of the restrictions, were referred to as 'agricultural tractors'. Much of this work seemed to be going on at the time, even in Essen, right under the noses of the Allied inspectors. In fact, in 1942 Krupps once boasted that all the guns used in the war up to that date, had been fully developed by 1933, the year Hitler came to power. The only problem lay in how to mass produce them. The 1918 gun 'Long Max' was hidden away by standing the barrel upright and building bricks around it, so it looked like another factory chimmney.

In 1934, Hitler paid his first official visit to Krupps in Essen. Some six years before, he had tried to pay a visit as a normal sightseer, but was turned away. He soon became a regular visitor, as did other Nazi leaders.

As well as gun barrels being made in Essen, Krupps was in the Kiel shipyards, behind screens, building U-boats, minesweepers, and destroyers en masse.

From the Nazis Gustav Krupps was decorated with both the low and high classes of the War Cross of Merit, and later the highest civilian honour the Nazi Party badge in gold by Hitler on his seventieth birthday.

As the war was about to begin in 1939, the Krupps shipyards at Kiel began launching U-boats at the rate of one a month. In and around Essen, factories were producing field howitzers and heavy mortars by the score. The mass production of the multi-purpose 88mm anti-aircraft tank gun, which had been tested in the Spanish Civil War, was also just beginning.

On the 8 August 1939, Reich Marshal Goering stated: 'We will not allow a single bomb from hostile aircraft to hit the Reich.' From this statement the defences of the Ruhr were considered virtually impregnable against air attack since it was obviously the most vital target in Europe.

The main industrial area of the Ruhr between Duisburg and Dortmund covered 250 square miles and had a population of about 3,000,000 people. Between December 1940, and February 1945, vast numbers of prisoners of war and foreign workers were employed in the workshops of the Krupps Casteel works at Essen. Slave labourers from countries occupied by Germany were used in the production of weapons and munitions. Turrets for tanks, carriages for heavy Army and Navy guns, and crank shafts for U-boats and aircraft, were also produced. In the middle of 1941, workers from Poland, Galicia and the Polish Ukraine arrived in Essen, having been transported by goods trains in cramped and filthy conditions. They were beaten and kicked by the Krupps overseers who were amazed at the speed in which people got in and out of the trains. Some of these people were sick and could scarcely walk, but were still taken to work. A Krupps memo dated 25 March 1941: 'By using all the forces at his disposal Krupps, and regardless of effort, costs and risk, considerable export contracts were secured when served to obtain foreign currency or raw materials and were at the same time politically desirable'.

In a speech dated 6 May 1941, Krupps declared: 'For one who, like myself, during the last few weeks, had the chance to visit and thoroughly inspect the fields where our superb troops made the breakthrough in the west, who could hear on that occasion the roar of your Air Force against England, who witnessed how our U-boats and speedboats distinguished themselves against the remains of England's sea might; such a person is bound to be thankfully proud to be able to contribute through his labours to ensure that our fighters have the weapons they need for their battles.' In an article dated the 1 March 1942, Krupps wrote: 'If Germany should ever be re-born and shake off the chains of Versailles one day, the Krupps concern had to be prepared again. I wanted and had to maintain Krupps in spite of all opposition, as an armament plan for the future. After the rise to power of Adolf Hitler, I had the satisfaction of being able to report to the Führer that Krupps stood ready. We are all proud of having thus contributed to the magnificent successes of our army.' On the 24 July 1942, he wrote to Hitler: 'My Führer! The big weapon, whose manufacturing is to be thanked to your command, has now proved its effectiveness.'

The Krupps armaments works at Essen covered about two square miles in the middle of the town. A subsidiary plant on its outskirts, covered another one-third of a square mile. These plants were to become one of the most important targets in the Allied bombing campaign against German industry. The plants included blast-furnaces, steelworks, press shops, forges, rolling mills, and machine shops for the manufacturing of guns of every size, tanks, locomotives, aircraft parts, and naval vessels, including submarines. Essen was the largest town in the Ruhr, with a population of 670,000 people, of which a large number were empolyed by Krupps. In addition, the mining industries employed about 16 per cent of the working population. After Essen and Cologne, the most important town was Duisburg, Sited on the mouth of the River Ruhr, it had the largest inland waterway harbour in Europe, and contained important heavy industries. The leading commercial city in western Germany and also its third largest inland port, was Düsseldorf. It was as equally important as Essen or Duisburg in the production of armaments, and also the administration HQ of nearly all the heavy industries of the Ruhr was located there.

From the beginning of the war Krupps had its own independent early-warning system, and an operations room which was in direct contact with the Air Force by telephone. This room was connected to every workshop and office by a duplicate telephone system, so that alarm orders and any other instructions could be given without delay. At the first sign of enemy air activity a black-out system was extended to all workshops, railway lights, street lights, and yard lights; any defects in the black-out were pointed out by roof spotters. If danger was imminent, a warning was given and all personnel, except a few key men, were ordered to the shelters below various workshops. The key men only went to the shelters when the final warning was given and bombing was certain to begin. The Krupps factory had its own fire brigade consisting of 21 engines, and several ambulances. All the staff workers were trained in fire-fighting.

In 1941 a decoy factory was built three kilometres south of the Baldney See in the open country. It consisted of a system of lights intending to simulate the effect produced by a Krupps plant if it was badly blacked out. The site also included stationary lights which imitated goods stations that were badly blacked out. This was taken over from the Air Force and controlled by a pill box in the middle. It was a success until radio aids were used, and in 1943 the German Air Force tried, without success, to supplement the decoy site by using decoy markers, but this was abandoned at the end of 1943, mainly because they could not get the right colours that would simulate the markers used by the Pathfinders of No.8 Group.

In addition to the Krupps factory on the fringe of Essen there were also hydrogenation plants, one near the Gelsenkirchen-Benzin works at Nordstern, and another near the Hydrierwerke-Scholven works at Buer. These two plants together produced some 575,000 tonnes of aviation fuel per annum.

Up to January 1943, 48 bombs were dropped on the Krupps plants and 70 bombs were dropped on the decoy site. The number of incendiary bombs dropped on the Krupps plants was 1515 and on the decoy site 5665. It can be appreciated that the industries of the Ruhr area would be a vital target to attack. If the Allies could stop the enemy moving or deprive them of weapons and ammunition, this would be even more effective than beating them on the field of battle.

5 The Bomber Offensive

On the 10 January 1943, a memorandum was drafted by the Air Staff. In this, a directive was given that all available heavy and medium bombers should be used for the forthcoming air offensive against Germany.

This was felt the only way to exert direct pressure on Germany in 1943, it would take away flak, guns and fighters from the Russian front making a third front for the Germans and also, keep the short range fighters away from the Mediterranean, at a time, when our superiority in the air had been vital to the success of our amphibious operations against Sardinia, and Sicily. If the US daylight attacks and RAF night attacks together, could keep up the conflict over twenty-four hours, three vital things could be achieved; 1: Accelerate the rate at which German military potential is being destroyed. 2: Draw the German Air Force away from Russia. 3: Advance the date of the invasion.

Until 1943, Bomber Command had not been in a position to carry out its long-planned policy of true strategic bombing, that is to say the bombing of selective targets on a scale sufficient to weaken the industrial capacity and undermine the morale of the enemy, rather than to perform an ancillary role in support of land and sea operations. The three main problems which had to be solved before such an offensive could be mounted were:

1. Finding enough suitable aircraft, aircrew and airfields.
2. Coping with the difficulty of hitting the target in the weather conditions which were having to be faced.
3. Counteracting the growing strength and effectiveness of the enemy's defences.

One factor which would contribute greatly to the Allied offensive would be the bombing raids by day of the United States Air Force. But it was not until the 27 January 1943, that the first American day attack on German territory took place. This was carried out by 64 'Flying Fortresses' against the North Sea coastal town of Wilhelmshaven.

Although 30 per cent short of the 4000 bombers which had been proposed in 1941, Bomber Command were now, in 1943, preparing to mount regular raids into Germany using between 500 and 800 aircraft for each operation.

The PFF now had the new standard target marker indicators replacing the old 'skymarkers'. On one occasion a representative of the firework industry, which were making all the pyrotechnics for the PFF, said to Don Bennett, the Air Officer Commanding (A.O.C.) of the PFF: 'You are using an awful lot of pyrotechnics.' Bennett replied as one would expect: 'Yes, I am proud to say we are.' The representative then asked: 'Do you known how many workers are employed in making them?' 'No', came the reply. 'Well its 42,000.' At that time the aircrew in the PFF numbered 21,000, so for every crew member there were two workers.

During the period January to February 1943, there were a number of raids which have become known as 'nuisance' raids, although to the commanders who were responsible for these operations, they were far more than this. Also *OBOE* operations were mounted against the Ruhr area, which included a raid on Düsseldorf on the night of 27-28 January 1943. This operation would have been yet another failure because of cloud in the target area, if it had not been for the use of *OBOE* and the new target indicators which were being used for the first time. During this period, there were no less than four attacks on Essen, making twenty in all since the outbreak of war.

There were 31 key cities and suburbs which contributed to the building of the German war machine. They fell into three main groups:

Western; which included Essen, Cologne and Düsseldorf.
Central; which included Bremen, Hamburg and Kassel.
Eastern; which included Kiel, Rostock, Stettin and Berlin.

The western areas were within 300 to 400 miles of London, central areas within 600 miles and eastern areas within 900 miles. To attack these areas required bomber aircraft with sufficient range to reach all targets and the bomb-load capacity to complete each operation successfully. On one occasion Harris said: 'If I could send 20,000 bombers over Germany tonight, Germany would not be in the war tomorrow; if I could send 1000 bombers over Germany every night, it would end the war by Autumn'.

While the Allies were preparing for an all-out bombing offensive, the Germans were setting up their defences to meet the coming onslaught. On the Western Front, Germany had 930 heavy guns, 3072 light and medium guns, 396 searchlights and 96 barrage balloons. Throughout the rest of Germany, there were 4491 heavy guns, 6456 light and medium guns, 3330 searchlights and 1680 barrage balloons.

In 1935, Germany had set up a section known as 'Air Protected Objective Charting Section' (*Luftschutzobjektkartei*). The responsibility of its operations and tactical deployment for air defence, was given to the German Air Force (GAF). The German anti-aircraft authority was called *Flakarilueri*, or Flak as it became known; its translated meaning was 'Defence Against Aviation'. The troops in Flak wore the grey uniform of the *Luftwaffe*, edged with red piping.

In 1943, 70 per cent of the total Flak personnel or 900,000 men and 75 per cent of the heavy guns available, mainly the 88mm flak gun, were located on the Western Front. The basis of the flak defences was to detect and locate enemy reconnaissance bombers or fighter aircraft and destroy them by ground-fire or aerial combat. It was not always possible to defend all vulnerable areas, as the force needed to do this was not available. On one occasion Goering said: 'Germany has the largest Flak force in the world but not enough guns to protect everywhere.'

All Germans between the ages of 18 and 60 were liable for service in the Home Guard Flak, the only exception were doctors. Civilians doing duty in the Home Guard Flak were known as *Flakwehrmanner*, and could include schoolboys, who were known as *Luftwaffenhelfer*. Women were only used on the staff side and not on the operational side.

The local Flak commander was responsible for the defence of the immediate target area. In areas where German night-fighter aircraft operated, flak could still be fired up to any height and the pilots had to accept the risk of some rounds bursting higher than 3200 feet, which was the minimum height the fighters operated at in the 'flak' areas.

In each Allied bomber group there was a 'Flak' Officer from the Royal Artillery, whose job it was to lecture crews on what to expect in the way of flak and how to try and cope with it. He, as did, for example, Major J B Mullock, who was No.5 Group Flak Officer, often went on operations to view the extent of the enemy flak and to constantly keep up-dating methods on how to cope with it.

At the beginning of 1943, the flak defences in Germany were in need of strengthening and reorganization; even more so when Bomber Command began saturation bombing tactics. The flak defences, which were employed in single batteries, could not cope with the concentrated attacks by the Allied bombers. Up to this time the defence system had been based upon a division of Germany's industrial towns into sectors, each containing up to 30 searchlights and about 60 heavy and light guns. Each sector had been responsible for its own area. The method of defence was to concentrate all searchlights in each sector on to a single hostile aircraft and to direct gunfire into the apex of the cone formed by the searchlights. During 1943, a thorough reorganization of flak defence methods resulted in the old scheme of 'sector' defence being discarded. Instead, flak was concentrated into *Grossbatterien* (large batteries) comprising two to three single batteries of the earlier pattern. At all large and important targets such as the Ruhr all reserve mobile including railway flak was brought in and the number of guns in single batteries was increased to six then eventually to eight guns. Increasing numbers of 105mm guns and the first 12.8mm guns also came into operation in 1943. The guns were adaptable and formidable. The 88mm gun with a 35mm calibre shell, had a maximum horizontal range of 16,600 feet, and an effective ceiling range of 34,770 feet. It could fire 15 rounds per minute and each shell weighed 20lb. The gun barrel's length was 16 feet 2 inches. The 105mm gun with a 41mm calibre shell, had a maximum horizontal range of 19,100 feet, and an effective ceiling range of 37,000 feet. It could fire 15 rounds per minute and each shell weighed 32lb. Its length was 20 feet 8 inches.

For the aircrews of Bomber Command who had to fly against the German defences, enemy searchlights were often feared more than the flak. The searchlights could be dipped to show German fighter aircraft the direction the bombers were heading, and used in such a way, so as to dazzle and confuse the pilots, bomb aimers and gunners. The bomber would be flying through the dark night when, suddenly, a large blue searchlight would shine on it. This 'master' searchlight would then attract maybe another twenty searchlights on to the unsuspecting aircraft. Then came the flak. On one raid, an Australian pilot was heard to say: 'Hell's Bells! How do we get through that?' While the rear gunner called out: 'Surely we are not going through that, are we? Think of my wife.' In a Canadian squadron, Squadron Leader Clive Sinton, remembers it as being similar to a fly buzzing around a dark room, trying to avoid the light-beams of a torch being shone. Sinton recalls: 'One was often blinded in the aircraft by the searchlights. Sometimes they were so bright, you could see to read the time on your watch. Then up came the flak like a fireworks display, but when you could smell the cordite, you knew it was getting too near for comfort.'

On cloudy nights the effectiveness of searchlights was reduced. In such conditions the searchlights were aimed so as to follow the bomber along the base of the cloud in order to indicate its course to the German fighters. On clear nights the searchlights were sometimes operated so as to produce a 'cone' of light in the sky, often directed ahead of the bomber which may then be visible to fighters attacking from the rear, so compelling the hostile bomber to run the gauntlet of light and to fly so close to one of the beams or group of beams that it may become visible from the ground, thus allowing other searchlights to focus on the bomber.

The standard size of searchlight used was 1500mm, which had a powerful narrow beam and was used for locating high-flying aircraft. The smaller 500mm searchlight had a broad beam and was used in conjunction with light flak guns to locate and attack low-flying aircraft. There were also a number of French manufactured 2000mm searchlights being used. These were possibly the 'Master' searchlights. The blue appearance of some searchlights when shone close to an aircraft was caused by the high density of current being passed through the arc of the searchlight which could be compared to the bluish flash of an electric train.

Up to thirty searchlights were used in 'belts' 1000 to 2000 yards apart, or in triangular groups 2000 to 3000 yards apart. In gun-defended areas, they were spread at a distance of 3000 to 4000 yards apart.

Some 68 per cent of the German fighter aircraft force was engaged in defending Germany and the Western Front, which left only 425 fighters to defend and patrol the Eastern Front, an area of 1650 square miles. In March 1943, Germany was producing 700 fighter aircraft a month, and re-equipping practically the whole of their single-engine fighter force with the latest Messerschmitt 109G and Focke-Wulf 190 fighters.

One problem for Bomber Command was to keep its intended missions a secret from the enemy right up to the last moment. The German Signals Intelligence Service monitored all RAF bomber airfields day and night. They observed, for example, that 'tuning traffic' or radio silence were indications of impending operations from certain airfields. The covering of radio-telegraphy (RT) traffic on airfield frequencies disclosed such things as the postponement of operations or very active take-off traffic. Weather messages could be picked up indicating which airfields were able to operate. The 'direction finder' tuning at airfields could also be picked up and indicated if an operation was on that night. The interception of signals from H2S was another.

An aircraft reporting centre in the vicinity of London with the call sign Q58 (known to the Germans as *Freischetz-Meldungen*) would warn anti-aircraft batteries and fighter aircraft units in the UK of impending operations by Allied aircraft, so that they would not attack them. The messages were passed in three–letter code. This code was never broken by the Germans but they worked out that the longer the message, the larger the bomber force and the longer the route. In the Paris area there was a similar radio station which repeated messages when the route passed over French territory. The Germans discovered that whenever Q58 passed a message in the late afternoon which was transmitted by the Paris repeater, there would be a major RAF attack that night, and that the bomber force would pass over France. The Germans set up the Bomber-Meldkopf reporting centre at Zeist in Holland. If Allied operations were indicated the control officer would release the cover word *Adler*, if no operation was indicated, the cover word would be *Taube*.

A WAAF checks a belt of cartridges to be used on a Halifax bomber. The WAAFs could load 50 belts of ammunition with 250 rounds in each per day. (Keystone)

An important lady in the WAAF, particularly to the navigators. Known as the Map Queen she looked after and kept stored all the available maps of Europe. Whenever an operation was on she would produce the correct maps for the area of the operation. (Imperial War Museum)

Another important group of WAAFs were the parachute packers. Each man who flew relied entirely on having a properly packed parachute. In Bomber Command there were over 9,000 prisoners of war who would vouch for their parachute having worked when required.
(Imperial War Museum)

On the Lancaster bomber there were over 96 spark plugs, 24 to each engine. Each had to be cleaned and tested before every flight.
(Imperial War Museum)

6 Twenty-Four Hours on a Bomber Station

To mount a bomber offensive such as Bomber Command began in 1943, relied heavily on many backroom staff. The task involved for each of the bomber stations in East Anglia, Cambridgeshire, Lincolnshire and Yorkshire, was to prepare for action some twenty aircraft and their crews of 140 men, for up to five days in each working week over a period of months. Doing this over a period of five months would amount to about 100 days of continuous operations and some 2000 sorties. It was rather like putting on a play or show in the theatre and on the opening night seeing the finished article, which to the layman looks so simple and easy to stage, but in fact requires months of planning with lighting, scenery, and rehearsals, to make it all come together. Preparing a bomber offensive was very much the same, with the aircrew as the actors, and the groundcrew as the stage-hands. A lot of thought and hard work went into planning the route, drafting the intelligence reports, and carrying out the maintenance, fueling, arming, and loading the bombs of each aircraft. All these supplies, of course had to be got to the airfields. Provision would have to be made for feeding and then transporting about 140 men to the bombers. Then there was the final briefing and weather reports to digest. All these activities had to be done before one aircraft could roll off the perimeter, on to the runway, and then take off when the green-light signal came. As soon as all the bombers had taken off, preparations would begin all over again for the next night.

The aircrew were like guests at a hotel, and a bomber station like a small self-contained town. On a bomber station there were a number of buildings over a wide area with considerable space between them, all connected by a network of roads. These buildings included the station headquarters, where the operations room was situated; the officers' mess, the sergeants' mess, and the airmen's and WAAF quarters; the sick bay; hangars for the maintenance and overhaul of the aircraft. The bomb dump was always set well away from the other buildings on the station. The airfield itself was surrounded by the perimeter track. All the buildings were camouflaged so as to blend in with the surrounding countryside. Aircrews were posted into a squadron on a bomber station, whereas many of the groundcrew were posted to a bomber station and became part of the permanent staff.

One night the aircrews might be in the local pub, and the next night over the heart of Germany fighting a battle for their lives. They were the infantry of the air. It placed great demands on the minds and bodies of men who had to prepare themselves to face the impending operation, and then try and unwind when they returned, mixing with people who could not possibly imagine what it was like over there in the hostile skies of Germany. A soldier in combat winds himself up to a certain pitch and stays at that pitch all the time he is in the battle-zone; he does not come back to the UK between battles. To give them something to look forward to, all aircrew were given six days leave every six weeks, but many never lived long enough to enjoy that leave. One Australian ex-airman commented: 'You had not paid for your training until you had completed five operations.'

At Bomber Command headquarters in High Wycombe, the day began at 9a.m. The work of the intelligence people was vital to the C-in-C. They had to know everything there was to know about German towns, industries, fighter squadrons, decoy sites and camouflage, aids to escape for aircrew. Every target had a map and photograph, and full details of its defences and vulnerability. All this information had to be available for the C-in-C at a moment's notice.

The C-in-C's operation room was protected by a layer of concrete and inside a green mound covered by flowers. The single entrance was guarded by sentries and no one was let in or out without the correct pass. On the main wall were three blackboards, each about 30 feet by 10 feet. The information on these blackboards told the C-in-C at a glance, the order of battle and strength of each Group, and the number of aircraft available. It was the duty each day of Dorothy Phipps, a WAAF Sergeant, to cope with the continuous number of 'Q' forms which arrived each day on the teleprinter from all Groups submitting the number of aircraft they had available. These details she then chalked up on the blackboard. To do this she had to climb up on a long ladder, which was not easy until you got the hang of it as it tended to slip back and fore. Her first duty each day was to make sure the C-in-C's desk was shipshape and that all the pens, pencils and the other things he would need, were in place.

When the C-in-C arrived he was escorted by members of the RAF regiment, who made sure he got to his office safely. His conference at 9a.m. each day was attended by all his staff and also by a Royal Navy officer and an Army officer. Each day a special code was passed and a scrambler telephone, manned by a WAAF, which had a direct line to Sir Arthur Harris's house at Springfield. A chart on the wall showed the periods of moonlight and darkness thoughout the month. The main targets were marked on a 1,500,000 scale map of Europe with pins which had a coloured label attached, giving the code formula for each target. A separate map showed targets in Italy. The naval officer would keep Bomber Command in touch with the Admiralty, enemy shipping and give advice on mining operations. He would plan all routes for mining ops, routes, targets, defences etc.

In the centre of the operations room was Harris's desk and next to it three large tables mounted on pivots so that they could be easily moved. On one table there were maps to do with operations planned for that night, and also a photographic mosaic of the whole of the Ruhr. Another table had a large map of Europe showing the routes to the target and places where German night-fighters were known to be. A third table had a display of graphs which showed the number of times a target had been attacked, a map of Berlin, and enlarged photographic reproductions of the most important targets. The type of target to be attacked that night or any other night was chosen by the War Cabinet, who determined the major direction of the Air Offensive. It was Harris's duty to implement these directions to the best of his ability.

The weather was an important factor, not only over the target area but also back at base for the returning aircraft. Although the weather was neutral in the war going on, time and time again it proved to be the enemy's greatest friend. If the 'Met-man' gave a wrong forecast, the crews called it 'Duff Gen' but if it was a correct one and all went well, it was known as 'Puka Gen'. The door of the Met officers' office would often bear the inscription 'Depression Villa'.

Once the target was chosen, the number and availability of aircraft was placed before the C-in-C. He then decided the proportion of heavy and medium loads to be carried, and after considering the hours of darkness available, would determine the number of aircraft to be used. And so the operation would be on or 'laying on', as it was known. On a form marked 'C-in-C, Daily Allotment of Targets', the C-in-C writes down the code formula for the target to be attacked, the number of aircraft from each Group to take part in the operation, and the proportion of incendiary and high explosive bombs to be carried. This form is then passed to Group Headquarters by the controller. In all, this has only taken an hour since the conference started at 9a.m.

Each Group was divided up into bases commanded by an air commodore, and each base would have satellite stations commanded by group captains. The group navigation officer would work out the distance and times involved for the squadrons within his group. The petrol required, was calculated in relation to the number of aircraft and the bomb load. A further message would come from Bomber Command HQ stating the number of 'waves' of aircraft and the number of each aircraft in each wave. The message also detailed the drill for the PFF, which would depend on the weather that could be expected over the target area. If there was 10/10 ths (of full) cloud up to 10,000 feet, then the PFF would lay flares above the cloud for the main force to bomb. If there was no cloud forecast, then they would ground-mark with target indicator markers which would burst at 3000 feet and cascade 60 roman candles, coloured red, yellow or green, for the main force to bomb on. If a dog-leg route was necessary then the PFF would lay flares at the turning points of each 'leg' to enable the main force to get their bearings.

The details of the operation for that night are then passed on to the men who are to do the job — the squadrons. The station commander would send for his squadron commanders and operations officer and would relate to them the orders he had received. This meeting on a bomber station was usually known as a 'prayer meeting'. The distance involved and the amount of petrol needed was worked out, allowing for weather conditions and the amount of time the bombers would be over the target area. If the route was a dog-leg to avoid known flak positions or searchlights, then more petrol would be needed. The northern part of Germany and the Ruhr area had a searchlights 'corridor', which was well known to the crews of Bomber Command.

The flight sergeant in charge of the bomb dump and his team would make up and load the required bomb loads on to standard bomb trolleys. Only one 4000lb bomb could be loaded onto a trolley at a time. Each 500lb and 1000lb bomb would have to have a bomb-carrier, which was left behind in the aircraft after the bombs were released.

In the bomb dump at Binbrook in Lincolnshire, the station armourers did all their own fusing. It was not left for the squadron armourers to do it when the bombs arrived at the aircraft. The detonator hole was tested, then the detonator about 2½ inches long put in, and so it went on until the bomb was fused. Every time he did this, Corporal Ted Loveridge recited aloud exactly what he was doing and this prevented any slip ups, which, of course, could mean disaster. On one occasion when a NAAFI waggon came to visit them at the Binbrook bomb dump, a NAAFI girl said: 'We keep coming down here but never see any bombs, where are they? All we have seen is some old boilers with valves sticking out.' When they were told that the 'old boilers' were 4000lb bombs (or 'cookies' as they were known) they never came again. It's worth mentioning that, when the bombs came into the bomb dump they appeared to be just solid blocks of metal and did not look like bombs. The armourers would have with them bags of nuts and bolts, and the 'fins' which they would then assemble on to the tail of each bomb. So they not only fused and maintained the bombs but also assembled them.

On one occasion, the A.O.C. of the Pathfinders Don Bennett, said: 'The amount of bombs that Bomber Command could drop was determined by how many the railways could deliver. This was our limiting factor.' After the bombs were fused, they would be taken by trolley to each aircraft for 'bombing-up'. Bombs of a weight higher than 1000lb were hung on hooks inside the bomb-bay of the aircraft; portable cranes were used to hoist the heavy bombs up. The fitting of the bombs into the rack took time as they had to be aligned with the lugs in the bomb hatches, otherwise the bomb would not fit. A 4000lb bomb was locked by a small lever on the side of the bomb release. An expert 'bombing-up' squad of twenty-eight men could load fifteen aircraft in two hours.

The map clerk, known to the crews as 'map queen', was responsible for issuing and looking after all the target maps. At Dishforth in Yorkshire this was the responsibility of Corporal Edna Skeen. She had in her charge thousands of maps and charts, and had to be able to put her hand on any one of them at a minute's notice; she also had to make sure they were kept in good condition. When she knew the target she would prepare the appropriate map or 'Gen' for the navigators who would come to collect them, saying for example: 'Let me have a 250,000 scale map of Bremen.' The maps would have coloured sections representing for example, woods, built-up areas, water. The target area was coloured in red. Because she usually knew the target before they did, the aircrews would ask her: 'Where are we bound for?' She always replied: 'Wait and see.'

The lives of the aircrews depended on the expertise and dedication, in all manner of weather and conditions, of the groundcrews whose motto was: 'Keep them flying at all costs'. On an average there would be about ten groundcrew to every aircraft. At Syerston in Nottinghamshire for instance, there were 2500 ground staff, though there was more than one squadron based there. On a Lancaster bomber, there were some 96 spark plugs — 48 on each side of the aircraft, with 24 in each engine. Changing these plugs on a cold winter's morning or in the rain, was a miserable task, but it had to be done day in and day out so that the squadron had the maximum number of aircraft available. On one occasion a bank of six plugs in an engine needed changing, but to wait until the engine had cooled down would be too late. Without a thought, the fitter put his hands in the engine and changed the plugs, in the process burning his hands badly. Each aircraft was given a complete inspection everyday before take-off. This took the groundcrew about three hours, each tradesman giving his own part of the aircraft an inspection. The electrical system, the controls, instruments, radio, auto-pilot, hydraulics, guns and the ammunition feed to the guns, were all inspected. If the aircrew were to make it to the target and back everything had to work 100 per cent. This, the groundcrew would endeavour to achieve and the admiration by the aircrew was unbounded. The engines for them were all thoroughly tested, each one given a maximum 'run-up' on the ground. A final check of the hydraulic system, serving the flaps and gun turrets was performed before the aircraft was handed over to the aircrew for an air test.

The aircraft, of course, as well as being 'bombed-up', must have enough fuel to get to the target and back, so the aircrew would often have some idea of their destination by the amount of petrol being pumped into the aircraft. The crew of the bowser lorries would for instance put some 2143 gallons of petrol into a Lancaster to get it to the target and back.

An important task was the stripping, cleaning and oiling of the Browning ·303 machine guns, which were installed in the gun turrets of the bombers. On one station this task was allotted to Leading Aircraftwoman Margaret Madden who, in her wartime service, served on four bomber stations and worked on Halifaxes and Lancasters. Each day she reported to the station armoury, where her daily task was to 'belt-up' the ·303 machine guns with ammunition ready for the squadron air gunners to collect. They would often help in this tedious but vital task. Every round had to be put in correctly to avoid stoppages. With a German fighter coming at you, the last thing you wanted was a stoppage. More than one romance between a gunner and a WAAF armourer started in the station armoury. Tracer, incendiary, and armour piercing bullets would be belted in sequence. The rear gunner would need 10,000 bullets and the mid-upper gunner 2000 bullets. One night on a station, some 36 aircraft could be operating, which would mean belting-up 432,000 bullets at the armoury! In Margaret's case, she did meet and marry an air gunner, Warrant Officer Bernard Dye, who flew with 622 Squadron at Mildenhall. He would wave to Margaret with a handkerchief, from his turret as the aircraft took off; for both of them it would then be a long night. He went on to complete his tour of 30 operations and then they married. This friendship was not encouraged and as soon as it became known, she was posted to a different station, but this did not stop them meeting, as Bernard would hitch-hike over to Margaret's new posting to see her.

The parachute store of a bomber station was also manned mainly by WAAFS, who not only looked after parachutes but also the inflatable dinghies and the famous Mae West life jackets. Inside the parachute store, there was a table 40 feet long and two stoves to keep the place warm. The parachutes, which would be hung on long pulleys for 24 hours before being packed, had to be kept in a warm atmosphere, something the packers also appreciated in the winter. Each chute had its own flying log-book in which all inspections and re-packing had to be logged and signed by the packer. Each man, rather like having a fitting for a new suit, would also have a fitting for his chute. If he was a little cheeky or over-zealous to the packer, she would soon get her own back by trussing up his chute a little tighter than necessary and when his voice went up an octave, she knew it was time to slacken off.

There were two types of parachute, the seat pack, which was usually worn by the pilots and sat on during flight; and the observer pack, which was kept stowed away during flight and became known as the 'chest pack' because it was clipped on to the chest by a clip on each side, and released by pulling a handle on the left-hand side of the chute. Every so often the chute had to be opened and re-packed. This was a great treat for packers like Liz Clark (who later married Wireless Operator Mike Bond) as she would pull the rip-cord and out would billow the chute across the room, and to the usual aircrew comment, 'it worked'.

The medical personnel of a bomber station were trained to rescue crews from crashed aircraft. The 'Albion' ambulance would standby on aircraft take-off and return landings. All injured or wounded crewmen would be taken to the crash theatre, and then if necessary, to the base hospital.

The motor transport, or MT section as it was kown, would be totally involved in bomber operations. Leading Aircraftwoman Peggy Brannan would collect mines and bombs and take them to the aircraft on her tractor. Spare parts had to be delivered to the groundcrew working on the aircraft and, of course aircrews had to be taken to their aircraft before take-off. More than one aircrewman later married the girl who drove him to his aircarft. At times, while driving her tractor, Peggy would look back and see a Lancaster bomber following her down the perimeter.

The catering for all these men, of course, was important, the whole organisation would fail if they were not fed. The operational supper of corn flakes and poached egg on toast alone, would involve some 140 eggs being cooked for the crews. While the WAAFS cooked and served the meals, there would be an air of expectancy, everyone speaking quietly.

The cameras that would bring back evidence of the success or not of the bombing mission were loaded with films and taken out to each aircraft. When the bombs were dropped, a high magnesium flash bomb (like a flash in camera) would fall with the bombs, and the camera shutter would slide away to film the impact of the bombs. This was the reason for the 30 second straight and level flying after the bombs had been dropped — the crew except the bomb aimer, wanted to get out of the target area as quickly as possible and then head home, but the bomb aimer wants proof that he has done his job.

The hub of any bomber station, particularly at aircraft take-off and landings, was the flying control tower, or watch-tower as some called it. Each squadron would have a code-name. For 115 Squadron at Witchford in Cambridgeshire, for example, it was 'Blackmass', and all returning aircraft of 115 Squadron would call in and say, 'hello Blackmass, this is A-able', or whatever the calling-in aircraft's letter identification was. The WAAF Operator's voice would be the last the crews would hear from home and the first they would hear when they returned. This was to be the role of Noreen Dunbar for some two and a half years at Witchford. She said it was the most worthwhile thing she has ever done in her life. Before the war she had been a model in London, but her job now was anything but glamorous. The clothes she wore on night-duty would be scarf and battledress jacket underneath which was a heavy pullover and trousers.

The watch-tower was a grey utility building on the airfield. On the first floor an office with a radio transmitter set, another room has a long table at which sat the radio officer, flying control officer, and radio transmitter operator, which at Witchford was Noreen Dunbar, and next door the MET office. There was a small kitchen to cook suppers in. The staff in the watch-tower also ate the aircrew diet of eggs, bacon and beans. There were always at least three RT operators, three officers, and three groundcrew on duty. The day shift worked from 8a.m. to 5p.m. and the night shift 5p.m. to 8a.m. They often kept themselves awake by drinking cocoa or tea, and writing letters. Once Noreen was asked by an aircrewman of 115 Squadron if she cared, as her voice sometimes sounded a little aloof. Recalling her memories of this time, Noreen said that she cared so much it hurt, but you had to try and not show your feelings on the radio, because it could affect the crews. A bomber station was at times a very tense and sad place.

When the bombers took off, it was all systems go. Radio silence was kept and the take-off signal was given by Aldis lamp by the controller, who had a caravan on the edge of the airfield. It went all quiet as the last aircraft's engines were heard going away. The duty officer went to get some rest; the fire engines and ambulances were stood down for a few hours, but the RT operator had to keep listening all night. When the bombers returned, the place came alive again and everyone was on their toes as the bombers were 'stacked' over the airfield, waiting their turn to land. If one was in trouble, it was given priority to land. The operations room was manned 24 hours a day, seven days a week, and 52 weeks of the year. It required a minimum of three WAAF watchkeepers rotating on a twenty-four hour shift. The incoming watchkeeper, was given details of aircraft flying and the operations planned during her shift by the off duty watchkeeper. Similar to today's flying controller at major airports.

On every bomber station there was the commanding officer (CO) of a squadron, who was not only responsible for his squadron, but also flew as an operational pilot. Although only required to fly about four operations a month, many COs flew much more than this. The CO of 427 Squadron at RAF Croft in Yorkshire, was Wing Commander Dudley Burnside, DFC. His day started at about 7.15a.m. when his batman would wake him with the usual, 'good morning sir' and a very welcome mug of steaming hot tea. The atmosphere in the officers mess later was a quiet one. He was usually joined by the adjutant, who would share a lot of the many jobs to be done that day. There was an airman to see about compassionate leave, as his mother had been killed in an air raid; there were two new crews to greet; a Sergeant pilot Cook to interview for a commission, and one or two airmen on minor charges. And so it would go on throughout the day, plus the inevitable papers to read and sign. But on this particular day, the 5 March 1943, a message came, stating that a maximum effort was required on Essen that night. All Burnside's plans for that day were now postponed. The main briefing for the raid was due at 6.30p.m. for take-off at 8.30p.m. He had decided to fly himself that night and so informed the crew of his intentions. Somehow he found time to do a short air-test of his aircraft before returning to the operations room to prepare for the briefing, and make arrangements for transport with the MT officer, and meals with the catering staff.

The briefing was where the crews would be informed of the target and the plan for that night's operation. For new, or 'freshman' crews, it would be their first briefing. However, when it came to missions against the Ruhr everybody had the same chance of survival. History would show that it took its toll of 'old hands' as well as new ones. In 426 Squadron one flight commander, Squadron Leader Clive Sinton (who later became CO of 433 Squadron) remembered the briefings as something he never got used to. It gave him a gut ache knowing what the crews would have to face, and how much 'lady-luck' would play in their survival.

In the briefing room, the station intelligence officer with the help of the map clerks, plotted the routes in and out of the target on a large-scale map of Europe. The routes were indicated with wide red tape. After this had been done, a screen was dropped down over the map, the briefing room was locked and the windows shuttered. At the allotted hour the aircrews would assemble in the briefing room. The doors were closed and guarded by the RAF police and no one else would be allowed in now. When the screen was drawn back to reval the map of the target, a general murmur would come from the men in the room with comments like, 'bloody Ruhr again' or 'not Essen again' being heard. The roll was called and each pilot, having assembled his crew, would shout 'here'. The complete outline of the raid would be given, such as intelligence about the target and its defences, and the weather conditions to expect. The flying control officer would give details of the runways to be used and the order of take-off for each aircraft. The main gist of the operation would be give by the CO of the squadron.

When the briefing was over, all those flying that night had to empty their pockets of anything that could be of use to the enemy; things like money, letters, bills of sale, etc. Each man had a personal bag for these items which was then put into a larger bag with the rest of the crew's personal bags, and then they were collected and placed in a safe place until the aircrew returned. Every crew member was issued with a perspex escape pack that contained glucose sweets, foreign currency, a small compass (some packs had the button or collar-stud type compass) and other things that were thought to help if your aircraft was shot down, or you were forced to bale out, such as water purifying tablets. Before take-off, Joan Thomas, a map clerk, would be given letters by the crews to post if they did not return, or messages to look after a dog, wallet or bike. At take-off time the WAAFS, who had done so much to organise the operation, would cycle across to the perimeter and watch the aircraft go away.

When the bombers returned, the 'map queens' would collect the maps and clean them if necessary, then file them for the next time. On some occasions they would even collect blood-stained maps and documents from damaged aircraft that, only some hours before, had been issued to the navigators. The blood on the maps told a sad tale.

After the crews had landed they were taken to the briefing room or operations room and interrogated by intelligence officers. Questions were usually asked concerning the type of flak encountered, any combat with fighter aircraft, and if the Pathfinders marked the target area correctly, and so on. The answers given by the crew were recorded. The crews would be sipping rum-laced tea or coffee, often served by the Padre on the station, who would be there at all hours to give a welcome word. The room would be full of comments about the raid like, 'I dropped incendiaries north of . . .' or, 'the fires looked like a heath fire to me', and so on. At least three WAAFS would volunteer to hand out sandwiches or drinks to the crews, and their welcome smiles were a tonic to the tired and weary men. When the last of the crew had been interviewed, the usual question from the WAAFS was: 'Are all the boys back yet?'

As soon as the aircraft reached the dispersal area, the magazines of film were removed from the camera and taken away to be developed as soon as possible. The photographs were sent to the intelligence section and from there to Group HQ, then finally to Bomber Command HQ at High Wycombe. The aircraft's engines and gun turrets were covered by tarpaulin by the night staff. At daybreak, the fitters and riggers would inspect the aircraft from nose to tail. The oil and fuel consumption were checked against the pilot's log. The spark plugs were carefully checked for oil. The wings and fuselage were checked for holes from flak and machine gun fire; the tyres were pumped up, the controls checked and special attention paid to the bomb-release gear.

For Dudley Burnside, this raid against Essen on the night of 5-6 March, had taken about five hours. Apart from a little damage to his aircraft, he had returned safely, but two of his aircraft and crews were missing. After waiting for some time it was evident that they were not going to make it home, so he returned to his room where his faithful batman was waiting for him. He slept for a few hours, had a late breakfast with the adjutant. Burnside said later: 'He did not have to remind me that I had ten letters to write to the next of kin of the two missing crews; one of these men was the sergeant pilot I was due to interview for a commission the day before.'

7 The Battle Begins

The month of March 1943, was to be the start of the Bomber Offensive, an offensive which would go on to the end of the war in Europe. On the 3 March, the following message was sent to Winston Churchill by the Russian leader Stalin: 'I welcome the British Air Force, which yesterday bombed Berlin so successfully. I regret that the Soviet Air Force is, for the present, engaged in a struggle against the Germans at the Eastern Front, so is not yet in a position to take part in the bombing of Berlin.'

At the time Harris sent a message to No.6 Group saying: 'As RCAF Squadrons you have done fine work already, as a RCAF Group we are proud to have you with us. Hail Canada, Hail Hitler with bombs.' They were to go on and carry 13,000 bombs, in 1943 to enemy targets, and its aircrew were awarded 700 decorations, including five CGMs and fifteen DSOs. The Battle of the Ruhr was fought by aircrew who came from countries all over the world, including Australia, Canada, New Zealand, South Africa, Jamaica, Rhodesia, Ceylon, Cyprus, the Falkland Islands to name but some of the 25 colonies that contributed. And to add to this, were men from eight European countries. Many of these men were trained under the Empire Training Scheme. On return to the UK they then went to Advanced Flying Units (AFU), and Operational Training Units (OTU) and finally to conversion units and operational squadrons. The exception to the rule was the flight engineers who were trained in the UK and did not go to conversion units. A long training which was never omitted throughout the war, despite the severe losses suffered. Each man was given full training before being expected to fly operationally.

The opening target for the offensive was to be that 'old chestnut', the Krupps factory in Essen, a target ten miles wide by twenty miles long and some 250 miles from the Norfolk coast. The operation on the 5-6 March 1943, was the 21st attack on Essen since the war started, and the 100,000 sortie carried out by Bomber Command since the war started. The code-name for Essen had been 'Stoat', but this was now changed to 'Bullhead'. All the targets in the Ruhr were named after fish, having previously been named after reptiles. All groups in Bomber Command were detailed for this operation, including No.8, the Pathfinder Group, who were to play a tremendous part in the coming months. The number of aircraft to be used for this raid was determined at 442 consisting of Halifaxes, Lancasters, Wellingtons, and Stirlings. For the Ruhr offensive, the engines on the Lancasters were changed from the Mk20s to the more powerful Mk22s.

The plan agreed for this raid on Essen, was that eight Mosquitos of No.8 Group would lead the attack using *OBOE*, and they would be followed by 22 Pathfinder Lancasters that would act as back-up. All the Pathfinder aircraft would drop yellow Target Indicators (TIs) on track fifteen miles short of the target, to guide the main force. The Mosquitos with *OBOE* were to mark the aiming-point with salvoes of red TIs. The back-up Lancasters were to attack at intervals of one to two minutes between zero and zero plus 38 minutes aiming green TIs and high explosives in salvoes at the red TIs with a delay of one second before releasing the incendiaries. The main force were detailed to attack in three sections:

Section 1: Halifaxes, zero plus 2 to zero plus 20
Section 2: Wellingtons, and Stirlings, zero plus 15 to zero plus 25
Section 3: Lancasters, zero plus 20 to zero plus 40.

For one airman it was to be his second period of attacking the Ruhr. On the first occasion, 'Goldie' Goldstraw was with 207 Squadron flying Manchesters, and had taken part in a raid on Essen on the 9 March 1942. On his tour with 207 Squadron he had to be a bomb aimer as well as a navigator, and much of his time was spent trying to identify the target, as there were no electronic aids in those days. Also in 1942, the aircraft could safely fly around the target again to enable one to get the bombing correct; but to try and do this in 1943 would have been suicidal, as there would be too many aircraft coming in towards the target at the same height. With the electronic aids available in 1943, however, it would not have been necessary to fly around the target again. He found the briefings in 1943 more detailed and professional than those of 1942. Navigation was more intense, with constant revision of the aircraft's ground speed, Estimated Time of Arrival (ETA) and so on.

At RAF Bourne, Lincolnshire, they were preparing eight aircraft from 15 Squadron for the 5-6 March. Their call-sign was 'Derby'. Petrol 1820 gallons, rations for 59 men, meal times were 1600 or 4p.m. and the briefing 1700 or 5p.m. The transport was detailed at the officers mess for 1645 or 4.45p.m. and the Sgts mess 1715 or 5.15p.m. At RAF Coningsby, Lincolnshire, the call-sign was 'Bozam', which aircraft from that station would use when calling the watch-tower at Coningsby. Their briefing for the raid was due at 2.30p.m. and the allotted take-off time 6.58p.m.

The crews that were operating that night had to perform their air tests. During this test, the flight engineer would check that the engines were operating smoothly. He kept a log, recording oil pressures and temperatures. He compared the petrol consumption with the engine at various r.p.m. and that the fuel system feed to each tank was in order.

After a meal and the briefing it was time to get ready for the mission ahead. The whole Battle of the Ruhr was to last some four months and this area became known to some crews as the RAF graveyard. The air in the locker room as the crews dressed would be of apprehension. Many wore a heavy, white roll-neck sweater, although some preferred to wear the service dress-jacket under their battledress. Over this went the Irvine jacket and Mae West, which would be needed in the case of a ditching in the sea. On their feet they wore silk socks under thick woollen socks over which they wore heavy, flying boots lined with lamb's-wool. Lastly, the flying helmet was put on complete with oxygen mask, which would be connected to the aircraft's oxygen supply. Then it was time to walk out to the aircraft. A check is made outside the aircraft that the pitot head cover is off, that the chocks are in position, fire extinguishers are available on dispersal in case of fire and the controls and tabs are serviceable. Form 700 is signed, then the men climb into the aircraft, where further checks have to be made.

Inside the aircraft, all the hatches are checked for security, and all the instruments are checked to see that they are in working order. Then it's time to start up the engines. The NCO in charge of the starting crew calls out: 'undercarriage locked down, brakes on, switch to ground, check bomb doors.' Then: 'contact starboard inner.' The starter-button is pressed, and when the engine fires, it is snapped on to 'slow-running'. The other engines are started in the same fashion. If it is at night, the NCO will indicate with a torch each engine to be started.
Before leaving the aircraft parking spot the following check is made: A.D.P.T. P.F.F.S.I.R.

A.— Auto Controls
D.— D.R. Compass (Distant Reading)
P. — Pitot Head Heater 'ON'
T. — Trimming Tabs
P. — Pitch Fully Fine
F. — Fuel
F. — Flaps
S. — Supercharger
I. — Intake
R.— Radiator Shutters Automatic

The pilot would taxi the aircraft by using the two outer engines to direct it to the right or the left as they moved along, and then on to the runway allotted, making sure the tail wheel was straight and the gyro compass on the correct magnetic heading. The flaps are once again checked, and then the WAAF in the watch-tower would give permission to take off. The pilot would stand hard on the brakes, push the control column forward, then push the throttles forward and release the brakes. Half-way down the runway, the tail wheel would rise, and the rudders were used to steer the aircraft. The flight engineer would often help the pilot to keep the throttles open by putting his hand under the pilot's. When the aircraft was airborne, the flight engineer would cause the undercarriage to be raised. The navigator would soon come on the intercom and give the pilot the course to steer.

The rear gunner, having settled himself in his turret and locked the turret doors behind him, would then swing his guns from side to side. This was done by operating a pair of handles which were rather like a bicycle's; the power to move the guns came from the hydraulic system. He then loads and cocks his guns, and reports all this to the pilot. From his position, the rear gunner sees nothing of the aircraft, as he faces the open sky. It is, as described by one gunner, 'like being suspended in space'. Once over the sea, he would ask to test his guns to make sure they work, although the attitude of most gunners was not to use them unless it was unavoidable. Never attract the attention of a fighter aircraft was the order of the day.

The night of 5-6 March. Target — ESSEN

The first red TIs were dropped at 8.58p.m. These were immediately attacked by the main force of bombers. Small marker bombs and sticks of incendiary were seen burning round them. The green TIs were laid very close to the red TIs and by 9.05p.m. the fires had begun to take hold in the target area. A few minutes later a tremendous explosion was reported. Most of the bombs fell within a two mile radius, and by the time the attack had finished at about 9.36p.m. the whole of the target area was covered in fire and smoke. The bomb aimers will have done their job keeping the pilot on the target, and then keeping him there for 30 seconds so as to take the bombing photograph. The pilot would then, to the relief of the rest of the crew, fly the aircraft out of the target area. Once the bomb left the aircraft, it would take approximately twenty seconds to reach its target, so to have a direct hit, the bomb would have to be released the same number of seconds before the aircraft flew over the target. It was also important to keep the aircraft flying straight and level just before releasing the bomb.

This was quite a different trip to Essen for 'Goldie' Goldstraw than the one he went on in March 1942. On this occasion he was with 467 Squadron flying a Lancaster ED543, piloted by Squadron Leader D. Green. They made their attack on a compass heading from the North and found the target area well illuminated, through a layer of cloud and haze, by flares, flak bursts and searchlights, which silhouetted other aircraft against the sky. 'Goldie' saw two aircraft destroyed on leaving the target. The enemy searchlights were used in a broad band to the north and west of Essen and in an inner ring around the town itself. The flak at the beginning of the attack was intense with some 27 aircraft being hit, and nearly all in the target area. In four incidents the aircraft were 'coned' by searchlights.

Aircraft of No.4 Group reported intense searchlight activity, and No.3 Group reported accurate flak up to 20,000 feet. 'Chandelier' flares, rockets and 'umbrella' flak were reported, also barrage balloons up to 8000 feet. Of the seven aircraft believed lost over the target area, five were stated to have been shot down by flak and all were seen to go down during the first half of the attack. In the Essen area some nine fighter patrols were observed; eleven pursuits were made resulting in one combat but no success claimed by the enemy. The bomber crews reported eight attacks and twenty-one approaches by enemy fighers. The fighter units (Night Fighter Geschwader) reported operating were NJG 1 and NJG 2 in the

Gilze Rijen area, and NJG 5 in the Lippstadt area. The Germans claimed they had shot down fifteen aircraft by fighter and/or flak.

Two Wellington bombers collided. The aircraft involved, were flown by Flight Sergeant Tozer of 466 Squadron, flying HZ 256, and Flying Officer Hope of 196 Squadron, flying HE 396-J. Tozer's aircraft was unable to continue and had to jettison its bombs in the sea and returned to base; however, Hope's aircraft was able to go on and complete its task. It is sad to have to record that Tozer was later lost on a raid against Pilsen on the 16 April; he was the first Australian to be lost from 466 Squadron. He was twenty-one years old.

The crew of Wellington bomber BJ 819-A of 199 Squadron, flown by Sergeant Harlem, found it an eventful night. They were attacked by a Focke-Wulf 190 fighter, which resulted in the port cowling being holed, the port tyre punctured and a large tear in the port side of the fuselage. At the time, they were flying at 11,500 feet when the fighter came in firing cannon-and machine-gun bullets at the Wellington's engine, cowling and wings. The rear gunner, Sergeant Finlayson fired no less than 750 rounds of bullets during the three attacks that the fighter made. Finlayson was sure he hit the fighter a number of times on the third attack, but no claims were made. In the recommendation on the 10 May 1943, for the DFM to be awarded to Finlayson, this action was mentioned. At the time he had only some thirteen operations under his belt. A Wellington of No.1 Group reported having destroyed a Messerschmitt 109 which had attacked them off the Dutch Coast.

One aircraft of 429 Squadron, BK 755-Z crashed on take-off. The navigator, Sergeant Bell of the RCAF, was killed and the rest of the crew, including the pilot Flight Sergeant Conroy, were injured. Bell was buried on the 8 March at Sutton-on-the-Forest. The inquiry revealed that the undercarriage had been retracted too soon during take-off. At the time, 429 Squadron were attempting to get aircraft off at 30 second intervals.

Back at base, at the ETA of the returning aircraft, the flying-control rooms became alert. When the first faint crackle of the station call-sign and aircraft identifications were heard, the watchkeeper immediately rang the station commander, squadron commanders and the intelligence officers. All fire, ambulance and MT officers would also be alerted. The returning aircraft would 'stack' over the airfield until they were given permission to land by a WAAF in the watch-tower. If an aircraft was in trouble or had wounded aboard, it would be given a priority landing before others. The station commander and others would assemble in the watch-tower. The watchkeeper would be logging the time when each aircraft first called in, and its time of landing. She would then telephone the Group controller to inform him of the number of aircraft that had arrived back, and to enquire if there was any news of missing aircraft having landed away from their own base.

Fourteen aircraft or 3.2 per cent of the total bomber force that took part in the raid, were lost on this night of the 5-6 March. Five were estimated to have been shot down by flak, and probably three or possibly five lost to night-fighters. The remaining losses were recorded as 'causes unknown'.

When reconnaissance flights were made on the 7-8 March, results showed that some 53 separate workshops in the Krupps factory had been affected, and thirteen main buildings destroyed or severely damaged. Other factories in Essen had been gutted. In all, an area of over 160 acres of Essen was laid to waste.

Some five aircraft had attacked other targets in the areas of Bocholt, Gladbach, and also Alkmaar, Leeuwarden, and Akersloot in Holland. The description given by the crews of the area they attacked included comments like 'an immense pot boiling over' and 'the glow from 150 miles away looked like a red sunset'. Seven aircraft of No.4 Group were detailed to lay mines off the Frisian Islands. Two returned with engine problems, but five managed to drop a total of fourteen mines.

In the log-book of Sergeant Percy Walder of 467 Squadron, a simple entry for this trip to Essen reads: 'Krupps works, big fires, 4 hours 25 minutes.' He had already completed operations against Berlin and Hamburg, and was to go on and take part in many more raids against the Ruhr.

Any luck that Sergeant Bakewell and his crew of 419 Squadron had, deserted them on this raid to Essen. Their aircraft first had engine trouble while crossing the English Channel, and then after successfully reaching and bombing the target they were caught by searchlights and engaged in heavy flak. This attack wounded in the eye, flight engineer Sergeant Alvin Turner, who was on his tenth operation. Their troubles were still not over as, when they reached the Zuider Zee over Holland, they were attacked at first by one and then three Junkers 88 fighters. Several times Bakewell was able, with the instruction of the rear gunner, to avoid being hit, but eventually the starboard wing was hit and caught fire. From this moment on, the writing was on the wall, and the order came to bale out. In his descent Turner was somehow knocked out and awoke, lying on his blood-saturated parachute, some two miles north of Amsterdam. Despite the presence of German E-boats on the Noord Zee canal, he managed to find a boat and get to the other side of the canal. Then first with the use of a bicycle and then by train, he reached Aachen, where he managed to gain admittance to a house. The owner gave him a mirror to look at his wounded face which was covered in dry blood. They gave him clothes and food and helped him on his way. With this help he reached Liège, Belgium on the 12 March. From hereon he was aided by an escape organisation and reached Gibraltar via Spain on the 27 June. Next day he was flown to Hendon in the UK.

The next raid on Essen was planned for the 7-8 March, but owing to adverse weather this was cancelled, so it would be a week before the next major raid on Essen. The Mosquitos of No.8 Group did attack Essen and Mülheim on the 10-11 March. These were known as 'nuisance' raids, but the men who flew them felt that they were more than this. Their A.O.C. agreed with them.

The night of 12-13 March. Target — ESSEN

On this operation, 457 aircraft consisting of Lancasters, Halifaxes, Stirlings, Wellingtons and Mosquitos, were involved. The Pathfinder aiming point markers aided by *OBOE* were accurately timed and concentrated. After the first quarter of an hour the fires merged into a huge mass of red flame. The crews of No.1 Group reported excellent bomb concentration and very few bombs being dropped outside the marked area. The largest explosion occurred around 9.33p.m. and was accompanied by an eruption of flames estimated to be as high as 1000 feet. The glare of these flames lit up the cockpits of aircraft flying at bombing heights of up to 18,000 feet. Even when passing over the Dutch coast on their return journey the aircrews could still see the glow from the fires burning in Essen.

Considerable opposition had been encountered from the ground defences. The flak was intense, sometimes reaching up to a height of 20,000 feet, and a large number of searchlights were in operation. The flak was directed mainly at aircraft that were held in searchlight 'cones'. One crew counted thirteen of the cones, each one being formed by some twenty to thirty searchlights.

The Berbeck area north-west of Krupps was hit in this operation, one *Kolonie* or housing estate being wiped out and another badly damaged. In the Krupps factories the damage was rather more severe than that caused by the attack of 5-6 March. This time the locomotive shops and the rolling-stock works were burned out. About one-third of the total built-up area of Essen was destroyed, including two-thirds of the city centres. Of the 300 workshops in Krupps, 54 had been destroyed and 80 damaged. All schools were closed and teachers were employed in first aid work. In many areas electricity supplies had broken down and there were no trams running. After the raid of the 5-6 March, work had seemed to continue, but after this raid on the 12-13 March, it appeared to stop completely. Reports showed the damage in the industrial areas to be twice as much as that in the non-industrial areas. As a result of these two raids on Essen, 27 per cent of the built-up areas of Krupps was damaged. A report from Sweden stated that the damage to Krupps was the heaviest inflicted so far by the RAF on works vital to the German war effort.

The enemy's defences had been strengthened between the two raids. There were estimated to have been up to 150 searchlights, which remained active throughout the attack, operating in groups of ten to fifteen. They were able to 'cone' up to ten aircraft at a time. The enemy night-fighters were heard operating in the Gilze Rijen, Leeuwarden, Laon, and Athies area. Of the 52 ground-controlled night-fighters logged operating that night, some 25 were in action against the bombers during this raid on the Ruhr. Some 49 aircraft were damaged by flak and three damaged by fighters. Twenty-three aircraft went missing. Out of the 879 aircraft despatched in these two raids on Essen, 37 failed to return.

For this operation of the 12-13 March, Percy Walder recorded in his log-book: 'Good trip. Fired at searchlights.' Recalling his memories of that period, he said: 'The master searchlight would pick, or try to pick you up, followed by the other searchlights around. As you flew on, you would be passed on to the next lot. In the meantime, the flak gunners would have a visual target, and a pick-up point for any fighters in the area. We usually went into a steep dive when coned by the searchlights; pull up at the bottom of the dive and open up with all guns. On the 12-13 March it worked, otherwise I would not be here today.'

For bomb aimer Tom Osborn flying with 460 Squadron, he found it the most heavily defended target that he had so far encountered, having to evade fighters on the way in and then come up against extremely heavy flak of all types. A piece of this flak penetrated the nose of the aircraft, just missed him at his bomb-sight, and lodged in the pilot's flying boot. For one moment, when he felt the draught of cold air on his face, he thought he had been wounded in the face.

Many crews were superstitious, maybe because it was a 'safety-valve', or something that made you feel safe, or gave you some comfort to think that you would survive so long as you kept to the same routine or carried some form of trinket or mascot. For instance, Andrew Black of 10 Squadron always wore his walking boots over his neck by the laces, in the way many of us have worn our football boots when going to a match. He felt that if he had to bale out of the aircraft, he would need these boots to enable him to walk and contact the underground Resistance. The issued flying boots would not be suitable for this. The oldest member of his crew was the navigator, Flying Officer Ted Kitchen, who was married and had rented a cottage on the road alongside the airfield. He would always wave to his wife from the aircraft's astrodome window provided, of course, there was enough daylight to allow this.

Andrew Black relates their experience of this operation against Essen:

> We were now at the end of the runway facing into the wind, suddenly the brakes were released, and with the engines at maximum power, the plane leapt forward as if anxious to get away from its earthly bond. In a moment the Halifax was off the runway and airborne. As we climbed higher, each one of us slipped quietly into our own 'office'. The navigator went to work immediately with his slide rule. We arrived in the target area ahead of ETA, Ted's navigation and George's flying had been spot on. The zero hour for bombing was some minutes off, although the Pathfinders' flares had been dropped. The target was relatively quiet. Over the intercom came George's voice, 'what do you think chaps, shall we be first tonight or should we stooge around for a couple of minutes?' After a discussion, it was decided to fly in and drop our bombs and head home p.d.q. We had just started our bombing run when a bluish-white searchlight locked on us, followed by about twenty to thirty more; we were well and truly coned. The pilot George Vinish put 'A-able' into a steep dive and commenced a corkscrew pattern, at the same time we heard the rear gunner, Flight Sergeant Jacques Barsalou firing his guns, then

> they stopped. We were coned three times and each time George skilfully evaded the searchlights although we were hit eighteen times. It was later found that the hits were on a propeller and the rear turret.

The pilot eventually got a reply from the rear gunner, who said 'carry on skipper, I can hang on till we reach the coast'. On hearing this, George sent Andrew Black back to see what was up. He found Jacques slumped over his guns, and the turret was covered in blood. Black recalls: 'I managed to man-handle him out of the turret door and got him back to the rest bed; got his clothing off and gave him first aid. He was in good spirits and insisted he could bear up until the English coast was reached.' The pilot instructed Andrew to send a message informing their base that they were returning with a badly wounded member of the crew. When the aircraft landed Jacques was quickly taken to hospital. He had suffered severe shrapnel wounds to the intestines and right buttock, and for a while was critically ill but later recovered. On the 14 March 1943, he was recommended for an immediate DFM. In the recommendation the pilot, in his personal report wrote: 'My tail gunner has more guts than he knows what to do with. I shall never fly with anybody of greater courage.'

As Lancaster R5749 and its crew of 106 Squadron approached the white TIs fifteen miles short of the target, the searchlights and flak became more intense than that experienced on the 5-6 March. They were hit by flak, but this only caused superficial damage to the aircraft, though two other aircraft were seen to explode over the target at a height of 20,000 feet. The bomb aimer Neil Lindsay, because of the box barrage of flak decided to put on his parachute. After the bombs had been dropped and the bomb doors closed, there was an explosion and a white flash in front of their aircraft. When he recovered, Lindsay found that he had been blown out of the front of the aircraft and was aware, as he came down in his parachute, of aircraft passing overhead, and of searchlights which were coning him; he pretended to be dead. When he hit the ground two figures approached him out of the dark. They were workers from Krupps, and one of them spoke the familiar phrase 'for you the war is over'. He was taken to hospital and here he learned that the rest of his crew, including the pilot Flight Sergeant MacDonald, had not made it. They are now buried in Duisburg War Cemetery. While in hospital he was able to see at first hand the effects of the Allied raids on the Germans. When he was interrogated by a German Intelligence Officer, he learned that around Essen there were 4000 heavy flak guns, and around the whole of the Ruhr area some 7000.

For Geoff Archer of 199 Squadron the main memory of the Ruhr raids was a feeling of sheer terror. He remembers their aircraft being coned by searchlights, then the flak coming up, followed by the dive to avoid the searchlights when the whole aircraft would seem to vibrate, and with the engine screaming, the altimeter unwinding like crazy as they descended with ever-increasing speed, and then the gunners blazing away at any nearby searchlights.

For Wing Commander Dudley Burnside, the CO of 427 Squadron, the trip to Essen on the 12-13 March was one he would never forget. His

Wellington bomber was hit by flak about eight miles from the target. The navigator who was standing next to him was killed instantly and Geoffrey Keen the wireless operator, had half his foot shot away. Despite this they kept going, descending to 10,000 feet over Essen to drop their bombs. On the return trip they were attacked by a night-fighter whose tracer bullets missed them fortunately. Despite the injury to his foot, Geoffrey Keen continued to work on, repairing the radio which had been damaged in the attack, and got the intercom working again; he also helped with the navigation. They eventually made an emergency landing at Stradishall, Suffolk.

For this operation Burnside was awarded a bar to his DFC, and the bomb aimer, Pilot Officer Reg Hayhurst, was awarded the DFC. Hayhurst had been covered in glycol almost to the point of suffocation; also his oxygen supply had been punctured and had failed. Despite this he had continued to direct the pilot to the target and give the normal bombing instructions (photographs developed later showed the bombing to have been perfect). Hayhurst also helped to navigate on their return journey, and gave first aid to the wounded. Wireless Operator Geoffrey Keen was recommended for the VC by Burnside but later was awarded the CGM, despite the A.O.C. of No.6 Group endorsing Burnside's recommendation.

Goebbels recorded in his Diary of the 13 March 1943, that the Krupps plant had been hard hit. He telephoned its Deputy *Gauleiter* Schlesmann, who gave him a rather depressing report. Some 25 major fires were raging in the grounds of the Krupps plant alone. On the 15 March he recorded that workers were having to be transferred to Essen and Munich to make essential repairs. He also wrote that the worst was still to come. On the 17 March he stated that the damage to Essen was very considerable and the evacuee problem there had assumed great proportions. There was also very little accommodation available. On the 20 March he mentioned the precision of the English bombers operating in Essen, but wrote that the report of 80 per cent of the Krupps factory being destroyed was exaggerated, although serious stoppages of production were to be expected.

A WAAF driver at the wheel of a tractor towing a Lancaster bomber into a hangar for a major service before going out again on operations. (Imperial War Museum)

WAAF Watchkeeper Cpl Mary Pratt in the operations room at RAF Scampton. (Mary Pratt)

The lull before the storm; a Halifax crew have their last cigarette and chat before climbing aboard ready for take-off. The operation was to Essen and the period April 1943. (Imperial War Museum)

The take-off and ahead lies a six hour or longer trip into the heart of Germany and the fighters and flak guns of the German airforce. (Imperial War Museum)

8 The Battle Intensifies

Because of bad weather conditions in the Ruhr area it was nearly two weeks before another operation could be mounted. About this time, a report was received that up to the 22 March no work progress had been made at the Krupps factories as a result of the previous two raids. In this area, 105,000 people had been made homeless which included 15,000 Krupps workers.

On the 22 March 1409 Flight were transferred from Bircham Newton, Norfolk, to No.8 Group (the Pathfinders) at Oakington in Cambridgeshire. No.1409 Flight consisted of eight Mosquitos and their role was to assess the weather conditions en route and in the area of the operation. These weather reconnaissance flights were code-named 'Pampa'. They were used in two ways, firstly, to obtain a broad survey of meteorological conditions over enemy territory in terms of cloud distribution prior to the selection of targets and secondly, to survey conditions over those areas of enemy territory which would assist the meteorologist most in forecasting cloud en route and around selected targets. In the latter case, weather reconnaissance by 'Pampa' was normally made up-wind from the geographical positions to which the forecast would apply. Each reconnaissance route proposed was examined by the Air Staff and compromises made between what was best meteorologically and what was desirable to avoid the most heavily defended areas and to ensure that the proposed target was not made obvious to the enemy.

The night of 26-27 March. Target — DUISBURG

For the attack on Duisburg, code-name 'Cod', 455 aircraft were despatched and all Groups involved. The attack itself was very scattered, the method of attack being 'wanganui'* or 'skymarking'. There was full-cloud cover up to a height of 14,000 feet over the target area. No back-up aircraft were used on this operation. Nine aircraft using *OBOE* were detailed to 'skymark', but only four were able to mount the attack when the other five aborted with technical trouble.

* A method of marking known as 'skymarking' where the markers exploded in the air in conditions of cloud found in the target area. The marker would explode above the cloud and illuminate the area for the following bombers. Although the target could not be seen the target would have been found by the use of electronics.

This was the first occasion that the Germans had used decoy flares. This tactic was successful because 100 Allied aircraft bombed them, and the fires thus started were later bombed, through the cloud, by other aircraft. The failure on this occasion was primarily due to there being insufficient flares, so that when the enemy put up its decoys, incoming crews had nothing apart from these on which to release their bombs. The recommendation for future attacks was that blind bombing attacks should have an ample supply of skymarkers rather than to hope for 100 per cent concentration, and risk technical failures and enemy decoys. It was also recommended that back-up aircraft be provided on skymarking operations.

Crew reports from No.1 Group stated that the flares were up to twenty miles apart, and that incendiary bursts were over a radius of about thirty miles. One crew reported 'a complete failure, PFF flares scattered', and another, 'a scattered show. Cloud conditions made it impossible to assess success of raid'. The flak was moderate to heavy. Enemy searchlights were unable to penetrate the cloud and the flak was mainly in the form of a barrage to the north, or north-west of Duisburg, or in predicted concentrations around the flares.

Flying Officer Fox in a Wellington bomber of 429 Squadron, was at 15,000 feet when, near Utrecht in Holland a salvo of four shells burst close by. The rear gunner immediately reported the aircraft being damaged. Flak then seemed to come from all directions. The port engine was set on fire. Then the order to bale out was given. In the space of fifteen minutes, the aircraft had been hit, set on fire and the crew forced to leave.

Sergeant Gordon Murray, a bomb aimer from Darlington, came down in his parachute near Voorschola south-west of Leyden in Holland. With the help of local people and later, Dutch escape organisations, he got into Belgium and then into Spain and finally arrived in Gibraltar on the 27 June 1943.

The first *OBOE* Mosquito to be lost in the Battle of the Ruhr was DK 318 of 109 Squadron, flown by Flight Lieutenant Leslie Ackland, DFC, and navigated by Warrant Officer Frederick Strouts of the RCAF, who was later commissioned but never knew of it. The last heard of them was when they sent out an SOS at 10.20p.m. from North Foreland. Neither their bodies nor their aircraft were ever found, so it must be assumed they went down in the sea. Both Ackland, who was aged 23 and came from Barnstaple in Devon, and Strouts have no known grave but are remembered for all time on the Runneymede Memorial.

When returning from this raid against Duisburg, Flight Lieutenant Bazalgette tried to land his aircraft with the wheels up, the undercarriage having been damaged by flak. On the first attempt he failed, on the second the aircraft hit a tree on the perimeter of the airfield, but they survived. Later, Bazalgette was to go on and attack a number of targets in the Ruhr and be awarded the DFC. In 1945 he was killed while serving with the Pathfinders and was awarded the Victoria Cross posthumously.

The night of 29-30 March. Target — BOCHUM

The town of Bochum was about the size of Hull in Yorkshire. The force sent on this operation was 149 Wellington bombers led by eight *OBOE* Mosquitos. The target had the code-name 'Quinnat'.

The attack itself was once again in the main a failure, due partly to weather — 'icing' on the aircraft being the primary problem. The flak was modest to intensely heavy and was the predicted type working in conjunction with the searchlight cones and also in a barrage form. Of the 128 night-fighter sorties recorded, 58 were directly involved in actions against the bomber force. The Germans claimed that 27 British bombers were shot down. In fact thirteen aircraft from the Wellington force failed to return to base, and fifteen were damaged by flak. There was no evidence of 'icing' being the reason for actual losses, although some 40 aircraft did return to base for this reason. Two aircraft were possibly coned and shot down over the target, and one may have been shot down by a night-fighter near Deelen. Squadron Leader Cairns, DFC, of 429 Squadron said: 'This was the worst operational trip I have ever completed owing to weather conditions.' He felt there were not enough aircraft on a target of this importance.

On the 30 March the doorbell of a house in Sydenham, Oxfordshire was rang by a telegram boy, who was holding in his hand the standard yellow envelope, which during the war, was dreaded by every household with a father, son, husband or brother in aircrew. It read on this occasion as on many other occasions before and after: 'REGRET TO INFORM YOU THAT YOUR SON SGT JAMES ROBERT ARTHUR HODGSON IS MISSING AS A RESULT OF OPERATIONS ON THE NIGHT 29-30 MARCH 1943 LETTER FOLLOWS. STOP. ANY FURTHER INFORMATION WILL BE FORWARDED TO YOU IMMEDIATELY.'

Nothing was heard until December 1943, although Hodgson's father had received a letter from the International Red Cross of Geneva dated 7 May 1943. He had kept the letter hidden and it was only by accident that it was found and the facts became known how Hodgson and his crew had lost their lives on the 29 March 1943. They had been shot down by a night-fighter flown by Oberst Werner Streib (the CO of NJG 1) at Venlo in Holland. Streib was the man behind the idea of the upward-firing cannon, known as 'Schräge musik'. The cannon was set at an angle of 45 degrees and fighters could approach bombers undetected and fire at them from below. He went on to become Inspector of Night Fighters in 1944 and ended the war as a Brigadier-General, having shot down 66 bombers, and been awarded the Knights Cross with Oak Leaves and Swords.

The Wellington flown by Bob Hodgson had crashed in the rear garden of a surburban house near Deelen airfield. The airfield fire brigade were unable to put out the flames, so the aircraft was left to burn itself out. On the 1 April the bodies were handed over to the Dutch authorities at Moscowa Municipal Cemetery and were buried in the central avenue which, unknown to the Germans, was a place of honour in the cemetery reserved for resistance fighters. Each day the graves were covered in flowers, much against the orders and wishes of the Germans. The date on the headstone was given as the 1 April but later changed by the Red Cross to the 29 March, the date they had in fact died.

One of the crew Bob Weese, was a Canadian and had only been married ten days. The father of Stan Farley the navigator, was very bitter when he received two letters at the same time, one telling him his son was missing and the other that his son had been commissioned to the rank of Pilot Officer. In 1945 the buried crew were split up. The graves of the two Canadians Bob Weese and Fred Dupré were exhumed and moved to the Canadian National Cemetery at Groesbeek some twenty miles away. And so the unique comradeship that aircrew had was split up. There is now a gap between the two British airmen Bob Hodgson and David Keenan and the third British airman Stan Farley, where Bob Weese and Fred Dupré were buried. In 1948 Bob Hodgson's mother and father visited the graves for the first time. Here they met a young Dutch girl called Riny Palm who had looked after their son's grave ever since.

The Wellington flown by Sergeant Owen Eastwood Collins, age 23 and from Tongaporutu, Taranaki in New Zealand, and of 166 Squadron went missing on this raid against Bochum. The aircraft was thought to have gone down into the sea off the Dutch coast. Collins has no known grave but his name is on the Runneymede Memorial.

In the month of March 1943, No.4 Group flew 660 sorties and its losses were 3.8 per cent. The newly formed Canadian No.6 Group flew 328 sorties and suffered a higher loss rate of 5 per cent.

There were a number of German fighter pilots who became 'aces'. One was Major Heinz-Wolfgang Schnaufer, who was stationed at St. Trond, Belgium. By August 1943 he had shot down some twenty bombers, and by the end of the war had 121 to his name. In 1950 he was killed in a car accident. He had been awarded the Iron Cross with Diamonds, Swords and Oak Leaves. Prince Heinrich zu Sayn-Wittgenstein, a Major and a Junker 88 pilot, was killed in January 1944, but not before he had destroyed some 83 bombers and been awarded the Iron Cross with Swords and Oak Leaves.

On the 2 April 1943, the first 'Pampa' flight by 1409 Flight took place, flying to France via Plymouth. This was the first of 1364 sorties over a period of 632 days that 1409 Flight was to make. Throughout this period, they suffered only three casualties.

The night of 3-4 April. Target — ESSEN

This operation, the third against Essen in less than a month, was the first in which over 200 Lancasters took part. It was a dark, cloudless night with visibility only moderate — the conditions were more suited for enemy night-fighters than they had been for some time. Ground-controlled night-fighters were heard operating in moderate numbers and seven bombers were claimed to have been shot down during this operation. The searchlights were intense and aircraft were held in cones and fired on by flak. Some aircraft were held at 20,000 feet and then forced down to the range of the light flak. In all, 42 aircraft came back with hits by flak.

The attack was led by ten *OBOE* Mosquitos using the 'musical parramatta'* technique. A further fifteen separate buildings at Krupps were damaged, of which three were main workshops. The housing space available for the essential workers at Krupps and Essen was reduced. Sixty-five per cent of the Goldschmidt factory which made soft metals and alloys, bearing metals and welding materials, was destroyed by fire. The destruction of the Wolff factory was likely to cause problems for the Germans. The Krupps harbour foundry works, which supplied the main Essen works with more than 1,000,000 tons of pig iron and steel ingots yearly, was damaged over an area of 100,000 square feet. Some 550 high explosive bombs and 526 incendiary bombs were dropped. Of these, 228 bombs were plotted and twelve were recorded later as not having gone off. This compared with the two previous raids in which 644 high explosive and 607 incendiary bombs were dropped on the 5 March, and 588 high explosive and 633 incendiary bombs were dropped on the 12 March. In these last two raids 180 bombs failed to go off.

After this raid on 3-4 April the Germans admitted for the first time that 'big damage' had been done to Essen. One big explosion at the time of the attack was recorded and another when the crew were near the Dutch coast on the return journey. No smoke was seen later coming from the chimneys in the Krupps works to indicate that they were working.

Sergeant Johnson and his crew of 419 Squadron were attacked by a Messerschmitt 110, which raked the Halifax with fire from nose to tail, wounding gunner Sergeant Thomson of the RCAT, who did manage to get a short burst of gunfire off before he was hit. The other gunner, Sergeant Wallis, was also wounded. Despite this attack Johnson did manage to land at Coltishall in Norfolk. Flying on this operation was the CO of 102 Squadron, Wing Commander George 'Spider' Holden, who was later killed while commanding 617 Squadron — The Dambusters. The bomb aimer, Sergeant Tom Wingham, remembers the flak being intense, but despite this, they bombed on the target indicators. The defences were so intense that Holden would not allow the use of 'George', the automatic pilot, until he was well clear of the target area. He was suffering greatly from sciatica at the time and had to relinquish command of 102 Squadron the next day.

The night of 8-9 April. Target — DUISBURG

Intense, heavy flak, coming through 10/10ths cloud and bursting up to 21,000 feet, was experienced on this operation. The Germans claimed that anti-aircraft artillery of the *Luftwaffe*, and the navy, and night-fighters,

* Was a method of marking a target blindly, without actually seeing it the flares were dropped and exploded so as the target could be identified. On this occasion they exploded on the ground as opposed to in the air and above the cloud.

shot down fifteen enemy aircraft. In fact, on this operation nineteen aircraft went missing and twenty-six more were damaged by flak.

The attack was led by three *OBOE* Mosquitos marking with the 'musical paramatta' and then later, the 'Wanganui' method. For this operation Sergeant Leonard Williamson was awarded the CGM. Despite his aircraft having been hit by heavy flak and badly damaged, he went on to bomb the target and made it back to base. At the time he was serving in 428 Squadron, who were still using Wellington bombers. A Mosquito of 109 Squadron, DZ 430, flown by Flying Officer Walker and his navigator, Flying Officer McKenna, took off from Wyton, Cambridgeshire, at 10.01p.m., for a 'marking' role on Duisburg but crashed two miles south-south-west of the airfield. It was thought that Walker, who was on his first operation, had got into difficulty while flying through cloud and executing a high-speed diving turn.

Thick cloud up to a height of 20,000 feet, was encountered on this operation. 'Icing' was also a problem with some aircraft becoming so heavy with ice that pilots had difficulity in controlling their aircraft. Pilot Officer Stovell was caught in a 'box' of flak, and when he took evasive action by diving, his aircraft was so heavy with ice that for a while he lost control, and gave the order to prepare to bale out. When they were down to 1000 feet, Stovell managed to re-gain control of the aircraft because three engines, which had stopped due to the effects of the ice, now re-started. He was then able to fly the aircraft back to base. For his efforts, he was awarded an immediate DFC.

The night of 9-10 April. Target — DUISBURG

On this operation the flak, which came through heavy cloud, was described as moderately heavy and accurate. It was predicted and also in barrage form. The Germans claimed to have shot down eight aircraft and this was in fact the number of aircraft that went missing on this operation. Four aircraft were damaged by flak.

In No.1 Group, 28 Lancasters claimed to have attacked the target dropping twenty-six 4000lb bombs, one thousand three hundred and forty-four 30lb incendiaries, plus one thousand one hundred and ten 4lb 'X' type incendiaries. The target was obscured by 10/10ths cloud and it was impossible to obtain ground detail. The first release point flares appeared to have been a minute or two late as a consequence a few aircraft bombed on their ETA. Other than this, the TI markers were punctually dropped and clearly seen, and there was evidence of a concentrated and well-directed attack having developed. The following are some comments from personal reports on this night's raid: 'A better effort than the previous night.' 'If the PFF were accurate, Duisburg should have had a nasty knock.' 'Excellent trip. Aircraft seemed to be well concentrated en route and over the target. Unfortunately PFF was not there at zero hour.'

When Flight Lieutenant Bickers's aircraft landed at Bodney, Norfolk, the undercarriage collapsed. All the trimmers had been shot away and the centre petrol tank holed and all the fuel lost. The fuselage was riddled with bullets, and the bomb doors had fallen open. The rear gunner, Sergeant Howell, had been killed and his turret set on fire. The mid-upper gunner, Sergeant Shaw, was half-way out of his turret when a second attack came and he was hit in the legs by the fighter's fire. The first attack had been so sudden, having come from below, that both gunners were too surprised to return fire.

Sergeant Broadbent and his crew of 57 Squadron reached the target and bombed it without any problems, but on their return trip, they were attacked by a Junkers 88 fighter which opened fire with cannon and machine guns from about 300 yards away. Both gunners returned fire, though the rear gunner's vision was partly obstructed by oil from one of the port engines, which had developed a leak on the outward journey. In the attack, the pilot's cabin was shattered. Broadbent's left shoulder was hit and three tendons in his left hand severed. The mid-upper gunner, Sergeant Young, was hit in the leg. The rear tyre had been punctured in the attack and the astrodome was completely blown away. Despite great loss of blood, the pilot made a good landing at Scampton in Lincolnshire. Both men were then taken to Rauceby Hospital. At the time, Broadbent had only five operations in his log-book, having only been with 57 Squadron for a month. For his efforts, he was awarded an immediate DFM.

As on the Essen raid of 12-13 March, bomb aimer Tom Osborn was once again lucky. When he inspected his aircraft the next morning, he found four holes in the front turret from flak hits. If he had been in the turret at the time, there is no doubt he would have been wounded or even killed. Whenever he visits the Australian War Memorial, the memory of those two operations come flooding back.

On the 10 April 1943, Goebbels visited Essen and described the damage from the three raids as: 'Colossal and indeed, ghastly.' When he visited the Krupps factory he demanded an increase in flak guns to defend the factory. The idea of moving the factory to another city or town was considered but soon dismissed on the basis that wherever it was moved to, the English would find and bomb it. He now admitted he had a real picture of the English air warfare, and what it meant.

The night of 16-17 April. Target — MANNHEIM

The raid on Mannheim in fact was a diversionary raid to the raid on Pilsen, code-name for the op was 'Mannheim Chubb'. The attack was highly satisfactory, the target having been accurately identified and marked by the PFF. Large fires were started and photographic evidence showed that considerable damage had been done. Hits were scored on the workshops of IG Farben, a synthetic-oil producer, and the works of Joseph Vogele AG, who produced components for tanks and tractors, and here the damage was devastating, with some five and a half acres being destroyed. Damage was done to the sheds and warehouses in the docks area, causing problems for the transport vessels using the River Rhine, and adding to the much greater destruction lower down the river at Duisburg, Düsseldorf and Cologne.

Of the 271 aircraft despatched, 225 attacked the target, and some 18 went missing and 30 were damaged by flak. The method of attack was 'musical parramatta' using green and red flares. Seven Stirling bombers were operating with H2S. The flak encountered was moderate to intense heavy and operating, as usual, with the searchlights. The bombers had been instructed to cross the English coast at a high level and then to drop down to 2000 feet to cross the known fighter area. This seemed to meet with the approval of the crews.

Sergeant Hartwell's aircraft of 214 Squadron was attacked by a Messerschmitt fighter on the homeward trip from Mannheim. During the attack the rear turret's hydraulic system was damaged, though the rear gunner, Sergeant Elliott did manage to fire off 200 rounds before his turret was put out of action. The mid-upper gunner, following the rear gunner's instructions, fired off 300 to 400 rounds. A crash-landing was made at base in which the pilot was injured.

As Flying Officer Upton's aircraft of 166 Squadron crossed the coast at Dungeness, it started to loose height as per instructions. But then the port engine cut out and then picked up again, the rear gunner hearing the pilot say: 'Oh Christ! The three engines are icing up, we'll have to turn back,' and then after a while: 'It's okay, they're picking up again.' However, all was not well, as the starboard engine began to stall and the aircraft lost height very quickly. When they were down to 200 feet, ditching orders were given. The aircraft struck the water nose first. Water began to enter the aircraft rapidly. The rear gunner and the navigator managed to get clear of the aircraft as it broke into two parts. The rear gunner arrived at the dinghy first and helped the navigator in. On hearing the shouts of the rest of the crew they paddled the dinghy towards them. The bomb aimer, Sergeant Merton, was supporting Upton in the water; both had broken their backs, and Merton also had a large hole in his forehead. They managed to get Merton into the dinghy, but he died three hours later and was buried at sea. Upton had failed to get into the dinghy and was drowned. As for Sgt William Whitfield, the wireless operator, there was no trace of him from the time of the crash. His and Sergeant Merton's names are recorded on the Runneymede Memorial as having no known graves. It was five days before they were spotted by Typhoon aircraft on patrol, who summoned up help in the form of an RAF Air Sea Rescue (ASR) launch, and guided them to where the dinghy was.

Flight Sergeant O'Connor's aircraft of 15 Squadron came back with 300 holes, having been attacked by a Messerschmitt 109 on the return journey. The rear gunner, Sergeant Sherar, and the enemy night-fighter opened fire at the same time, at a range of 500 yards. The fighter's attack damaged the starboard inner engine. They were then attacked by a second Messerschmitt 109 from dead ahead and at the same time, the first Messerschmitt 109 attacked from below and further hits were scored on the British plane. The mid-upper gunner, Sergeant Gayler, managed to get a burst in on one fighter as it passed below. The second Messerschmitt 109 had scored hits on three propellers and the front turret; the gunner had returned fire and managed to avoid being hit, although one bullet was deflected by some coins he had in his pocket. In a third attack, the front gunner managed to hit the fighter and claim it as damaged. In yet another attack, no further damage was done to the British plane, but Sergeant Gayler was able to fire 400 rounds and saw a fire break out in the fighter's nose. The rear and mid-upper gunners saw it go down in a steep dive and explode on the ground. This was confirmed by the rest of the crew as they saw it burning on the ground.

Pilot Officer White and his crew in 90 Squadron were not destined to be so lucky. At 2.11a.m. and three minutes flying time from Laon in France, there was a sudden explosion in the bomb aimer's position, and at the same time the navigator felt a sting on his hand as his instrument panel fell to pieces in front of him. They were then picked up by a searchlight. Rear gunner Sergeant Fitzgerald asked: 'Shall I shoot?' He was then heard to fire and the searchlight went out. The pilot had been wounded in the wrist and the wireless operator Sergeant Gaisford went forward to bandage it for him. When one of the engines stopped after overheating, they had to crash land. The pilot and second pilot were thrown out through the windscreen. The rear gunner was hanging by his oxygen mask, it was still connected to the oxygen supply. They had crashed on a sloping field, one of the aircraft's wings having hit a tree; the tail unit had broken off and the port wing was on fire. Sergeant Wallace Phillips the second pilot, had been knocked out in the crash and injured his ear. He was given first aid by the French in the area and a doctor later stitched his cut head. He was kept in a house at Chauny till the 15 May, but did get to Gibraltar on the 23 June and Hendon in the UK on the 25 June. Sergeant John Ford the mid-upper gunner, arrived in Gibraltar on the 17 July and from there after travelling by ship, arrived in Liverpool 24 July. Sergeant Gaisford arrived at Portreath in Cornwall, on the 23 June. Sergeant Fitzgerald remembers seeing a stream of bullets sweeping across the Stirling, wounding pilot Officer White, who was also hurt in the chest by the aircraft controls. White was on the last trip of his first tour of operations. the rest of the crew Pilot Officer Ross, the bomb aimer, Sergeant Smith, the flight engineer and Flying Officer Everiss, the navigator all evaded capture and got back to the UK; but White, probably because he was weak from his injuries, was taken prisoner.

The night of 26-27 April. Target — DUISBURG

A force of 561 aircraft was launched on Duisburg. It was the most concentrated air attack yet made. Nearly 1500 tons of bombs fells at the rate of more than 30 tons a minute on to the smallest area ever to receive such a load. The flak was moderate to intense and assisted by the large number of searchlights in the town. The Germans claimed to have shot down 31 bombers, but in actual fact the figure was seventeen shot down and 54 damaged by flak and four more damaged by night-fighters. Of the seventeen lost, the causes were thought to be nine lost to flak, five to night-fighters and three to unknown causes. By 2a.m. the night-fighter system was already reacting strongly. Patrols from Alkmaar, Amsterdam, Arnhem and Venlo were airborne in close succession. From one of the Alkmaar patrols the following message was picked up to translate to: 'Have you a hostile for me already?' The fighter went on to chase a bomber for eleven minutes before the bomber was able to shake him off. As a result of this chase, the fighter went out of its area of patrol, which allowed a number of other bombers to slip through successfully.

The whole of the central town of Duisburg was wrecked and numerous warehouses, factories and colliery buildings were gutted by fire in the port area and elsewhere. One Lancaster pilot who took part in the raid reported: 'The whole Duisburg area seemed ablaze with incendiaries. The glare from them was so intense that it was difficult to pick out ground details. We dropped our bombs as the white glare was turning to red, showing that the fires had caught and were beginning to spread.' Another pilot who bombed towards the end of the raid said: 'The fires in the port area gave it the appearance of a cauldron bubbling with angry molten metal which spurted up every now and then as more and more bombs exploded.' The ground marking was recorded as being fairly accurate. This was undertaken by nine *OBOE* Mosquitos at 2.13a.m. from a height of 2800 feet, using the 'musical paramatta' method with Green TIs on Red. Crews were able to identify the target visually despite 5/10ths cloud at 1000 feet.

For Pilot Officer Frank Plumb of 115 Squadron it was to be an eventful start to his 24th operation. Immediately after take-off, the aircraft's constant speed unit on the starboard outer engine failed, and this increased the engine's r.p.m. The pilot reduced the r.p.m. by using the propeller decrease switch which enabled the aircraft to continue climbing, and once at a safe height, he returned this switch to the automatic position, as by now the engine was getting hot and the oil pressure dropping. Despite all this Plumb decided to continue, reducing the engine's r.p.m. by throttling back. He managed to complete the sortie despite the aircraft flying on only three engines. On his return he was recommended for an immediate DFC.

The Wellington BK 619, flown by Pilot Officer Peter Buck of 75 Squadron, and on his 26th operation, was actually on its bombing-run when it was attacked by a night-fighter. In the attack, the rudder and tail were hit and damaged, and the rear gunner, Sergeant Rogers, mortally wounded. Two other members of the crew suffered minor injuries. One of them was Pilot Officer Symons, a Canadian, who was hit in the hand and in considerable pain but still managed to tap out messages with his damaged hand for the rest of the flight. These messages enabled the aircraft to be guided home on the shortest route, a distance of 300 miles. During this flight the starboard engine failed but they still managed to reach their home base in Newmarket, where a successful crash landing was made.

Wing Commander Leslie Crooks took over 426 Squadron after it had suffered serious losses, and by his leadership and untiring work, the squadron was able to reach a high standard of operational efficiency. In the month of March it had maintained a daily aircraft serviceability of 100 per cent. On the operation of 26-27 April, he was about twenty miles short of the target, when his aircraft was raked by cannon fire from an enemy fighter. By evasive action he shook off the fighter and continued towards the target, but when Flight Lieutenant Francis Marsh, the squadron signals leader, inspected the damage he found it was impossible to release the bombs, so the attack was abandoned. The damage sustained amounted to one aileron and half the port tailplane shot away, and the hydraulic and electrical systems put out of action. Coffee from the thermos flasks and oil from the rear turret was poured into the emergency hydraulic system. Flight Lieutenant Marsh spent over an hour trying to fix the hydraulic system and to pump the wheels down by hand into the locked position for landing. This attempt failed and as the bombs were still aboard, Wing Commander Crooks gave the order to abandon the aircraft, which eventually crashed at Stonegrave in Yorkshire. When landing by parachute Crooks sprained his ankle, and Pilot Officer Power also hurt his foot when landing. For their efforts on this operation, Crooks was awarded the DSO and Marsh and Flying Officer Donald Simpson the navigator, were awarded DFCs. This abortive raid was a fine example of how a crew fought to survive and tried to bring their aircraft back to base.

On this operation against Duisburg all the aircrews had to cope with a 60m.p.h. gale tailwind, with occasional gusts of up to 100m.p.h. recorded.

The night of 30 April-1 May. Target — ESSEN

Of the ten Mosquitos detailed to mark the target on this operation, only seven were successful. Every effort was made at the briefings to ensure the crews knew that the 'skymarking' method was to be used. All aircraft were detailed to climb before crossing the English coast and fly above the thick cloud expected between the Dutch coast and Essen. The 'skymarking' was to be performed at five-minute intervals.

Full cloud cover over the target rendered the enemy's searchlights ineffective, though the flak was heavy, both predicted and in barrage form. Although the searchlights failed to penetrate the cloud, they were very active and illuminated the cloud layer.

It was in the Egmond/Amsterdam area that a night-fighter was patrolling the inward route of the British aircraft. At 2.18a.m. the same pilot claimed that a bomber had crashed in flames. In all some 34 sorties were flown by ground-controlled night-fighters, of which 14 were heard operating in connection with Bomber Command activities, and 12 interceptions were made. One other German claim made, and intercepted was at 3.23a.m. south-east of Deelen. In each case the British aircraft was stated to be burning. In all, the Germans claimed to have shot down only six aircraft whereas in fact twelve went missing, seven of which were thought to have been shot down by flak in the target area and five to night-fighters. Thirty-seven aircraft were damaged by flak and one aircraft was lost to causes unknown.

The No.1 Group pilots reported that the technique used by the PFF was admirably suited to the conditions and their timing was excellent. At 3a.m. a large explosion was seen by crews already twenty minutes away from the target area on their way home. One aircraft of 103 Squadron collided with another aircraft over the target area, but on this occasion both aircraft got away with only slight damage. During the period of Bomber Command's operations against the Ruhr, it was thought that many aircraft were lost due to colliding with one another.

In the reports from Australian squadrons it was stated that no fewer than eight aircraft were hit by barrage-type fire while over the target, two being thrown over on to their backs by the blast. Flight Sergeant Christenson of 460 Squadron was forced to dive down to 1500 feet before regaining control of his madly plunging Lancaster. Flying Officer Thomas Archibald, who was only on his fourth operation and flying in a Halifax of 77 Squadron, was able to bomb the target from 19,000 feet but in so doing was repeatedly hit by flak, one burst rendering his starboard inner engine unserviceable. It was also discovered that when the bomb doors had been closed a 1000lb bomb was still inside, this was known as a 'hang up'. Archibald immediately turned to port and attacked the target once again, bombing the skymarkers from a lower height of 17,000 feet. His return trip was uneventful and he made an excellent landing with only three engines in use. When the aircraft was inspected, extensive damage, which had been caused by flak was revealed. The tail-wheel, fuselage, starboard mainplane, port elevator and port outer main plane plus the engine, were all badly damaged. The recommendation for his DFC was made on the 2 May 1943, and countersigned by Air Commodore GA Walker, known to all as 'Gus' while he was commanding at Pocklington, Walker remarked: 'This officer displayed courage and devotion to duty of the highest order. He is an officer who will lead and inspire others. Recommended for the immediate DFC.' This was high praise from a man who had done it all way back in 1940/41 as a bomber pilot with 50 Squadron.

For another crew there would be no accolades or awards. Sergeant Glotham and his crew, flying in Lancaster ED 706, took off from Scampton, Lincolnshire, bound for Essen. They were known to have come under attack while over Holland and came down in the Zuider Zee area to the east of Amsterdam. No trace was found of the crew or aircraft, until in 1987, when land was being reclaimed from the sea in the area now known as South Flevoland, a drainage engineer came across fragments of metal. A recovery team from the Royal Netherlands Air Force excavated the site and found the wreckage of Lancaster ED 706. Human remains were also found and interred in the Canadian War Cemetery at Groesbeek which is south of Nijmegen. Up to that time the names of Sergeant William John Glotham and his crew were inscribed on the Runneymede Memorial, panel 150, as having no known grave. In 1987 a service of remembrance was held at the Cemetery and attended by members of the crew's families. They laid wreaths, as did the RAF, Bomber Command Association and the RAF Escaping Society, a Society founded in 1945 for men who had evaded or escaped capture.

This raid on Essen brought the total tonnage of bombs dropped on the city to 10,000 tons, the greatest tonnage dropped on any town or city in the world to date. In this attack the Krupps factory was again hit and damaged. On this operation this ice was recorded by crews up to 20,000 feet, the temperature down to 28 degrees below freezing on the outside of the aircraft. The ice was so severe that many aircraft had their trailing aerial snapped off, and this was in the month of April.

Sergeant Ronald Goddard of 78 Squadron, who came from Tilbury, was navigator of the Halifax bomber which, when on course to Bochum, developed trouble with its outer starboard and port engines. The port engine also caught fire. The pilot, Sergeant Bane, gave the crew the order that they hoped they would never hear or have to obey, 'bale out'. They were at the time south of Louvain. Sergeant Goddard was the first to leave the aircraft. He landed in a cornfield near Hamme Mille, in Belgium. During the afternoon of the next day he was approached by two peasants. Goddard recalls as per his report:

> They asked me if I was RAF. I admitted that I was and one of the peasants went away and later returned with beer and food. They later told me to go after dark, to a farm about a mile away. The farmer took me in and gave me a meal, he also found me a linen coat, a pair of pin stripe trousers and boots but would not take any payment. That night I slept in the farmhouse, and next morning he gave me a flask of coffee and food and told me to hide in the cornfield which at the time, had not been cut. Later that day the farm was visited by a Belgian policeman, and on a bicycle loaned by the farmer, I set off behind the policeman to Pietrebais and his home where I spent the night. The next day he took me to another village and from here my escape was arranged for me.

Goddard arrived in Gibraltar on 8 July, and Hendon, by air, on the 9 July. On the 29 July, for successfully evading capture, he was recommended for the DFM.

The last place a crew saw on the station after take-off was the Control Tower, in this case at RAF East Kirby in Lincolnshire. This is still preserved and can be visited. Today it is owned by Mr Panton, a farmer, whose brother was killed flying on his twenty-ninth operation with Bomber Command. (Author's collection)

One of those always waiting with a kind word and a cup of tea laced with rum was the Station Padre. In this photograph he is talking to a Halifax pilot. (Imperial War Museum)

Krupps factory in Essen 1945 showing the extensive damage from the RAF attacks from 1943 on. (Mike King)

The cost was high as seen by the rear turret of a Stirling the day after returning from an operation. (Norman Didwell)

9 A Bloody Battle

The sorties or operations mounted by No.4 Group in the month of April 1943, totalled 755, and the losses to night-fighters 6.22 per cent. In No.6 Group the sorties totalled 197, much lower than No.4 Group, but their losses were higher at 7.6 per cent. Overall aircraft losses in Bomber Command were steadily increasing. In March 51 aircraft were lost and 26 damaged, whereas in April 67 aircraft were lost and 33 damaged. But one has to take into consideration the greater number of operations and aircraft involved during April as opposed to March. To only lose 51 aircraft out of 755 sorties against an area like the Ruhr, says a lot for the dedication and skill of the operating crews.

In the Canadian 429 Squadron, four aircraft were lost in March and the same number in April. It's not only the number of crews lost which is detrimental, but who one loses because if, as this squadron did, you lose the commanding officer and a flight commander within a period of two weeks, then it is quite a blow, and naturally morale will be affected, particularly among the new 'freshman' crews who must have wondered what chance did they have if such experienced men were getting the 'chop'. Warrant Officer Eddie Edmunds (who had already completed a tour way back in 1940 when it was not unusual to fly to Berlin with no more than a force of four aircraft) remembers that morale among the crews was low and they were also superstitious. One example of this was the case of an attractive WAAF driver who, after going out with a few crewmen, was branded a jinx by everyone when it was suddenly realized each one of the crewmen had not returned or had got 'the chop'. Eventually she was posted away from the squadron.

The night of 4-5 May. Target — DORTMUND

The town of Dortmund had the code-name 'Sprat', and was attacked on this occasion by the largest four-engine bomber force so far despatched in the war. It was also the first major attack on Dortmund. The force consisted of 596 aircraft led by ten *OBOE* Mosquitos which dropped yellow TIs en route and Green TIs on the aiming point. This was backed up by red TIs dropped by Lancaster and Halifax bombers. However, these fell short by up to a mile north of the green TIs, though 50 per cent of the attacking aircraft still managed to bomb within three miles of the aiming point. Damage was widespread and severe caused mainly by fire. Some 45 acres of the industry of Dortmund, including 28 factories, were destroyed.

Two of the factories were priority targets — Dortmund Union and Hoesch Iron and Steel. The Germans called this raid *Grossangriff* (Big Raid).

The German estimation of the number of aircraft involved in this raid (120 to 150) was inaccurate. They also estimated that the weight of bombs dropped was 1750 tons, whereas it was in fact 1500 tons. The Germans stated that 693 people were killed in the attack, including 220 POWs and 75 foreigners. There were estimated to be 4193 fires of which 379 were classified as *Grossbrande* (Big Fires). In the town itself 1218 houses were destroyed and 88 industrial plants were hit.

The flak encountered was moderate to intense, in a predicted and barrage form. There was also considerable light flak up to 13,000-15,000 feet used in co-operation with 20 to 50 searchlights. In all it was estimated that some 200 searchlight, were active, mainly north and north-west of the town. The Germans reported that: 'British bombers attacked west German territory, mainly the town of Dortmund. Night-fighters and anti-aircraft guns of the *Luftwaffe* shot down 38 of the attacking aircraft, which were mainly four-engined bombers. Five were brought down by defensive fire from units of the German Navy, three multi-engine bombers being shot down over the Netherlands alone. The number of enemy aircraft shot down by naval anti-aircraft guns has risen to eleven. In fact thirty aircraft went missing, 29 aircraft were damaged by flak and three damaged by enemy aircraft. Of the missing aircraft it was estimated that sixteen were lost to night-fighters, nine to flak and the rest to unknown causes.

The night photographs plotted confirmed the crew reports, the largest concentration were in the centre of the town in the closely built-up area. There was also a large concentration about two miles north-east of the town centre. This covered an important group of industrial targets, namely Hoesch-Koln-Neuessen AG. The steel works of this firm had an annual capacity of 1,500,000 tons and produced shells and forgings for tanks. In the same area were extensive marshalling yards and a benzine plant. The German communiqué admitted that considerable damage had been done to buildings in the town. There was every reason for Bomber Command to believe that the attack had been successful and that another Ruhr town had been disabled for some time.

Sergeant Powell finished his training at the end of April 1943, and was posted to 102 Squadron at Pocklington, Yorkshire. Within two days he had taken part in a mine-laying operation off the Dutch coast. His 'baptism of fire', however, came on the trip to Dortmund. Powell recalls: 'As a "fresher" crew, we set out in a confident mood, the light of the shell-bursts from the intense heavy flak barrage appeared like a wall of cascading water in their density and one was suddenly aware that we had to run the gauntlet, and somehow penetrate the barrage successfully in order to deliver our bomb load on the chosen target — a terrifying ordeal at the time.' He and his crew survived their first real experience of bombing against the Ruhr with little more than slight damage to the aircraft's bomb doors, received on the homeward journey over Den Helder from an ack-ack unit on the Dutch coast. Continues Powell:

Each round trip to the Ruhr took on average five to six hours flying time and at least three hours of this was over enemy territory. Although the flak barrage was usually as fierce on each 'op', the more experienced you became the more you realized that there was ways of avoiding flak and searchlight beams, such as by jinking your aircraft from port to starboard and back, or gaining and losing height. These were just some of the manoeuvres we carried out in a battle of wits with the gunners on the ground below, in a effort to stop them gauging our range. At the same time you had to keep a sharp look-out for enemy fighters and friendly bombers in the area to avoid collisions. I think an even more terrifying experience than the flak barrage, was to be caught and coned by searchlights which swept across the sky in conjunction with the anti-aircraft guns. As soon as one beam locked on to an aircraft, as many as up to 30 or more would converge to form a cone. Suddenly your own little bit of sanctuary in the sky where you thought you were safely hidden, was engulfed in brilliant and dazzling light. For a split-second you were paralysed with fear until the fight for survival took over. The aircraft was caught like a fly in a web trying desperately to extricate itself before the gunners could get a bearing on it. Not many survived such attention from searchlights and flak. The only hope was to get clear before the searchlights could form a cone. On a number of occasions I observed bombers held in cones of searchlights and watched helplessly as the shell-bursts got nearer the aircraft until suddenly, flames appeared and sometimes a violent explosion; sometimes you would see parachutes open and flutter away. Then it was back to the empty blackness in that spot in the sky as the searchlights sought out more prey to pounce on.'

Of the 15 raids that he had made on the Ruhr, the one that Flight Sergeant Rowe of 103 Squadron remembers most vividly was the Dortmund operation of 4-5 May. He recalls:

> Our crew, being inexperienced, went to the target. The fires were unbelieveable, I could see Wellingtons silhouetted against the glare of the fires, probably a mile or a mile and a half away and below us. A couple of days after this raid I was having a night vision test, and with me were a few Wellington crews from 166 Squadron. I said to them how sorry I felt for them on the Dortmund raid as they appeared to be right on top of the fires. They replied by saying they had felt sorry for us as we had received all the flak, and they had a free run.

Tom Thackray of 10 Squadron remembers this period well because it was after the Dortmund raid that they began formation-flying training, and they assumed they would be joining the Americans on daylight operations. Recalls Thackeray: 'The crews seemed to come and go, the only ones you got to know were the lucky ones who got to stay alive for a few weeks. The route to the Ruhr was always the same, in and out on the same track, flying over the huge searchlight cones at Amsterdam and Rotterdam; but they did have their advantages to navigators who could use them as pin-points for the journey. In Tom's crew, rear gunner Jock MacFarlane from Glasgow always made the same remark before an operation: 'Oh well, here we go again arse first into the Third Reich.'

For Flight Sergeant Bowman, flying in Halifax W 7820 of 102 Squadron, this was to be a very eventful night. After they had successfully bombed the target from 17,000 feet (Sergeant Tregunno saw the bombs burst near the green ground-markers) they were hit by heavy flak and lost an engine. They proceeded for some while on three engines, but then the starboard outer engine also gave up. Despite being reduced to two engines, Bowman was able to keep the aircraft at 8000 feet until they were about 100 miles off Flamborough Head, when the port outer engine also failed. The pilot was then compelled to ditch the aircraft into the North Sea some 75 miles off Flamborough Head; the time was 3.14a.m. They were later picked up unhurt by the RAF Air Sea Rescue.

One crew of 196 Squadron were known as the 'Veterans Wellington Club'. This crew of five young men with an average age of 23, had between them, completed no less than 236 operations. The pilot, Warrant Officer T Mellor, a former accountant from Derby aged 25, had 29 operations in his log-book. The bomb aimer, Flight Sergeant H Webb, a former clerk from Market Harborough had, despite being only 21, no less than 56 operations to his credit. The navigator, Warrant Officer Leslie Quick from Taunton and aged 23, had completed 54 operations. Flight Sergeant L Alison, the rear gunner, and a former glass worker from Chelmsford, had 51 operations to his credit, and wireless operator, Flight Sergeant R Williamson, a former shop assistant from Darlington aged 21, had completed 46 operations. Later, Warrant Officer Quick was commissioned and awarded the DFC in September 1943. As a crew they went on to complete another three operations making a total of 239. On the trip to Dortmund they flew Wellington HE 980. This bomber was later lost together with another crew on a raid to Cologne in July 1943.

On this operation to Dortmund a Lancaster of 103 Squadron, ED 888 and called M for Mother, became known as 'Mother of them All'. This was M for Mother's second operation and for Flying Officer Nick Ross, the pilot, it was his fortieth. Nick had also flown it on its first operation — the Essen raid of the 30 April. He remembers the aircraft being very new and smelling of new paint and camouflage. All the controls were stiff and needed running-in, very much like a new car. This aircraft went on to fly no less than 140 operations, something Nick forty years later was surprised about but also very pleased that the 'old lady' had done so well, and survived the war. He remarked, 'it makes my own effort of 77 operations seem very meagre'. He remembers the Ruhr as being 'one hell of a place'. He said: 'It didn't matter which town or city was the target, you were pooped at by all the other surrounding communities on the way in and out. I found this medically beneficial, as a trip to the Ruhr did more for me than a packet of All Bran. I also had a love for the smell of cordite and I used to fly through as many flak puffs as I could find, which wasn't too hard.'

This operation was the first one for Sergeant Noble, flight engineer with 78 Squadron. He recalls:

> Prior to take-off I felt a little nervous but this soon disappeared when the Halifax thundered down the runway and took off. Except for a little flak on the way the trip was uneventful until we approached the target, then all hell seemed to let loose. There seemed to be searchlights everywhere, we were almost caught by one on the run-in. When we had released our bombs we were caught in a cone of searchlight beams. Our pilot tried all the manoeuvres in the book to dodge them, but there was no let-up. Eventually we went into a spin from 17,000 feet ending up at a height of 2000 feet and with one engine on fire. I remember the dreadful pain in my ears and the problem of trying to regain my feet. Somehow we were able to feather the engine and put out the fire. Then we were again coned and fired upon by the flak gunners, but Sergeant Kent the rear gunner, was able to fire on the searchlight and put it out.

Wing Commander John Searby, who had taken over from Wing Commander Guy Gibson as CO of 106 Squadron, recorded that the course taken to Dortmund was bad, but the raid itself successful though the flak had been heavy and accurate. For some crews the weather on the return to the UK was worse than coping with the guns and fighters in the Ruhr area. In No.3 Group the airfields at Graveley in Cambridgeshire were closed at 2a.m. because of fog. For its Station Commander, Group Captain Menaul, DFC, AFC, the morning of the 5 May proved to be quite a headache. At 2.10a.m. a Wellington reported being in difficulties and asked to land. At 2.45a.m. Wyton airfield reported a hostile aircraft flying towards Graveley. At 3a.m. an unidentified aircraft landed without permission and crashed through the fence at the end of a runway which was in use at the time, though now it would have to be closed. At 3.23a.m. more aircraft were coming in; F-Fox had only two engines working, S-Sugar was short of petrol, Q-Queenie of 35 Squadron, whose home base was Graveley, had its engine overheating, and K-King, also of 35 Squadron, was short of petrol. Visibility was now down to 1200 yards. At 3.28a.m. it was down to 800 yards. At the time, FIDO* was not completed on the airfield, and so could not be used to help the aircraft in. S-Sugar landed at 3.30a.m. F-Fox landed at 3.50a.m. but got stuck at the end of the main runway. Y-York was given permission to land at 4.05a.m. only to crash four minutes later into trees by the old Elizabethan manor house called Toseland Hall. The aircraft burnt out. No one saw or heard the crash, owing to the fog. Only one of the crew, Sergeant Robertson the rear gunner, survived. He was

* FIDO (Fog Investigation Dispersal Operation)

found still in his turret which had broken away from the main body of the aircraft.

By now the strain on the Flying Control Staff at Graveley was immense. In addition to the intense radio traffic from aircraft in distress, all the telephones were ringing, with calls coming from Group HQ requiring information, and distant stations enquiring about their own aircraft. Also, visiting aircraft had to be guided to dispersals in the bad weather conditions. At 4.13a.m. K-King, flown by Sergeant Wright, landed with only fifteen minutes petrol left. At 4.20a.m. E-Easy and C-Charley of 35 Squadron were instructed to divert as the runway was blocked, but owing to difficulty in receiving, they did not appear to get this instruction, as E-Easy made two attempts to land, then nothing was heard of this aircraft as it climbed towards the west. In the meantime C-Charley had landed at Oulton, Suffolk. Then a message came at 7a.m. from RAF police to say they had picked up an NCO who had baled our from E-Easy. At 7.30a.m. a message came from Chelverston to say that the other six members of E-Easy had also baled out and were safe. The aircraft had crashed near Waraton in Northamptonshire.

There was a humorous side to this very serious and harrowing night. Shortly after these events, the school of Flying Control in Watchfield, Oxfordshire, gave every pupil an extract from the log-book dealing with this night, and then asked each of them if they wished to proceed with the course.

A member of 405 Squadron, Dennis Whittaker, has vivid memories of this night:

> When we arrived back over our base, we were told it was shut down owing to dense fog. After trying another airfield and failing to land, we returned to our own base once again but it was still shut down. So we then went to a FIDO drome which was Graveley but as we tried to land, a 'darky' distress call came from another aircraft. This aircraft came to land and crashed a few miles from the runway. [Probably Y-York which crashed near Toseland Hall]. We were now short of petrol and so decided if we were to get in we should send a 'darky' call, which we did. On came three SANDRA [Contact Airfield Lights] lights over the airfield. We were asked if we could see them, and replied 'Yes', also that we could see the watch-tower. We were then give permission to land but still we could not get in. So we set off towards the east. Later, as we came out of the cloud there, as clear as bell, lay an airfield with its lights on, but as we made for it we nearly collided with a Stirling who was obviously hell-bent on the same thing. Somehow we missed each other. By now our pilot was very tired and suddenly dropped twenty feet as we came into land; this threw me on to my back but I suffered no injury.

During the month of May 1943, there was a moon period stand-down. The moon was the last thing that the bombers wanted because in clear visibility and moonlight, not only were the night-fighters up looking for prey but so also were the day-fighters. This would mean heavy casualties and so a stand-down order was given until moonless nights were forecast.

On occasion crews would arrive at their aircraft and be told that the mission was aborted. On one occasion a crew were actually on the runway and ready to take-off when it was called off. All they wanted to do was get off and get the operation completed or, if it was cancelled, to get off down into the town. Life was simpler then, it was one thing or the other.

The night of 12–13 May. Target — DUISBURG

This was to be the fourth attack on Duisburg during the Battle of the Ruhr. Some 562 aircraft attacked on this night. Zero hour was 2a.m. The initial marking was done by nine Mosquitos dropping red TIs backed up by five Stirlings, five Halifaxes and fifteen Lancasters aiming green TIs at the red TIs. Eighty per cent of the red TIs fell within the aiming point and 85 per cent of the green TIs within three miles of the aiming point.

The weather was ideal and the attack centred squarely on Duisburg itself. In 45 minutes, 1600 tons of bombs were dropped, and 48 acres entirely burnt out. It was thought to be the *coup de grâce* for Duisburg. The whole of the city area was an inferno with smoke rising in great billows into the night sky. Great damage was inflicted in the suburb of Meiderich, and the main Duisburg railway station was destroyed. Considerable damage was done to important boiler works and many other factories including coke and benzol purifying plants, and chemical works. A shipbuilding yard was damaged and barges in the dock area were sunk; railway tracks were smashed and rolling-stock scattered. It was estimated that over 2000 buildings were destroyed by fire or made uninhabitable. So heavy was this raid, that the reconnaissance planes which went to Duisburg the next day found many of the fires still burning and a column of smoke rising to 10,000 feet over the dock area. One Halifax captain describing the operation said: 'As we turned away the place was filling up with fires, and when we reached the Zuider Zee, some 150 miles from Duisburg, on the way back home, the rear gunner could still see the fires.' Special rations were rushed to Duisburg by Nazi welfare organisations and some 2000 prisoners of war were to be used as forced labour to made necessary emergency repairs.

En route, many guns were observed at Amsterdam and some 50 searchlights at Egmond and Utrecht. The intelligence people reported some 160 sorties by ground-controlled night-fighters, all of which were directed against the bombers. Patrols were put up in no less than ten areas. Of the bombers missing, at least twelve were shot down in the Rotterdam and Arnhem areas. The German claim of having shot down 33 aircraft was in fact just one short of the actual figure, 34 or 6 per cent of the total force. Of these, eight were observed to have been shot down by flak in the target area. Overall, eighteen to twenty aircraft were observed shot down by nightfighters and fourteen to flak. This successful attack on Duisburg would now allow a transfer of effort to its two important satellite towns of Oberhausen and Mülheim.

Squadron Leader Keith Thiele, DSO, DFC, was on his second tour and on this operation was flying a Lancaster of 467 Squadron. He had nearly reached the target, when his aircraft was hit by a shellburst underneath the fuselage causing severe damage. This did not deter him however, and he carried on to bomb the target. While on the bombing-run and at 16,000 feet, the aircraft was caught in a cone of searchlights. Usually he would have taken evasive action, but in order to give his bomb aimer a chance of bombing successfully, he kept the aircraft flying straight. Just as the bomb aimer let the bombs go, the aircraft was once again hit by a shell, putting the two starboard engines out of action. The bursting flak also smashed the entire perspex on the starboard side of the pilot's and the bomb aimer's cabins. A shell splinter hit Thiele on the side of the head, dazing him. Despite being in a dazed condition and with two engines out of action, he still managed to elude the searchlights and got the aircraft back to base in Coltishall, Norfolk, at 3.55a.m. where he made a successful 'belly-landing'. For his efforts he was awarded an immediate bar to his DFC.

Whilst on their way to the target, Pilot Officer Young and his crew of 90 Squadron were attacked by a night-fighter. During the attack, rear gunner Sergeant William Devine was badly wounded in both legs, and his turret put out of action. Despite his wounds he was able to give his pilot detailed instructions as to where the fighter was during the four further attacks it made. Sergeant Devine was awarded an immediate DFM and Pilot Officer Young, the DFC. They eventually made a 'wheels-up' landing with its aircraft running along the ground on the belly at Stradishall in Suffolk.

Sergeant Francis Compton's aircraft was attacked with cannon fire by a Messerschmitt 110 which resulted in damage to the rudder, bomb doors and Nos.2, 3 and 4 petrol tanks. He returned fire and saw his tracer bullets enter the enemy aircraft which then reared up, stalled and disappeared out of sight through the clouds. This was witnessed by the flight engineer and it was claimed as probably destroyed. Some thirty minutes later they were again attacked by no less than four Messerschmitt 109s. A running battle proceeded with Compton coolly taking evasive action, until cloud was reached and the fighters lost at a height of 5000 feet.

Over Amsterdam, Warrant Officer Lee's aircraft of 35 Squadron was hit by flak and lost its starboard inner engine. Three of the crew were wounded. For Flying Officer Hale and his crew of 9 Squadron, it was a night of success. When they were attacked by a Junker 88, the two gunners, Sergeant Clark and Jones, both managed to get a good burst of fire into the belly of the enemy fighter.

Another crew of 35 Squadron had taken off at 12.23a.m. from Graveley and were flying on a gentle, weaving course when a twin-engine fighter was seen below them. The pilot, Flight Lieutenant Julian Sale, tried to manoeuvre the aircraft away from the enemy's fire but was still hit by the first burst. The intercom was put out of action, and the port petrol tanks and engine set on fire. The elevator control got jammed, the central column could not be pulled back and the aircraft went into a slight dive. The fire became more fierce and appeared to come from the vicinity of the rear spar. The crew attempted to open the front hatch but were unable to do so, probably because it had been damaged in the attack. So then they decided to go back to the rear exit. Suddenly as Sale was taking off his helmet, the port wing exploded and he hit his head on the roof of the aircraft. He regained consciousness as he was coming down in his parachute and landed in a tree at Oldenzaal in Holland, about eight miles from the German border. After he had landed he saw seven aircraft shot down and on the following night, while still hiding out, he saw five more shot down, all by fighters. He was the only member of his crew to evade capture. Two of the crew were killed and the remainder made prisoners of war. He arrived in Gibraltar on the 5 August 1943, and reached Liverpool six days later. On the 12 September 1943, he was recommended for an immediate DSO. In his recommendation, it was mentioned that in evading capture he had passed through Germany, Holland, Belgium and then crossed the Pyrenees mountains into Andorra, before arriving in Barcelona, Spain. In all, he had covered 1252 miles, of which a great part was covered walking or riding a bike. It is sad to have to relate that nearly a year to the day later, Julian, who came from Toronto, was once again shot down on a raid to Leipzig. On this occasion his luck ran out and he died of his wounds in a German hospital.

This raid on Duisburg was Sergeant Joe Clark's second operation as a flight engineer with 100 Squadron and coincided with his 19th birthday. Sergeant Fred Fennel was the pilot of a Stirling that was flying at its maximum height for a full load of bombs — 12,000 feet. At this height, it was soon picked up by the flak gunners. A burst of flak and the subsequent splinters resulting from the flak, smashed the windscreen. As soon as the searchlights began to seek out the attacking bombers, Fennel lowered his seat and kept his head down below the windscreen to concentrate on the speed, height and course of the aircraft. This also prevented him from being blinded by the searchlights.

On the 14 May 1943, Goebbels recorded in his diary: 'During the night there was another exceptionally heavy raid on Duisburg. Even though it did not prove quite as disastrous as we had reason to assume it was, nevertheless, an exceedingly heavy bombardment. An unspeakable sorrow and great distress has come to the sorely tried city. Our technical development as regards submarine missions and air warfare is far inferior to that of the English and the Americans. During the past five months the enemy has had the upper hand, almost everywhere he is defeating us in the air.'

The night of 13-14 May. Target — BOCHUM

The attack on the 13-14 May was the second on this town during the Ruhr campaign. The plan of attack was to drop yellow TIs between Düsseldorf and Cologne as a navigational aid and then to drop red TIs on the aiming point at intervals throughout the attack. The red TIs were to be backed up by green TIs dropped by Stirlings of 7 Squadron. Of the ten Mosquitos detailed from 109 Squadron, only five were actually able to attack the aiming point owing to a considerable amount of technical trouble. The first two markers were dropped successfully but there was a gap until towards the end of the raid. The backing-up was well spread-out during the raid and tended to be short of the aiming point. Some green TIs were dropped as much as two miles short of the red TIs and with no further red TIs to 're-centre' the attack, the green TIs tended to creep back well short of the target. This accounted for considerable damage being done on a concentration two miles from the aiming point, and five miles to the south of Bochum. It was thought that crews were mistaking fires for red TIs, which had happened before in other raids.

Considerable activity from heavy flak and searchlights could be seen over the whole of the Ruhr area, and from the northern defences of Cologne over 150 searchlights were observed. The flak was presumed to be from 105mm or even larger guns. Few searchlights and very little flak was found over Bochum itself. The bombing-runs were carried out from south to north.

Very extensive damage was revealed by day reconnaissance photographs. From this time, until the end of the war, the productive capacity of Bochum was on average 45 per cent less compared with its pre-1943 level. This raid was timed so as to prolong the interruption to eastbound traffic caused by the Dortmund raid some ten days earlier. Both Bochum and Dortmund were key railway points into which the Ruhr complex of tracks met up before leaving eastwards via Hans Soesot and Schwerte. It was doubtful whether any appreciable quantity of freight would have been able to avoid these two bottle-necks until the block caused by the bombing had been removed. There were many hits on tracks and embankments and to the main passenger and goods stations.

A German report stated: 'During last night British aircraft penetrated into Reich territory on a broad front and attacked some places in western and central Germany, including small rural communities, with incendiary and high explosive bombs. The population suffered losses. Thirty-four enemy bombers have so far been reported shot down. Hauptmann [Flight Lieutenant] Lutje scored six victories as a night-figher pilot.' The official figure for missing aircraft was 33, of which ten were lost on the alternative target for that night, Pilsen. Some aircraft flying towards the target at Bochum were observed to be shot down by flak and by night-fighters. On their way home, 55 aircraft were damaged by flak and three by fighters.

A Stirling flown by Sergeant Griffiths of 149 Squadron was attacked by a Focke-Wulf 190 which opened fire when 800 yards away. Both gunners, Sergeants Price and Malley returned fire. In the course of the violent evasive action taken by Griffiths, it appeared that a flare came out of the aircraft's flare-chute and exploded, setting the aircraft on fire. The rear turret became useless as rounds of ammunition in the servo-ducts were exploding and jamming in the ducts. The heat expanded the rear gunner's doors and he was unable to get out of his turret. It was left to the flight engineer to put out the fire and then with the aid of an axe, force the jammed doors open and get the rear gunner out.

Another Stirling bomber, this one of 218 Squadron, was attacked on the outward route to Bochum. The enemy's cannon-fire killed rear gunner Sergeant Howard and wounded the mid-upper gunner, Sergeant Cleaveland. The aircraft was badly damaged in this attack. The intercom was put out of action. By the time the aircraft reached home base at Chedburgh, Suffolk, they were short of petrol, and when attempting to land, hit a tree and crashed. Four of the crew were killed instantly, including the wounded Cleaveland. The navigator, Pilot Officer Ted Pierce, was thrown clear and only suffered a sprained ankle and shock. The pilot, Sergeant Nichols and the flight engineer Sergeant Warre, later died in hospital.

For Sergeant Hicks of 428 Squadron who, only a month before had been awarded the CGM, the trip was once again to be eventful. After bombing their target successfully, they had trouble on the way home with a port and then a starboard engine. Despite having the use of only two engines, Hicks was able to fly the aircraft to the UK. He then gave the order to bale out, and alone crash-landed the aircraft at Winterton, Norfolk.

Pilot Officer Douglas Moulden of 149 Squadron was awarded an immediate DFC following this operation against Bochum. After crossing the enemy coast, his aircraft was attacked by a Messerschmitt 109 and then a Junkers 88. Both these attacks were beaten off by his gunners. Later, when about four miles from the target and without any warning, his aircraft was coned by searchlights. Then came the expected flak barrage, which ignited their incendiary load, wrecked the navigator's cabin and damaged the controls. The aircraft went into a steep dive, and the bombs had to be jettisoned. Only with the help of the bomb aimer was Moulden (with aircraft now down to 5000 feet) able to regain elevator control, but another 1000 feet was lost before he was able to pull the aircraft out of the dive. From there until the coast was reached, his aircraft was attacked no less than six times. Despite all this they were able to reach the English coast, and then their home base, where Moulden made a skilful landing, even though he had no aileron controls, his port outer engine was at full throttle, and his port tyre was punctured. His performance was all the more praiseworthy by the fact that this was only his fourth operation.

Between Cologne and Düsseldorf, the aircraft flown by Wing Commander McIntyre, the CO of 100 Squadron, was hit by flak and its port inner engine set on fire. When this fire was extinguished, the port outer engine then caught fire, but this fire was also put out. Not until after the target had been bombed did Flight Sergeant James Renno, an Australian, report to the pilot that he had been wounded in the stomach and thigh. Despite his injuries he insisted on staying at his radio, and was able to send out an SOS and obtain no less than six fixes. This enabled the pilot and navigator to make for the nearest point in the UK, which was Coltishall, and here a crash-landing was made. Once the aircraft was down, James succeeded in getting himself out of the aircraft and was taken to a Norfolk hospital.

At 8a.m. on the 14 May, a solitary pigeon returned to base, Wickenby, Lincs. This pigeon had been aboard the aircraft flown by Sergeant Scott of

12 Squadron which had gone missing the night before. The pigeon had been released by a member of the crew from the dinghy that they were in, having had to ditch into the North Sea after being hit by flak. They were to be adrift for the next five days before being picked up by a mine-sweeper which took them to Dover. After a check-up, the men returned to their squadron three days later and were given seven days 'survivors' leave.

As Fred Fennel's Stirling left the target area it was caught by a mass of searchlights and was coned for no less than twenty minutes. The navigator told him later that he had to hold his trembling right hand with his left, so that he could write an entry in his navigator's log. Fennel had learnt his apprenticeship on targets such as Hamburg, and it was this experience that he now called upon to 'turn the aircraft on its nose then on its tail'. As he did this, he told the gunners to look out for the positions of the flak barrage which arrived above, well below, well behind and in front of their aircraft. It seemed to work, as the aircraft was not hit at all during the twenty minutes that the searchlights shone on them. Sergeant Mitchell and his gunners, Sergeants Newman and Shinn of 75 Squadron, gave as good as they got after a Messerschmitt 110 had attacked them. It was seen to crash and explode in flames as a result of their return fire.

The destruction of Duisberg as seen from the air in 1945. (Mike King)

One Lancaster that would not be returning to its base. This is just one of many that failed to return and whose crews are buried all over Europe, or have no known grave.
(Author's collection)

A great fear of all crews was having to ditch in the sea. Knowing what to do and how to do it if they had to ditch was important and here in a practice tank a crew finds out what it is like to get into a dinghy. (Owen)

Pilot Officer Eddie Edmunds sitting with a colleague on a 4,000lb bomb before it is loaded into a Wellington for the operation that night. (Eddie Edmunds)

10 The Dams Are Breached

On the night of 16-17 May 1943, nineteen modified Lancasters of the newly formed 617 Squadron were made ready to set off for an attack against the Möhne, Eder, Sorpe and Ennepe dams. Between them, these dams controlled the rivers Weser and Ruhr, supplying the energy for power stations in the Ruhr area. Although this was a precision-target bombing operation, it was still in tune with Bomber Command's offensive policy against the Ruhr.

The nineteen Lancasters would attack in three groups. The first group would consist of nine aircraft and would be led by Wing Commander Guy Gibson, DSO, DFC. The second group would be led by Flight Lieutenant Joe McCarthy, and the third group or reserve wave, by Sergeant Townsend. After the first wave had taken off, the tension in No.5 Group HQ was felt by all the staff though they did not know the reason for this mission, as little was known about it outside the people directly involved. The C-in-C of Bomber Command was there, along with the A.O.C. of No.5 Group and the Senior Air Staff Officer. This indicated to the staff that the operation was something big, and not just a run-of-the-mill. Along with these senior officers was a slightly built civilian in a grey suit; he had greying hair and was wearing spectacles. He found it very difficult to keep calm and wandered around aimlessly, often staring at a map on the wall but with unseeing eyes, his thoughts obviously elsewhere. His name was Barnes Wallis.

At ten minutes past midnight the shrill pips of Morse rang out from the signals officer's phone. Everyone in the room looked towards Wing Commander Wally Dunn, the chief Signals Officer from No.5 Group. He begun to write on a note pad, but it was only a flak warning from Gibson's aircraft. Another long, thirty minutes went by before the Morse started again, this time the signal was 'Goner', which meant that at 12.37a.m. Gibson had dropped his bombs on the Möhne dam. The tension in the room continued. Then the signal 'Goner' came again, and this was to be repeated twice more until the message they were all waiting for came. Suddenly Dunn shouted out 'Nigger', which meant that the Möhne dam had been breached. This relieved the tension and the mood changed to one of jubilation.

At the scene of the Möhne dam, Gibson was communicating to the crew of the other attacking aircraft, 'okay chaps, come into attack when I tell you, I'll attack first.' He banked his aircraft, narrowly missing the tops of fir trees and descended to the attack height of 60 feet. The Australian voice of Pilot Officer Frederick Spafford came over the intercom, 'left a little, more left, steady, steady, bombs gone'. Then the voice of Flight Lieutenant Trevor-Roper, in his rear turret, was heard to say, 'I'll get those devils', as he fired back at the enemy ground defences. The dam was still intact but the water around it was foaming in a fury. The next Lancaster came in, supported by the fire-power of Gibson's aircraft, but for some reason the bomb was dropped too late and instead of hitting the wall of the dam, it bounced over the top and blew up the power house on the other side. The blast from this damaged the Lancaster which later went on and crashed, killing five of the crew. A further two attacks were made before water was seen to be rushing through a breach in the dam wall. The remainder of the force went on to attack and breach the Eder dam. The third dam, the Sorpe, was damaged but not breached. The Sorpe was an earth dam with a concrete core and was not really suitable to be breached with the 'bouncing-bomb', as Barnes Wallis its inventor, often said after the war.

When the returning crews landed they were met by the C-in-C of Bomber Command, Sir Arthur Harris, and other senior officers. Flight Lieutenant Mick Martin's own comments on the raid were: 'Rear gunner fire on two searchlights. Front runner shot-up other flak posts and searchlights. Navigation and map reading wizard. Formation commander did a great job by diverting the gun-fire from target towards himself. Whole crew did their jobs well.' Maltby said: 'In two cases a second aircraft flew alongside the one bombing and machine-gunned the defences on the north side of objective. The crews could not speak highly enough of the scientist who had designed the weapon, the people who had devised the modifications on the Lancaster, and the men and women who had manufactured them. And also the civilian test pilots who flew the aircraft, and the staff who planned the operation.' The final draft for this operation had been written in longhand by the Senior Air Staff Officer, Robert Saundby and was not typed until the evening of the raid. The secret of the operation was so well kept, that when the aircraft took off at about 9.30p.m. there was no reception committee, as was normal for bombing operations on take-off.

The attack on the Möhne dam had an important short-term effect on Dortmund owing to the flooding of the pumping stations which caused a shortage or water, especially for industrial use. The post-war German records show that production was reduced by between 10 and 15 per cent and was not back into full-swing for six months. The main railway line leading eastwards from the Ruhr to Kassel was out of action for several months. Shipping traffic on the Rhine was said to have been held up for five to six days after the dams raid. Information received from the USA, where railroad engineers had much experience of repairing tracks after flooding, indicated that it took an average of 25,000 man-hours per mile to restore washed-out tracks.

Goebbels recorded in his diary that British bombers had been successful, and that the Führer was exceedingly impatient and angry about the lack of preparedness on the part of the *Luftwaffe*. The *Gauleiters* in all the areas containing dams were worried because the anti-aircraft defences there were quite inadequate. When Dr Albert Speer landed at Werl airfield near the dams the next morning, he was confronted with the shattered Möhne dam and could not believe how much damage water could do. When he reported to Hitler the damage inflicted, it made a deep impression on the Führer. Experts were summoned from all over Germany to deal with the problem. They had the electrical installations dried out and confiscated motors from factories which were of the type used in the power house at the dam. A few days later some 7000 men were transferred from building work on the Atlantic Wall to the Möhne and Eder dams to help with their repair. The repair work was completed on the 23 September 1943, just as the rainy season began. It has always been a mystery to the Germans and many people in the UK why the dams were not attacked with conventional weapons and kept breached, at least until it was too late to collect the winter rains, and in so doing deprive the Germans of having enough water for steel-making.

At the end of May 1943, marshes and dykes about 100 miles away in Holland and Belgium were full of water. The locals said this was caused by the breaching of the Ruhr dams.

On 427 Squadron based at Leeming in Yorkshire, they learned that the MGM film company were to visit them on the 23 May, as they wanted to adopt the squadron. It was to become known as 427 (Lion) Squadron. On the afternoon of the 23 May, the whole squadron was assembled outside one of the hangars where a Mr Eckman, Managing Director of the MGM film company in the UK, presented the CO of 427 Squadron, Wing Commander Dudley Burnside, DSO, DFC, with a bronze lion of 18th century design. On the lion was an inscription commemorating the occasion. At a later date, all members of the squadron were presented with lion medals which would give them certain privileges at any MGM theatre. The squadron had also been told that each MGM film star would adopt one squadron aircraft. A vote was taken as to which star got what aircraft. Lana Turner topped the list followed closely by Greer Garson and Hedy Lamar. A draw took place and seventeen names were drawn. It was Sergeant EA Johnson's aircraft, DK 186 letter L, which would be adopted by Lana Turner, and became known as 'London's Revenge', signed Lana.

The night of 23-24 May. Target — DORTMUND

It had been nine days since an air operation had been mounted against the Ruhr area and this one contained the heaviest bomb-load dropped in one attack. The raid was to be launched in three waves. Of the thirteen Mosquitos of 109 Squadron detailed to mark the target, four returned with technical trouble, but the remaining nine successfully marked the target. Of the 826 aircraft which took off, 662 were four-engined bombers and it was the largest none- 1000 (since 1942) bomber raid yet despatched. The bombers were loaded mainly with incendiary and high explosive bombs.

The first wave of about 250 aircraft, consisting of heavy and medium bombers, were manned by the best crews of all groups. They were followed by all the remaining Stirlings, Halifaxes and Wellingtons and then the third wave comprising the remaining Lancasters.

The Mosquitos dropped yellow TIs north of the target on route as an aid to navigation. Other Mosquitos marked the exact aiming point with red, ground TIs between 12.58 and 1.08a.m. and thereafter at six-minute intervals until the end of the attack at 2a.m. They were backed up by other Pathfinder aircraft which dropped green TIs. The main force of bombers aimed their bombs at the red TIs, where visible, otherwise at the estimated centre of the area covered by the green TI markers. All crews were ordered to bomb from maximum height.

The Lancasters of No.1 Group had gathered above Sheringham, Norfolk, at a height of 16,000 feet. From there they climbed further so as to be at maximum height on reaching the enemy coast. They then flew to the target and bombed from the maximum height. After dropping their bombs, the Lancasters then increased their speed as quickly as possible so as to clear the area for the next wave of bombers. The Wellingtons in the group also met above Sheringham. They were to bomb from 12,000 to 16,000 feet over the target. All the crews in No.1 Group were instructed to take the minimum of evasive action over the target area, particularly on the bombing-run, to reduce the risk of collision, in view of the huge number of aircraft involved in the attack.

No opposition was observed until the aircraft were within 40 to 50 miles of Dortmund, where the defences of the target seemed to be very active and the glow of the fires considerable. A vast number of searchlights were in operation and up to eight perfect cones were always in existence within 25 to 30 miles of the centre of Dortmund. One cone of 52 beams was seen to 'hold' an aircraft for at least ten minutes, and another of 32 beams to hold an aircraft for five to six minutes. Apart from these two enormous cones, most of the others consisted of 15 to 25 beams. Despite considerable flak, both heavy and light, no aircraft were seen to be shot down; the defences were not particularly accurate.

Some 69 sorties were flown by ground-controlled night-fighters, of which 30 were active against the bomber force. Eight bombers were claimed to have been shot down by these fighters. The German report for this operation was as follows: 'Enemy bombers dropped numerous high explosive and incendiary bombs on Dortmund, causing considerable damage. Thirty-three of the attacking aircraft, mainly four-engine bombers, were shot down.' In actual fact the number of aircraft missing was 38. Forty-seven aircraft were damaged by flak and five damaged by fighter attack. The losses appeared to have occurred principally in the target area, in which eleven were shot down, and on the homeward journey. Only one of the losses occurred during the last twenty minutes of the attack confirming opinions that the defences were swamped. Other losses to flak were observed at Münster and off the Dutch coast at Egmond, where one aircraft was known to have been shot down by a flak-ship.

The smoke rose to 14,000 feet over Dortmund itself and the glow of the fires were still visible as the returning aircraft crossed the Dutch coast. The waterworks was put out of action and 34 factories were damaged, plus two collieries. One of the main steelworks, Hoesch, had no less than 48 buildings hit and the other main works at Verinigte Stahlwerke were also badly hit. The raid was particularly severe in the north and north-east of the city, but overall, it was considered that no district and few industries escaped unscathed. Some 2000 residential and commercial buildings were assessed as hit. It was estimated that 30 per cent of Dortmund's houses had been damaged. The reduction in public utility services were estimated as a 25 per cent loss of gas, 30 per cent of water and 50 per cent of electricity. The total loss of production in the industries was 15 to 20 per cent. Some 629 people were reported killed, this included 21 POWs and 53 foreign workers. Approximately 1340 people were injured which included 43 foreign workers. It was estimated that 90,000 people were made homeless. There were no less than 4470 fires of which 770 were known as *Grossbrande* (Big Fires). The weight of bombs dropped by the 764 aircraft which attacked Dortmund totalled 2248 tons.

Concerning this raid on Dortmund Fred Fennel simply wrote in his log-book: 'Again not funny, but we got away with it.' Warrant Officer George Barker of 90 Squadron remembers: 'Seconds after releasing our bomb-load, we ourselves were hit by falling bombs from another Stirling immediately above us. A large hole appeared in our aircraft from my mid-upper turret toward the tail.' Joe Clark recalls it as: 'Quite a good trip apart from being coned by searchlights for a short while and suddenly feeling naked and totally lit up at 19,000 feet. Thanks to some good flying by Les [the pilot] it didn't last very long, but it leaves you with a very dry mouth for a while.'

Tom Osborne of 460 Squadron, remembers this raid as: 'My first trip with Wing Commander C E Martin, DSO, DFC, the CO of 460 Squadron. He always flew in his dress uniform, or at least when I was with him he did. The usual flak and searchlights but an uneventful trip for us.' Tom Wingham of 102 Squadron relates: 'Bombed first on initial *OBOE* markers. Just after finishing-run, and while taking a photograph of aiming point, we received a direct hit by flak and lost all power in three engines, and fell 10,000 feet. At 7000 feet, the engines began to pick up again and although coned by searchlights and subjected to light and heavy flak, we eventually climbed out and made for home. Later, we discovered that a large chunk of flak had cut pipes on three extinguishers and flooded the engines with foam.'

A member of 426 Squadron, Sergeant Stanley Gaunt was awarded an immediate DFM for his efforts on the trip to Dortmund. He recalls:

> We were badly shot up and caught in a large cone of searchlights west of the target. The shell of the undercarriage was practically shot away. We took evasive action but several searchlights followed. After a while we got away, and then the front turret caught fire. As things

> looked grim I gave an emergency signal to the crew to bale out. The wireless operator saw the rear gunner, Sergeant McCraken and the air bomber, Sergeant Fadden immediately bale out. Shortly after, due to the back-draught of the escape hatch, the fire went out, but our troubles were not over as we were shadowed by a Messerschmitt 110 which tried to get underneath us. I corkscrewed most of the way and lost the fighter east of Rotterdam.

Gaunt's Wellington HE 995 crossed the North Sea and crash-landed at Martlesham Heath in Suffolk.

Sergeant Ken Brecken of 103 Squadron, was also awarded an immediate DFM and Sergeant George Ferrel recommended for the CGM but this was later lowered to the DFM. Sergeant Lloyd Collins of 432 Squadron was navigator to Sergeant Dingwall when their aircraft, Wellington HZ 272 letter W, was hit by heavy flak over Dortmund. Collins suffered a fractured skull and lost a great deal of blood.

The flight engineer of a Stirling aircraft, Sergeant Dickinson of 75 Squadron, remembers when they were engaged by two Junkers 88s at a height of 11,000 feet:

> We were approaching Dortmund from the north and could see the target, which was already burning. There was no moon or cloud, and it was possible that we were silhouetted against the light from the target. I was standing in the astrodome searching for fighters when the rear gunner's voice came over the intercom, 'fighter, turn starboard.' The Stirling was a very manoeuvrable aircraft, and our skipper's reactions were as good as any fighter pilot. He almost stood the old girl on her wing-tip. The fighter came in from the starboard quarter and he and our two gunners fired at the same time. I saw the tracer coming towards us, it appeared to be floating like a string of brightly-coloured balloons, until it passed over the top of us. A flame suddenly shot from the top of the fighter and he dived down under our port side. Our bomb aimer in the front turret also managed to fire at the diving fighter. We were still in a tight turn when the rear gunner and mid-upper gunner began firing again at a second fighter. This one broke off his attack and did a sharp climbing turn to port, exposing his underside which both gunners said they hit. We claimed both fighters damaged. Another crew in the area reported a combat and seeing an aircraft go gown in flames and blow-up.

Goebbels recorded in his diary on the 25 May: 'The night raid by the English on Dortmund was extraordinarily heavy. Probably the worst ever directed at a German city. Reports from Dortmund are horrible. We have received reports from Bochum and Dortmund indicating that morale was lower than ever before. The reports are somewhat exaggerated but we must recognise that the people in the west are gradually beginning to lose courage. The fires were under control by the afternoon, destruction, however, is initially total. *Gauleiter* Hoffman informed me that hardly a house in Dortmund is habitable.

After the attack Air Chief Marshal Sir Arthur Harris sent the following message to all squadrons of Bomber Command: 'Yes in 1939, Goering promised that not a single bomb would reach the Ruhr. Congratulations on having delivered the first 100,000 tons on Germany to refute him. The next 100,000 if he waits for them, will be even bigger and better bombs delivered even more accurately and in much shorter time.'

The night of 25-26 May. Target — DÜSSELDORF

The code-name for this operation was 'Perch'. During the attack, 759 aircraft dropped some 2000 tons of bombs with the 4000lb bombs falling on the target area at a rate of five every minute for a period of 50 minutes. In this attack 8000lb bombs were also used. Thousands of buildings were either gutted by fire or blasted by explosives. Rail and river traffic was disrupted. Gas, water and electricity supplies cut off, and the whole commerical and industrial life of the city brought to a standstill.

Despite this success, however, the attack was very scattered owing to large amounts of cloud, mainly 7/10ths and in two layers between 10,000 and 20,000 feet. The marking was carried out by nine *OBOE* Mosquitos, six Stirlings, nine Halifaxes and two Lancasters, operating with H2S. The cloudy conditions also prevented the searchlights and heavy flak which was mainly predicted* through cloud, and only moderate and inaccurate preventing an effective defence. Some 42 sorties by ground-controlled night-fighters were recorded, of which 23 were against the bomber force. The German claim of 24 aircraft shot down was three less than the actual figure of 27. Forty-six aircraft were damaged by flak and three damaged by enemy fighters. It would appear that the bulk of the losses suffered by the bomber force were away from the target area, en route to Düsseldorf and on their homeward journey.

In the record book of 426 Squadron, it was recorded that 'the Pathfinder marker flares were scattered, as were the fires — a disappointing night. The flak was heavy but inaccurate. Reg Lew, a navigator flying with 214 Squadron, recorded in his log-book: 'attacked by a fighter 30 miles from the target. Returned on three engines to prang on landing'. A Stirling bomber of 149 Squadron, flown by Flying Officer Williams, was attacked by a twin-engine enemy fighter, later identified as a Junker 88, which was then fired upon by the rear gunner. It was not seen again, but some six minutes later another fighter was seen by the mid-upper gunner, Sergeant Cutler, while they were on their bombing-run. As it closed and got to within 800 yards, Cutler opened fire and strikes were seen on the fighter's port engine, which then burst into flames. It was seen to dive out of control and crash in flames on the ground. This was a splendid piece of markmanship as both gunners between them only fired 400 rounds.

* To plot the range and height of the aircraft. Being through cloud it was only moderately successful and somewhat inaccurate.

Another aircraft of 149 Squadron was also attacked by a twin-engine aircraft. The enemy fighter was hit by fire from the rear gunner, Sergeant Williams and the mid-upper gunner, Sergeant Curtis, and this caused it to burst into flames and dive down out of control. In the log-book of Tom Wingham it is recorded: '8/10ths cloud in target vicinity, and as I recollect we bombed on ETA. The weather forecast being way out.' Fred Fennel recorded in his log-book: 'Not funny but we escaped.' On the German side, Hauptmann (later Major) Walter Ehle, already with 35 'kills' to his credit and awarded the Knights Cross, shot down no less than five aircraft on this operation.

One aircraft which was not destined to return was Stirling BK 611 letter U of 15 Squadron. The rear gunner, Sergeant 'Joe' Edgley, remembers:

> We took off from Mildenhall at 11.20p.m. As we crossed the North Sea, I saw from my turret other Stirlings above and below. On approach to the target at 1.35a.m. our aircraft was hit in the starboard engines by flak and both were put out of action. The mid-upper gunner, Sergeant Seabolt of the RCAF asked permission to bale out; the pilot, Sergeant Wilson of the RAAF said 'okay'. This was the last I saw or heard of him. The rest of the crew stayed until 2.12a.m. then the navigator, Pilot Officer Cooper from Chile left. I opened the escape-hatch panel on the starboard side and put on my chute. As I went to bale out, I looked forward and the Stirling seemed to be fairly level, so with a mighty effort I pulled myself back into the aircraft and plugged in my intercom and spoke to the pilot. He seemed to think we may make it to the sea, then ditch. I got into the mid-upper turret and had a look around the Stirling, from this point I could see what bad shape it was in on the starboard side. When we got down to 700 feet the pilot said we shall have to bale out. I went to the front escape-hatch in the aircraft's nose and pulled the escape-hatch lever to open it. However, this came off in my hand, so I returned to the rest escape-hatch aft of the mid-upper turret and undid it. The flight engineer, Sergeant Pittord, baled out but was later recorded as having been killed leaving the aircraft; the aircraft was at the time only twenty feet from the ground. As I prepared to bale out, we hit the ground at 2.15a.m. We had crashed at Venlo in Holland. I shouted to the rest of the crew and got a reply from the wireless operator Sergeant Maxted; we could not find the pilot or the bomb aimer, Sergeant Arnott. We succeeded in evading from the area and got to Antwerp, then Brussels and stayed here until the end of June. From here we were taken to a hotel in Paris and stayed the night. The next day we were escorted en route to the railway station to board a train for Bordeaux, and finally, if we were lucky to Spain. Suddenly, we were surrounded by six men armed with revolvers, and one said: 'Hands up! You are British airmen.' With this, our guide ran off and we did not see him again. We were taken to Fresnes prison, where we were interrogated by a civilian who was about six

feet six inches in height, and spoke with an American accent. We had been free for six weeks and were destined to spend the next six weeks in prison. On the 23 August 1943, along with thirteen other airmen, I was taken by train to Dulagluft prison camp at Oberursel near Frankfurt, and from here to Stalag 4B at Muhlberg which was situated between Berlin and Dresden. Here I stayed until the 23 April 1945, when the Russians liberated the camp. I left the camp with two companions and we were picked up by an American convoy and taken to Brussels, reaching here on the 17 May 1945. From here we were flown to the UK. We had been away nearly two years.

The night of 27-28 May. Target — ESSEN

This was the fifth raid on Essen during the Battle of the Ruhr. Some 518 aircraft were despatched and zero hour was set at 12.45a.m. Despite many aircraft under-shooting the aiming point by several miles, the Krupps factory was severely damaged and a large number of buildings in the north of the city were destroyed. The marking was undertaken by eleven Mosquitos using the 'skymarking' method. The enemy searchlights were generally hampered by the cloudy conditions. The red TIs were accurately placed by the eleven *OBOE* Mosquitos and although the timing was not as planned, the target was almost continually marked. The backing-up by the following aircraft was well-timed and unbroken. The bombing of the main force was concentrated within a narrow strip about one and a half miles wide, stretching back from the aiming point just south-west of Krupps for about four and a half miles along the line of approach and including the whole of the Krupps works. The Stirlings and Halifaxes which bombed four to eight miles short of the target, appeared to have been decoyed by imitation red TIs.

The damage to Krupps was vast, with 1600 tons of bombs dropped and over 200 fires started. The devastation was reported to have been equal to the whole of that caused by all previous raids on this target. Of the 190 workshops in the Krupps factory, 110 were hit. The havoc wrought by fire was immense and buildings were still burning two days after the attack. Billows of dense smoke rose to 1000 feet, and huge eruptions were seen from a distance of 100 miles by the aircrews on their homeward journey.

Some 78 aircraft were damaged by flak and three by fighters. The night-fighter activity was less than normal, only 28 being active against the bombers. One of the missing bombers was seen shot down by a flak-ship off Texel, near the Dutch coast. Of the remaining losses, eight were attributed to flak, ten or eleven to fighters and the remaining two or three to causes unknown, such as mid-air collisions. Despite the fighter activity being less than normal, the fighters that were operating made their presence felt and a number of combats were recorded.

Sergeant Percy Walder of 97 Squadron remembers tangling with a Junkers 88:

> We ran into a Ju 88 along the track home. He had shot someone down on the starboard side close to us, which I reported over the intercom. I then heard over the intercom someone else in the crew say 'he's not getting us'. It was probably the pilot, as the nose of the aircraft soon went down. Things were happening so fast, my torch suddenly was on the top of the turret, so I assumed we had looped the loop. When we landed at base my parachute bag was smothered in Jeyes fluid from the portable toilet known as the Elsan — I never did get the stain out. For this to have happened we must have been upside down. Anyway we got away with it and carried on our way home. About 30 miles off the English coast another Ju 88 opened-up on us with cannon fire. I saw tracer coming towards us. I told the skipper to 'weave' and then opened-up and returned fire. He then replied again and so did I with my four Browning machine-guns, using up no less than 500 rounds. Did I hit him? Who can tell, because that's the last we saw of him.

George Calvert 106 Squadron, narrates:

> This was our crew's third visit against Essen and our sixteenth operation completed during the blitz on the Ruhr. Things got off to a bad start as our usual mid-upper gunner, Bert, wasn't fit to fly and we were given permission to take our CO's gunner. This was our first time with a different member in the crew since training. After crossing the enemy coast we had an unusually quiet time until, approaching Essen, we saw the usual reception of heavy anti-aircraft fire and searchlights and below, the bomb bursts of previous crews exploding among the devastation. We began our level run-in for bombing and eventually came the words: 'bombs gone' but even before the bomb doors could be closed we were rocked by a shell-hit on our port wing. The outer port engine stopped and the inner engine set on fire. The pilot, Ted, put H-Harry into a steep dive which extinguished the fire, but in so doing we had lost a lot of height and were unable to climb anymore. Then the inner port engine stopped and so we worked out the shortest possible bearing for our trip home. However, we were still losing height and to try and gain height or maintain what height we had, we threw out everything we could to lighten the load. This included the bomb-sight, ammunition, some of the guns and even the ladder which we used to ascend and descend from our aircraft. Our route home took us over Amsterdam where we took another pasting from the anti-aircraft batteries. The aircraft suffered more hits but none of the crew were hurt. By now it was obvious we were not going to make it to the UK and prepared to ditch in the sea for the second time. We were already members of the 'Goldfish Club', a club which any crew who had come down in the sea were eligible to join. With his usual skill, Ted took us down and we finished up on a tiny reclaimed island, only feet from the water. We

released the pigeon carried for this very purpose, we thought at least one member of the crew should have a chance to make it to the UK. We never got to know, as the next two years were spent as POWs.'

In Goebbels's diary of the 28 May 1943, read: 'The English wrested supremacy from us not only as the result of tremendous energy on the part of the RAF and the British aircraft industry, but also thanks to certain unfortunate circumstances and to our own negligence. Why cannot we, in time, wrest it back from the English, if once we abandon the thesis that the war in the east must be ended first? It seems to me that the air situation should be considered one of the most critical phases of the war and that it should be conducted quite independently of developments in the east.'

The night of 29-30 May. Target — WUPPERTAL

The twin cities of Barmen and Elberfeld were amalgamated in 1929 and became known as Wuppertal, which was situated on the River Wupper, approximately fifteen miles south-east of Essen. It covered an area measuring two and a half miles by one mile and had a population of about 400,000. It was not a large industrial centre like Essen or Duisburg but still important in that it produced small component parts for tanks, guns, vehicles, aircraft and engines. Among its other industries were tube and sheet-metal works, wire-rolling mills, and the making of artificial silk. In size, Wuppertal was comparable to the city of Coventry.

The code-name for this target was 'Sprod'. Zero hour for this operation was set at 12.45a.m. Of the 719 aircraft despatched, 611 attacked the Barmen district of Wuppertal with great success. The fire-raising technique was effectively employed as a complement to ground-marking, resulting in the best concentration yet achieved by the PFF. Over 1000 acres of the town was damaged, affecting 113 industrial concerns, including two large textile works that manufactured parachute material. The transport system was totally disrupted and over 118,000 people were left homeless. In this attack some 2000 tons of high explosives and incendiary bombs were dropped.

En route to the target four special 'Y' aircraft — two Stirlings and two Halifaxes — dropped yellow TIs. This marking was maintained by thirteen 'Y' type back-up aircraft dropping their yellow TIs blindly with H2S. Of the eleven *OBOE* Mosquitos sent on this mission, three had to return to base early because of technical problems. The remaining eight aircraft dropped red TIs in salvoes of six minute intervals, between 12.42 and 1.28a.m. This was followed by 37 back-up aircraft which dropped green TIs timed to overshoot the red TIs by one second. The main bomber force crews were instructed to aim at the red TIs if visible, otherwise at the centre of the green TIs.

From reports, it appeared that the Mosquito timing was very poor, both ground stations bringing in their aircraft almost simultaneously with the result they attacked in pairs making long intervals between the red TIs being dropped. At 12.47a.m., 55 fire-raisers of the PFF and the four special 'Y' type aircraft, carrying mixed loads, attacked the red TIs. This fire-raising and the backing-up was of high quality, perhaps the best concentration yet to date. Fifty-one red TIs were plotted within a mile of the aiming point, while the unmistakable cascade of green TIs nullified the effect of the enemy decoy flares. The area most affected was Barmen which, when the bombers finally turned for home, was a mass of flames. One fire alone spread over three square miles. Some 2450 people were killed and a similar number injured. The flak defences were strongest after leaving the target area, particularly when flying over Düsseldorf, Cologne and Bonn. Intense flak was also experienced at Aachen near the Belgian border. A continuous belt of searchlights operated from Cologne to Dortmund, and 118 ground-controlled night-fighters were heard by wireless intelligence of which 37 were set against the bomber force.

A German report stated: 'Enemy air formations bombed several west German localities and considerable damage was caused, particularly in Wuppertal. Fifty-seven enemy aircraft, most of them with four engines, were shot down.' In fact, 33 aircraft went missing. the German claim included the losses for night and day, in which 47 aircraft were lost. Fifty-four aircraft were damaged by flak and two by enemy fighters. Most of the aircraft lost to flak were considered to have been in the area between Düsseldorf and Dortmund. It was estimated that 22 aircraft were lost to night-fighters. Five night-fighters were claimed as being destroyed in combat by the bomber force aircrew.

One pilot of a Halifax said of this raid on Wuppertal: 'We dropped our bombs and just as we were leaving there were two huge explosions and a mass of flames soared 800 feet into the air, followed by great clouds of smoke that glowed red from reflecting the flames below. In this curiously red light I could see all sorts of bombers — Stirlings, Halifaxes, Lancasters and Wellingtons, the sky seemed to be full of them.' Joe Clark, a flight engineer with 100 Squadron, remembers that the raid on Wuppertal went well and that the Pathfinders seemed to be getting better at their marking operations, which were not always as good as they should be.

Flying Officer Andrews of 115 Squadron was returning to base after bombing Wuppertal, when his aircraft was hit with a burst of cannon-fire that stopped the port outer engine and damaged the starboard rudder which caused the bomb doors to open and also put the hydraulic system out of action. This burst of cannon-fire also damaged the tail turret extensively and fatally injured the tail gunner, Sergeant Glazzard, who later died in hospital without ever regaining consciousness. The attack had come from dead astern and slightly below their aircraft. At the time of the attack, the tail gunner had his turret rotated fully to port. The mid-gunner, Sergeant Skriey, was able to return fire and score hits on the enemy fighter which was not seen again. The aircraft then resumed its course to base and made a successful crash-landing.

Alec Smith, also in 115 Squadron remembers:

> On our bombing-run we saw one of our own aircraft above us and also one on each side. A sudden shudder in our own aircraft was thought to be due to the close proximity of a 'cookie' from the aircraft above as it sped on its downward journey. Shortly afterward, white smoke was seen coming from the port outer engine but after a minute it ceased and the engine seemed unaffected. However, next day when the aircraft was examined, the tail of a 30lb incendiary bomb was found in the wing, near the port engine. It had passed through the wing shearing the side of an auxiliary petrol tank and releasing some 30 gallons or so of petrol in the form of white vapour. 'Lady-luck' was on our side.

Sergeant Newby, a navigator with 207 Squadron remembers that just before they dropped their bombs, the flight engineer noticed that the temperature of the starboard outer engine was rising rapidly, then shortly after, flames started to spout from the engine's nacelle. The bomb aimer, Sergeant Craig, then declared: 'Bombs gone.' After the pilot, Sergeant Fred Richardson, switched off the starboard outer engine the propeller started windmilling and would not feather. This meant that the extinguisher in the nacelle could not be used because of the rotating propeller. The flight engineer pressed the feathering button three or four times but the engine would not stop; this prompted the pilot to say: 'Right lads, parachutes on.' Sergeant Newby recalls:

> I remember looking out of the side blister or window and downwards over Wuppertal and thinking its a hell of a way down. At the time we were at 19,000 feet. I noticed the flames were streaming out as far as the tailplane and the leading edge of the starboard wing was beginning to glow red. Fred was battling to get us out, when the engine finally feathered and the extinguisher was activated; out went the fire just like a candle being snuffed. During these few minutes we must have looked like a great torch in the sky to the Germans, it seemed like every searchlight was on us. Somehow we limped home on three engines and landed an hour late at 4.15a.m., just in time to stop the next of kin telegrams going out to say we were missing. The next day we visited the hangar to look at Lancaster ED 550 K for King, our aircraft. We found a piece of shrapnel had punctured the feed-pipe from the glycol (coolant) tank to the engine, which caused the engine to get hot and catch fire. This had happened on our approach near Düsseldorf. The flight engineer went to see the CO and asked to be taken off operations. He told us he was not dicing with death for two shillings and sixpence a day and that he could go back to his old trade of engine fitter 2E and get eight shillings and sixpence a day. He was only twenty years old and had a wife and child, so who could blame him? Needless to say he vanished off the Squadron the same day.

In the month of May 1943, there had been a total of ten major operations, in which 228 aircraft were lost, 48 of them were twin-engined and 180 four-engined. The aircrew losses amounted to 1497 men. Aircraft losses in No.4 Group were 6.3 per cent based on 778 operations. In No.6 Group, the losses were 8 per cent on 175 operations. This means the number of aircraft despatched in the month of May was 4912.

On the 3 June 1943, a draft directive from Air Vice-Marshal Norman Bottomley, who was Assistant Chief on the Air Staff (Operations), was sent to Air Chief Marshal Sir Arthur Harris the C-in-C of Bomber Command. It was basically a reminder of the directive issued by the Combined Chiefs of Staff and dated 21 January 1943, in which the role of the bombers was defined. The primary objective remained, that is the destruction of the German aircraft industry and its associated industries.

DRONTEN

We did not weep nor count the cost, as one by one, our friends were lost.

Nor did we when the war's great toll took all the best of our young men. We did not weep as we saw them go down to the storm of the mighty foe. We did not weep — not once — not then, nor in the years to come, when on parade to do them honour, came Kings and Queens and Chiefs of State in pomp and splendour to relate how their cause was just, and justified by the freedom bought as they fought and died.

We did not weep — not once — until, in a little Dutch town, in a silence, the children came to honour our dead. Quietly, from out of the crowd with just a few flowers, their little heads bowed, in a line they came to lay them down by the Lancaster prop in Dronten Town. And then — and then — despite our will, we felt our watching eyes o'erfill with tears, and yet we smiled. How great the power of an innocent child.

Harry Brown ex 50 and 233 Squadrons.

11 The Battle Continues

The night of 11-12 June. Target — DÜSSELDORF

The second attack on Düsseldorf in two weeks. Zero hour was set at 1.20a.m. This attack was led by thirteen Mosquitos, of which only six were able to attack the target. In the Düsseldorf and Oberhausen areas, the flak was intensely heavy and predicted, but at the end of the attack it became a barrage defence. There were many searchlights in operation, which at the end of the attack became more active. En route from base to the English Channel there was 10/10ths cloud, and icing conditions. In the Düsseldorf area the weather conditions were good. The pathfinder technique was very well timed. Most of the 655 aircraft which attacked the target, out of the 783 despatched, got within three miles of the aiming point with their bombs. One Mosquito, however, released a load of TIs fourteen miles north-east of Düsseldorf, and part of the main force attacked this area and bombed in what was open country.

In the raid some 64 factories were damaged, including machine tool and heavy armaments factories, one of which employed some 36,000 workers. Another factory that was making torpedos and parts for U-boats, was also badly damaged. In all 2000 tons of bombs were dropped, and 1500 acres of the city and main industrial areas were demolished. Fires in the centre of the town destroyed the chief business and administration buildings and swept on unchecked; seven days later they were still smouldering. One pilot said: 'The smoke was absolutely pitch black'. The admin centre was destroyed along with its data relating to industries throughout Germany. The gas network was put out of action for seventeen days, and 20 per cent of the water system for some sixteen hours. Some 30,000 dwelling units were destroyed and a further 20,000 heavily damaged. The dock area was also badly hit.

Some 73 ground-controlled night-fighters were heard, of which 29 were in action against the bombers. A German report stated: 'British bombers flew over west German territory, in particular the town of Oberhausen. Twenty bombers were shot down.' In fact the figure was 38 aircraft missing. The pilots of No.1 Group reported: 'If the PFF were on the mark, indications are that the attack would be a success. Very concentrated attack comparable with Dortmund; PFF accurate yellow TIs helpful. Terrific fires — very successful. Very good prang — plenty of fires, and smoke fires well concentrated.'

For Geoff Archer of 199 Squadron, the trip to Düsseldorf was to be his last. He had started on operations against the Ruhr on the 12 March 1943, and had gone right through the Battle. On the 11-12 June he flew in Wellington HE 919 letter T for Tommy. After this operation 199 Squadron converted to Stirlings. After the war Archer flew for an air survey company and spent some time in the Ruhr, based at Düsseldorf. His role was taking aerial photographs to assist with the rebuilding of the area.

Joe Clark, flying with 100 Squadron, remembers the Düsseldorf trip as being a good one, and actually getting an aiming point photograph. 'We saw a lot of aircraft shot down by flak and night-fighters, and felt sorry for the Wellingtons and Stirlings who were bombing at heights many thousands of feet below us. I am convinced that there has never been a great concentration of flak and searchlights anywhere, before or since.' Tom Wingham of 102 Squadron remembers that although the 'skymarking' technique was being used, the indicators burst very high at 16,000 to 17,000 feet, about the height his aircraft was flying at the time. He also recalls their bomb-sight ceasing to function and having to aim by judgement.

The aircraft in which Sergeant Easby and his crew of 100 Squadron flew, was scheduled to fly with the last wave of bombers to attack the target and did not take off until 12a.m. For most of the trip they were flying through cloud, but long before they got to Düsseldorf they spotted a red glow in the sky and when they did get to Düsseldorf, the cloud had gone, giving a bird's-eye view of what looked like to them the crater of a volcano. The whole town appeared to be one mass of flames, and one column of smoke rose to a height of at least 18,000 feet. The defences did not seem to be particularly strong. The flak was in barrage form and there were some searchlights, but neither were considered to be dangerous on this occasion. The return flight was quiet and as they crossed the Dutch coast, the fires burning in Düsseldorf could still be seen in the distance.

For Sergeant Arthur Garlick of 102 Squadron, this was his 24th operation. three to four minutes before entering the target area, his aircraft, JB 150 Letter A, flown by Flight Lieutenant Ingram, was hit by splinters of flak. At the time, Sergeant Garlick was manning the under-blister and was struck and seriously wounded in the face and neck, suffering a broken jaw and great loss of blood. Despite his injuries, he refused to disturb the rest of the crew because the aircraft was entering the target zone at the time to drop its bombs. He carried out his own first aid, and not until the bombs had been despatched and their aircraft had cleared the target area, did he inform his crew that he was wounded. For his efforts he was awarded an immediate DFM.

On the 11 June, Flight Sergeant Collins of 51 Squadron was flying Halifax DT 742 which shortly after take-off, developed trouble in its port outer engine. Collins decided to jettison his bombs and abandon the sortie, but in the area of Sheringham, Norfolk they were suddenly engaged by light and heavy flak which came from an Allied convoy with a heavy escort, that they had previously observed. The aircrew had been given no information that this convoy was in the vicinity, so they decided not to jettison their bombs in case the ships were hit. Instead, as they turned away, they fired the colours of the day, which only made matters worse as every ship in the convoy fired up at them. Once again the aircraft fired the colours of the day and put all its lights on but by this time the aircraft had been hit by flak in several places and was in fact on fire. The petrol tank in the starboard wing had been holed and the leaking fuel had caught alight and blazed a long trail from the aircraft wing. The pilot endeavoured to start the port engine, which then also caught fire. By this time the aircraft was about 50 feet above the water and flying among the ship's balloons; it was only at this time that the bombs were jettisoned. It was obvious that the aircraft was going to ditch, yet still the ships in the convoy continued to fire on them. A direct hit was sustained by the aircraft in the rest area, which killed the wireless operator Sergeant Spreckley instantly, and also seriously wounded in the stomach, the bomb aimer Sergeant Parker. The ditching was successful but the dinghy failed to release. and it was only extracted with great difficulty by the mid-upper gunner. They managed to get the body of Sergeant Spreckley out of the stranded aircraft, and it was not until they got into the dinghy that Parker revealed that he had been wounded. After 45 minutes they were picked up by a trawler that was in the area. The Halifax was still afloat but burning furiously. Later, the aircrew were transferred to a destroyer which landed them ashore at Harwich. It was learned later that the convoy escort had seen the aircraft in the light of its own fire and although having recognized it as friendly, they were unable to stop the ships in the convoy from firing. Both Collins and Parker were recommended for immediate DFMs.

In 35 Squadron, Pilot Officer David Codd was flying as navigator in Halifax HR 798-A. He recalls:

> Little did we know it, but this was to be the last operation for Norman Williams our rear gunner from Australia. On the final-leg, about twenty miles from the target, we were attacked by two enemy fighters in succession. In the first burst of fire a cannon shell went through the mid-upper turret, hitting Des Smith a glancing blow above the eye, temporarily blinding him. The second fighter came in for the kill and its fire severely damaged the rear turret, and badly wounded Norman in the legs and abdomen, but despite this he continued to give the pilot directions to evade the fighters' attack. The first fighter came in for the second time, its burst of fire hit the aircraft in several places, causing the starboard wing to catch fire. As it turned away, Norman opened fire with his four Brownings and scored a direct hit, the fighter going down in flames. By now we were ten miles from the target with the wing still on fire. The skipper gave the order to jettison the bomb load, he then dived at speed and succeeded in putting out the fire. As we turned for home the second fighter attacked once more, with Norman still continuing to guide the pilot. Finally, as it came in, Norman got it in his gunsight and pressed the

> firing button. The result was the fighter blew up, and so close was it at the time that the aircraft was rocked by the blast. Norman yelled out: 'Got the bastard skipper!'

Only when they reached the English coast would Norman allow them to try and help him. The damage to his turret doors was so bad that they had to be chopped open with an axe to get him out. On being got out of the turret he was given a shot of morphine to ease the pain. A later inspection of the aircraft revealed the port undercarriage was damaged and also that the port tyre had burst. This meant the landing at Graveley had been made on the starboard wheel and held on this side until enough speed had been lost for the aircraft's weight to be distributed on to the port wheel as well. When this was done, the aircraft slewed away to port and came to rest on the grass in what was a splendid piece of airmanship by Pilot Officer Cobb. Both gunners were taken to the RAF hospital at Ely, Cambridgeshire. For his tremendous bravery and devotion to duty and consideration for the rest of the crew, Norman was awarded the highest award, other than the VC, that a non-commissioned officer can be awarded, the CGM. Only a matter of sixteen days later, on an operation to Cologne, Cobb's aircraft was hit by flak and the crew had to bale out, only for Cobb to die in the aircraft when it blew up before he could get out. In the meantime, Norman was fighting for his life in Ely hospital, to the extent that on one occasion a priest was sent for to administer the last rites. Somehow, in the same way he had stuck to his guns in the air, he stuck to surviving on the ground, and by the end of July he was back flying on operations. After the war he took part in operations in Malaya and then Korea. He was the most highly decorated NCO in the RAAF at the end of the war, having been awarded not only the CGM, but the DFM and bar as well.

For one crew of 12 Squadron, this was their third operation. The Australian pilot, Sergeant Danny Thompson, reached the target area (in Lancaster ED 537) where they successfully dropped their bomb load, but as they left the target area, the aircraft lost the use of an engine when it caught fire. Somehow the flight engineer and Danny Thompson managed to get the fire out and feather the propeller. However, they were not able to maintain height so the pilot decided to try and get the aircraft lower to the ground and 'crawl' home. The mid-upper gunner, Sergeant Bill Pingle remembers:

> I don't know how low we got before all hell let loose when a night-fighter hit and raked the aircraft in front of the mid-upper turret. The last I heard from the front of the aircraft was Danny saying 'bale out'. I got out of my turret and went to the back of the aircraft and opened the door, the fire by now was coming back all along the side of the aircraft. I couldn't see 'Sparky' Sparling, the rear gunner, so I went to the rear turret and opened the doors. He was stuck, so he pushed and I pulled and out he came. We went back and put on our chutes and shook hands. Before we had chance to bale out, somebody, I think it

> was Sergeant Bowers, the navigator, jumped out, without a chute I feel. I then went to the door and jumped out. As I floated down, I saw what I thought was sand, suddenly I was in water and it came over my head. My chute had wrapped itself around my legs, so I pulled the bottle on my Mae West and came up to the surface. I had come down near a tug towing a barge. They pulled me aboard and gave me a shot of Schnapps, (guaranteed to revive anyone). The next morning a sweep was made of the area and we came upon 'Sparky' being dive-bombed by sea gulls. We were taken to Amsterdam and handed over to the German army, and for the next 23 months we were prisoners of war. The old man on the barge had wanted to had us over to the Dutch Resistance, but the younger members of the crew were scared and insisted we be handed over to the Germans.

Sergeant Campbell, the wireless operator and a Scot, was washed up on the Dutch coast on the 17 June, followed by the remainder of the crew on the 21 June. In 1964, when the Zuider Zee was reclaimed from the sea, the wreckage of Lancaster ED 357 was found. One of the propellers was embedded in concrete as a memorial in a new town named Dronten which was built after the land had been reclaimed from the sea. In this new town, eight streets were named after the aircraft and crew of ED 357 — Lancasterdree, Pinglestaat, Sparlinghof, Thompsonstrad, Osbornehof, Campbellhof, Wardhor, and Bowershof. The streets were unveiled by Bill Pingle. On the 4 May every year in Dronten, a memorial service is held to honour the flyers of all Allied Air Forces who gave their lives for freedom. A former air gunner, Mick Smith, now a member of the Air Gunners Association (AGA), which has branches all over the UK, stumbled upon the memorial by accident in the 1970s, and then in a book, read more about the memorial. In 1975 he was invited as a special guest by the Burgomeister of Dronten, and again in 1976. After this last visit, he was asked by the Burgomeister to organise a party of former air gunners and their wives to attend the service in 1977. A party of about 50 was suggested, and so in 1977, the pilgrimage of the AGA to Dronten began. While they are there, they are hosted by the families from the three villages of Dronten, Swiftebank and Biddinghoizen that make up the district. This was such a success that the number of people attending these reunions has been increased to 150. On one occasion, Prince Bernhard of the Netherlands attended. He was given an AGA tie and wore it proudly, he himself having served as a pilot in the RAF during World War II.

When Sergeant Blanchard, of 77 Squadron, who hailed from Lincolnshire, walked into the briefing room at RAF Elvington Yorkshire, on the 11 June, he saw the target for that night was Düsseldorf. For him and his crew it was to be their second operation; their first had also been Düsseldorf. This first operation had painful memories for them, and they did not relish a return. On the first occasion they had limped home on three engines, having been badly hit by flak. On their second operation they reached the target successfully and Sergeant Blanchard was happy to say 'bombs gone' from his prone position in the nose of the Halifax. Suddenly, the flak stopped and the searchlights came on and this usually meant looking out for fighters. Soon they came — three Messerschmitt 110s — that attacked the Halifax bomber, setting it on fire. The order to bale out was given. Blanchard landed in a potato field near the village of Harcourt in Belgium. Later that day he met two elderly people who told him to stay in the field and they would return with food for him. This was brought by a woman of about thirty and a six-year-old child. Later, a farmer who spoke English told him to head for Liège. This he did and reached the town on the 18 June. Here, Blanchard stayed with the Maeger family. Mr Maeger was the Commissioner of Police, so he was in pretty good and powerful hands. From here, he travelled to Brussels in a car driven by a Belgian army captain. In Brussels he was taken to a flat, said to be in the grounds of the Swiss Legation. He stayed here until the 3 July, when he and five other evading airmen were taken to Paris, but now their luck ran out and they were arrested by the Gestapo and taken to Fresnes prison. It would appear there was a serious breach in the resistance organisation, as many airmen were arrested and sent to this prison around this time. Blanchard was kept here for six weeks, then taken to Dulagluft and finally to Stalag 4 at Fallingbostel which was his abode until liberated in May 1945. Evading capture depended on a lot of luck as well as help from many brave people.

This operation against Düsseldorf of the 11-12 June, was also the beginning of operations of Fighter Command in support of large-scale night raids by Bomber Command. This was now possible owing to fewer enemy raids on the UK by night. These operations were given the code-name 'Flower', and were carried out by Mosquito aircraft, whose role was to patrol enemy night-fighter airfields, and to cover them during the period that the Bomber force was operating in the area of the German fighter bases. As well as this, Beaufighter aircraft of 141 Squadron, based at Wittering, Lincolnshire, carried out operations known as 'Serrate'. They carried special apparatus for detecting and homing on to enemy AI transmissions. They also carried Mk IV AI, to enable the aircrews to find the range of the enemy night-fighters which it was pursuing in order to complete the final stages of the interception. The Beaufighter aircraft also patrolled in the vicinity of the bomber stream.

Each morning these operations were planned and controlled by the night operations branch of Bomber Command. They would pass on to the intruder controller the target or targets for that night's operations. He, in turn, would inform the intruder squadron involved and also the controllers of Nos 10, 11 and 12 Groups that aircraft would be required for 'Flower' and 'Serrate' operations. In the afternoon, the detailed Bomber Command program was once again passed to the controllers by scrambled telephone communication. A tactical plan would then be prepared by each CO of the squadrons involved that night. In the case of 141 Squadron, it was Wing Commander Bob Braham, DSO, DFC, who himself took part in many of the patrols. The two Mosquito squadrons 139 and 105, were often involved in 'Flower' operations.

The night of 12-13 June. Target — BOCHUM

The third attack on Bochum during the Battle of the Ruhr. On this occasion, 503 aircraft set out, of which 430 attacked the target. En route 11 target Mosquitos marked with red TIs. At 1.40a.m. a salvo of red TIs were dropped in error by a Mosquito about fourteen miles north-east of the aiming point, followed by green TIs two minutes later. About 50 aircraft of the following force attacked these target indicators, but the majority of back-up and the main force aircraft bombed the correct concentration. Over 14,000 square yards of the upper-storey of barrack buildings at a large, new military camp north-west of Kornharpen were gutted. One hundred and thirty-four tons of bombs fell on the built-up area of Bochum, and about 425,000 square yards of the target was seen to be damaged. The German casualties were 400 killed and 400 seriously injured.

The aircraft of No.1 Group reported the cloud cover as varying throughout the attack from 3/10ths to 8/10ths. The attack opened well and all the crews of the first wave were confident that the marking was accurate and that the first Pathfinder markers were well concentrated. The second wave, however, found the markers scattered, and in the final stages of the attack, two distinct concentrations of fire on the ground had been started, with a distance between them of four to eight miles. The flak was moderate to intense and operating with considerable searchlight activity. The number of German night-fighter sorties recorded was 68 of which 44 operated against the bomber stream. The Germans reported: 'British bombers attacked west German territory, particularly the town of Bochum. Twenty-nine enemy bombers were shot down.' In fact, 24 bombers were lost and a further 33 damaged by flak and two damaged by enemy fighters.

Tom Wingham, flying with 102 Squadron, remembers a deal of fighter activity as Northern Lights gave a great display to the north and a moon to the south — he had always wanted to see the Northern Lights but not under these circumstances. He saw aircraft shot down on the way to the target, but most of them appeared to be outside the main bomber stream. His aircraft was hit by flak, with one piece of shrapnel just missing the navigator, who, had he been in his usual position at the time, would have been hit. Sergeant Easby of 100 Squadron, remembers the way in over Holland as being reasonably quiet, despite the cloud being low and the moon bright — ideal conditions for fighters. Easby narrates:

> We soon realized that what first appeared to be the target, was in fact, a decoy. Once we had decided, we turned towards the target; it was then that the searchlights picked us up. We soon had not one but ten beams on us. Despite all the pilot's efforts to evade the searchlights, we could not lose them and the flak began bursting around us. It seemed like every gun in Bochum was concentrating on us. The only thing to do was to get rid of the bombs, especially the 4000lb. The pilot put the aircraft into a 'screaming' dive which proved

> highly successful, but only after we had dropped from 20,000 to 10,000 feet. On landing back at base, we found a piece of shrapnel had passed through the perspex in the bomb aimer's panel and had struck the lamp-holder which, in turn, hit the bomb aimer in the eye. But except for a bruised eye, he escaped injury. I did not think many had been fooled by the decoy so I think we can safely assume that Bochum had been fairly well pranged.'

When Dennis Whittaker of 405 Squadron and his crew got out to their aircraft, they found the groundcrew taking out black boxes, these held the scientific equipment in the aircraft. When asked why they were taking this out, they were told that the aircraft was to be screened the next day, and to save time were taking out some of the equipment. They were asked to stop doing this and to leave it until they had returned from the operation.

When they had successfully reached the target and bombed it, they decided to climb as high as they could to avoid the slip-streams of other aircraft. Whittaker relates:

> As we were climbing, we were hit by a shell which hit one of the starboard engines and it caught fire; also the starboard outer engine began to give trouble and so the order was given to bale out. When I tried to open the front hatch, it would not budge because the navigator was standing on the door putting his chute on. We then argued about who should bale out first. The rule was that in a non-emergency situation, the navigator was supposed to go first, and in an emergency situation such as this, I was supposed to go first. In the end we decided that I would bale out first. However, in leaving the aircraft I had forgotten to undo my oxygen lead which was still plugged into the aircraft. Fortunately I had taken off my helmet and this saved me from breaking my neck as the lead went off with a big bang, to such an extent, the navigator thought I had hit my head on leaving the aircraft. I landed in a cornfield and after three days I was captured on a farm. The Germans took me to an airfield for interrogation, then by bus to the local station. The bus was crowded but no one took any notice of me despite being in flying jacket and RAF uniform. At the railway station we got on a train which was going to Frankfurt, en route for Dulagluft. I was put in a reserved compartment, though the people who had occupied it first refused to budge, until an officer in jackboots arrived and roared at them to move, which they did. Because of an air raid on Essen the train had to stop and we sought refuge in the air raid shelters. At the first one my guards and I tried, we were refused entry, but eventually we managed to get in one and I found myself standing next to a man in a black leather coat who, addressing me in perfect English said: 'You're British aren't you?' I replied: 'Yes'. He then said that the raids on London were just as bad, having been there recently. Maybe he was Swiss who knows, as I never found out. When the raid was over I was

> taken back to the train station and kept away from the main body of people. I noticed a number of German soldiers around. After a few hours wait we boarded the train. One of my guards said later: 'It was a good job we had got on the train when we did, as a Sergeant-Major back there was going to form a lynching party for you.

On this operation Sergeant Aaron, who later was to be awarded the VC, was attacked by a Messerschmitt 109. Major Werner Streib of the *Luftwaffe*, who was to end the war with 65 'kills' and the Knights Cross with Swords and Oak Leaves, claimed no less than five bombers this night.

The industrial output from Bochum was reduced by 45 per cent after this raid. In the town, there were ten bunkers and five underground shelters which could take 20,000 people, and up to the first big raid on Bochum, the Civil Defence had coped quite well, but now they were overwhelmed. It was after this attack that Goebbels informed Hitler that he had told the people of Bochum of his personal interest in their welfare.

The night of 14-15 June. Target — OBERHAUSEN

The code-name for this target was 'Gillaroo', with 203 aircraft being despatched to attack Oberhausen, which was about the size of Plymouth. The marking was undertaken by six *OBOE* Mosquitos, of which four marked within two minutes of each other, leaving a gap owing to the first Mosquito being a little early in marking. The timing of the main force was good: 123 bombed out of 142 within the planned period of 1.15 to 1.34a.m. It was a well timed attack the method used being skymarkers. Mosquitos were reserves and not used in the marking plan. A reconnaissance on the 18-19 June showed heavy, concentrated damage. The output from the iron and steel works was reduced by 5 per cent. On their return journey, the aircrew could see the fires resulting from the attack, from as far away as the Dutch coast. The German claim of having shot down twenty multi-engine bombers was three more than the seventeen aircraft actually lost. Thirty-seven aircraft were damaged by flak.

Pilot Officer Robert Taylor of 1409 Reconnaissance Flight, set off at 11.30p.m. on the 14 June, but en route to the Ruhr, their aircraft was attacked by two fighters, reported to be Focke-Wulf 109s. In the attack, a shell went through the fuselage and Taylor was thrown forward, and suffered cuts to his eyes and neck. The aircraft then went into a spin and completely out of control. The pilot of the Mosquito, Flight Sergeant Durrant, told Taylor, his navigator, to bale out. But when Taylor tried to do so, because of his stout build, he got stuck in the entrance to the bomb aimer's compartment. Durrant meanwhile, went out of the top hatch of the aircraft. Somehow Taylor managed to connect his parachute to his harness and leave the aircraft. It was believed the perspex had blown away giving him just that bit more room to free himself from the aircraft. At the time, the aircraft was at 2000 feet, so within two or three minutes he was on the ground. He landed in a wheatfield near the village of St-Perre-La-Reviara in France and was approached by four farm labourers and a boy. They took his parachute away and buried it. With the help of a number of French people he was able to get back to the UK within ten days. On the 10 August he was awarded the DFC. The account of his successful evasion was included in the recommendation.

'Serrate' operations by Beaufighters of 141 Squadron were active in intercepting enemy fighters in the vicinity of the bomber stream. Wing Commander Braham, DSO, DFC, and his navigator, Flight Lieutenant Gregory, DFC, DFM, took off at 11.35p.m. for an intruder patrol off Deelen. At 2a.m. when over Stavoren, Holland, Gregory saw an enemy aircraft coming up behind them to attack. A dog-fight followed until Braham was able to get on the fighter's tail and rake his fuselage from tail to cockpit with cannon and machine-gun fire. The fighter was seen to go down, in a vertical dive and crash in flames. It was identified as a Messerschmitt Me 110.

The night of 21-22 June. Target — KREFELD

The code-name for this target was 'Mahseer'. Krefeld, with a population of 170,000 was a modern industrial town in the Rhine provinces and situated on the west bank of the Rhine, about three miles from the river itself and fifteen miles north-west of Düsseldorf. Krefeld was the largest producer of high-grade steel in Germany; one of its plants, the great Deutsche Edelstahlwerke combine, turned out nearly 200,000 tons of high-grade steel annually. This steel was sent to Krupps where it was used in the manufacture of aero-engines, engine crankshafts and machine tools. Apart from its steel industry, it had been famous since the seventeenth century for the manufacture of silks (an industry started by the French Huguenots) which, in wartime, was used to make silk parachutes. The town also acted as a railway junction for goods and passenger traffic travelling north to Holland and south to Cologne, and central Germany. Krefeld had been attacked by bombers in October 1942, and again in January 1943 when its marshalling yards were damaged.

On this raid of the 21-22 June, 705 aircraft were despatched, of which 561 aircraft attacked the target. The remainder aborted or just did not make the target area. The marking was done by nine Mosquitos dropping red TIs at intervals. Four of these Mosquitos carried one-minute delay TIs so that the marking would be continuous. The backing-up was excellent with 75 per cent of the markers falling within three miles of the aiming point. In order to saturate the German defences along the chosen route into Krefeld, the bomber crews were instructed to make every effort to keep together in a concentrated stream. In the time allotted, which was 53 minutes, it would mean an average of fourteen aircraft flying over the target every minute. In the third wave, timed for 1.49a.m. to 1.57a.m., the target was entirely allocated to 98 Stirlings of No.3 Group.

Two thousand tons of high explosives and incendiaries were dropped on Krefeld. This included 4000 bombs, which were released at a rate of five every minute. The raid had been highly concentrated in the centre of the town, doing extensive damage around the Adolf Hitler Strasse, and the West Wall. Fires raged unchecked and 900 acres out of a possible 1100 acres of fully built-up areas, were gutted. Some 23 factories or industrial concerns and 6200 houses were destroyed, and 14,000 damaged, leaving 72,600 people homeless. In the attack 1036 people were killed and 4500 injured. Great confusion reigned for many weeks in the commercial and administrative part of the town. This raid became known by the people as 'The Terror Raid'. The people were left nervous and apprehensive, but they showed no particular animosity toward the enemy airmen. Six months engineering production and ten months textile production was lost as a result of this raid.

The flak was heavy at the beginning of the attack, but fell away later. Sixty-two night-fighters were heard, of which 27 were active against the bombers. The Germans claimed 44 aircraft shot down, but the actual figure was 42, of which 30 were estimated to have been lost to night-fighters, four to enemy flak, and eight to unknown causes. One aircraft of 419 Squadron shot down a Focke-Wulf 190 which was seen to hit the ground and burst into flames.

Sergeant Murdock was commended for his action on this, his first operation, in which his Halifax JD 250 R of 51 Squadron was attacked no less than twelve times. The pilots who arrived over the target at the end of the attack reported a pall of smoke three miles high. One of them said: 'If you can imagine a blaze five or six times as big as the Coventry one, you can get some idea of what Krefeld looked like last night.' Squadron Leader Derbyshire and his crew of 9 Squadron survived the battle and were awarded two DFCs and five DFMs between then. The rear gunner, Fred Parsons, remembers seeing a single-engine biplane above them, but when they reported this back at base, they were not believed. One of the Mosquitos, for some reason not known, bombed Hamborn that night.

The raid on Krefeld was disastrous for 35 Squadron who lost six crews in all. On their outward journey, Sergeant Milne and his crew, in Lancaster BB 368 Letter H were hit by flak south of Rotterdam and the starboard outer engine was put out of action. Despite this, they went to bomb the target from a height of 13,000 feet. On their return journey just after crossing the Dutch coast, the port inner engine failed, then half-way across the North Sea, the starboard inner engine also gave out. The decision to ditch was made and the aircraft was brought down on the water at 90m.p.h. It was 3a.m. and they were about seven miles north of the Cross Sands lighthouse. Their dinghy was first sighted by two Mosquitos. As a result, two Walrus seaplanes of 278 Squadron came out and landed on the water at about 9a.m. Between them, they rescued the seven men and took them to Coltishall.

The aircraft flown by Pilot Officer Hickson and his crew was shot down by a Halifax aircraft which had either been manned by a German aircrew, or by an Allied aircrew that thought the aircraft they attacked was a German night-fighter. Two of the crew were killed outright but the remainder got out of the aircraft safely. Flying Officer Patrick Croft, the bomb aimer, managed to get to Paris via Holland and Belgium, but when he and other aircrew evading capture were taken to a hotel, they were promptly arrested by the Gestapo and taken, as were others during this period, to Fresnes prison in Paris. Here they stayed for a month before being taken to Dulagluft, the *Luftwaffe* interrogation centre. From there they were taken to Muhlberg POW camp, where Croft was to remain until the 25 April 1945.

One happier event for 35 Squadron, was that Flight Lieutenant Alex Cranswick completed his 96th operation and was awarded the DSO. Also Flight Sergeant Kenneth Greene was awarded a bar to the DFM he had been awarded two years before. Greene was in Lancaster ED 499 flown by Flight Lieutenant Robertson, when, over the target and having released their bomb-load, a 4lb incendiary bomb from another aircraft flying above them fell, through the astrodome, lodged in the heating apparatus and ignited. Promptly, Ken Greene picked the bomb up and threw it, with the help of the navigator, behind the main spar of the aircraft, which successfully extinguished it. He was on his 41st operation at the time.

For Keith Ryrie, the Krefeld raid was his second trip as second pilot to Second Lieutenant Jack Russell of the US Army Air Corps, but who was flying with the RAF in 57 Squadron. The help that Jack Russell gave Keith was of the greatest use when he eventually got his own crew. On this operation, Jack said it was quiet compared with some targets, although to Keith it seemed more than enough was going on.

The German radar station fifteen miles north-east of Brussels and with the code-name 'Tomtit' was on full alert. However, the bomber stream was passing 40 miles to the north of the station, but they did pick up a lone Allied aircraft, Stirling BK 712 of 218 Squadron, and flown by Pilot Officer William Schillinglaw who came from New South Wales in Australia. He also carried with him a second pilot, Flying Officer Arne Helvard, a Dane who was there to gain experience, much as Keith Ryrie was doing with Jack Russell. Schillinglaw's aircraft had strayed over Belgium and was heading towards 'Tomtit'. Orbiting over the radar station was Leutnant Heinz Wolfgang Schnaufer, a twenty year-old pilot who had joined the *Luftwaffe* in 1942. He received a radio warning from Leutnant Kuhnel, who was commanding 13/211th *Luftwaffe* Signals Regiment, that told him: 'A courier or target is approaching from the west.' In their cabin the giant Würzburg set was painstakingly tracking the Stirling bomber, giving Schnaufer its height and bearing. In the rear of the Messerschmitt, Leutnant Bard, the radio operator, suddenly saw on his screen what he was looking for, a small speck of light which became bigger and bigger as the unsuspecting Stirling came nearer, until at 1.30a.m. and when 500 yards away to the right and above them, Schnaufer caught sight of the flames from the Stirling's exhausts. As he closed in beneath the bomber, he was seen by one of the Stirling's gunners, probably the rear gunner, Edgar Hart. Schillinglaw put the Stirling into a violent corkscrew manoeuvre but despite this, Schnaufer was able to get the bomber in his sights and after being hit by cannon and machine-gun fire, the Stirling burst into flames. It flew on for a while and then plunged into the ground. The attack and destruction of Stirling BK 712 had taken exactly three minutes.

A search was made at first light that morning for the wrecked bomber. It was Kuhnel who set out to find it, which he did, at the village of Langdorp. All that was left of the aircraft was twisted metal. The bodies of Schillinglaw and his crew were among the wreckage. A message was sent to the International Red Cross in Switzerland, which in turn, sent a telegram to the UK. The crew were buried at Langdorp. Edgar Hart, Tom Bunn, Arne Helvard, William Schillinglaw, Ray Goward, Arthur Gurney, Pat McArdle and Doug Ashay had made their last flight. It was Schnaufer's thirteenth 'kill' out of a total of 121 he was to make by the end of the war. He was to add Diamonds to his Knights Cross, already having the Oak Leaves and Swords. He was the world's highest-scoring night-fighter ace. In 1950, aged 27, he died in hospital after a road crash in which his car was hit by a lorry with faulty brakes. The tailplane of his Messerschmitt 110 now resides in the Imperial War Museum, London, UK.

Sergeant Frank Hugo was flying with 7 Squadron as a bomb aimer. The pilot was Pilot Officer Meiklejohn, an Australian. On the outward journey their aircraft was attacked by no less than three Junkers 88s. The aircraft was bady damaged and Meiklejohn who was wounded, gave the order to bale out. Hugo recalls: 'I finally opened the escape hatch and said to the pilot: "Goodbye Skipper". When I thought I was clear, I felt for my chest-pack but could not find it, looking up I could see the chute-pack attached by only one hook, I pulled it down, found the handle and pulled the rip-cord.' After safely landing, he made off and was helped by three local people to get to Brussels. Continues Hugo:

> This was our downfall. We were a group of aircrew and sent to a home run by Prospiv de Zitter (The Captain). Later we found out he was one of Harold Cole's* mob. From Brussels we were taken to Paris, and after a few nights in so called 'safe houses', I went off with a fellow who spoke good English (I wonder if it was Cole) who asked a lot of questions about target marking. We were on our way to the station to catch a train to Biarritz before getting to Spain, when on passing the Gobeln Tapestry factory, we were arrested and taken to Fresnes prison. Here, after a period of solitary confinement, followed by a lot of unpleasant interrogation and many threats, myself and others were sent to Dulagluft. Forty of us were locked in a cattle truck for three days as we travelled to Stalag IV B at Muhlberg.

During his time at Fresnes Frank Hugo had his twentieth birthday. It was April 1945 before he was released from Stalag IV B by the Russians, and with the help of the Americans he got to the UK in early June. At the

* Harold Cole was an army deserter who absconded with the Sergeants' Mess funds in France in 1940. He stayed on the continent helping airmen to escape, but he also was later known to be helping the Germans as well. He himself was later shot by the French police.

end of the war Zitter was caught and killed himself while in prison. Cole died in a gun battle with the French police in 1946.

On this operation, Sergeant George Honey and his crew of 102 Squadron were in Halifax JD 206 when the aircraft was hit by flak. The hydraulic system and three engines were put out of action. The bombs and leaflets were jettisoned, but, having done this, the bomb doors would not then close, so at 16,000 feet and still losing height, Honey decided to ditch the Halifax. This he did successfully, coming down on the North Sea eighteen to twenty miles north-west of Over Flakkee, Holland. The aircraft's emergency dinghy inflated automatically and came out of its storage compartment the right way up. The last man had evacuated the aircraft before the water in the fuselage had reached a depth of three feet. Some 30 minutes after ditching, the bomber sank. Fortunately for them, they were observed by bombers returning from the raid, and then by Mustangs at 6.35a.m. and then again at 3.30p.m. by Typhoon aircraft. At 4.40p.m. the controller of 277 Squadron informed a Flight Lieutenant Brown that a dinghy had been sighted perilously near the Dutch coast. The plan devised, was for two Walrus seaplanes to be sent to rescue the men. These seaplanes would be escorted by Typhoons who would, in turn, be relieved by two Spitfires of 277 Squadron, and they would be relieved by another two Typhoons of 198 Squadron. In this way, there would be a total fighter coverage throughout the rescue.

The two Walrus seaplanes were piloted by Warrant Officers Greenfield and Ormiston. When they arrived near the area, a red Very light was fired from the dinghy and this was seen by Greenfield, who in turn, dropped a smoke-float and then landed on the sea. He took aboard Sergeant Honey and two others. At the same time, Ormiston was landing but by now the sea was rough, and getting worse. Greenfield was able to take-off, but not before he had been taxiing some 30 minutes, and after two bounces off the sea. They were escorted to base by the two Spitfires and landed at 9.10p.m. where upon the rescued men were taken by ambulance to the station's sick quarters. The second Walrus, however, was not able to take-off because the sea conditions had got worse and they were now only fiften miles from the Dutch Coast and in danger of attack. This came when two Focke-Wulf 190s were seen and a warning given to Ormiston to take evasive action. Flying Officer Hessleyn in one of the Spitfire escorts, sped towards one of the German fighters and as they approached each other, both opened fire. The German missed but Hessleyn hit the German fighter's engine and the pilot's cockpit. The enemy fighter was claimed as damaged in Hessleyn's combat report.

Because of the sea conditions, Ormiston decided to taxi the Walrus all the way back to the English coast. This, they attempted to do from 7.50p.m. to 2a.m. in the following morning when the Walrus ran out of petrol, still several miles short of the coast. The waves were nine to ten feet high and the visibility so bad that the escorting Spitfires had to warn them of mines and other obstacles. The escorting aircraft were relieved by surface craft that were engaged in seeking out the struggling Walrus. When at 2a.m. the Walrus ran out of petrol and the engine stopped, the waves were by now ten to fifteen feet high, and it took twenty minutes for a tow-rope to be attached to one of the escorting vessels, motor torpedo-boat D16. It was towed for one hour, during which time the sea was so rough that the boat became invisible to the Walrus's crew when it dipped in the trough of the sea. The Walrus was taking heavy punishment from the sea and liable to break up, so Ormiston asked the escorting boats to take his crew and himself off. This was accomplished only with great difficulty, but they were finally taken to Felixstowe, Suffolk where they arrived at 6.30a.m. By this time, the Walrus had beached itself, but a party from 277 Squadron led by Flight Lieutenant Brown on board a high-speed launch were on their way to try and salvage it. Brown succeeded in boarding the Walrus and with the help of two sailors, started to bale out the water inside, before towing it to the hangars at Felixstowe. It was in a sorry state, and with the engines caked in salt deposit from the sea. The only injury to the Halifax crew was Sergeant Tugberry, the bomb aimer, who had a cut face. This was the third successful ditching carried out by 102 Squadron during the period April to June 1943.

In Germany, Dr Karl Holzammer, the German radio 'Home Front' reporter stated after the Krefeld raid: 'The damage is enormous, this is a spectacle of destruction and immense devastation. This madness does not deserve a full description. Delayed-action bombs which were mistaken for "duds" caused many losses.'

The night of 22-23 June. Target — MÜLHEIM

The congested town of Mülheim, which was about the same size as Wolverhampton, was sandwiched between Essen, Duisburg and Oberhausen. Up to the 22 June it had not been attacked before. The importance of the target was in its foundries, furnaces, rolling-mills, engine workshops and also its position as one of the principal outlets of the Ruhr to southern Germany. The code-name for this target was 'Steelhead'.

Of the 557 aircraft despatched on this operation, 499 attacked the target. The target was marked at 1.20a.m. by eight *OBOE* Mosquitos, and then two more Mosquitos attacked the red TIs with 500lb bombs for training purposes. In all, 1500 tons of bombs were dropped by the bomber force. At the end of the attack, more than two acres of the main workshops of the Vereinigte Stahlwerke AG was burnt out, and other buildings in the works were demolished. The main railway station was completely destroyed. In all, five large steelworks were hit.

The target was described by one Australian as: 'The hottest target yet encountered'. Both here and at Oberhausen, the local defences were joined by those of Duisburg, Essen and Düsseldorf. Heavy flak was reported as moderate in the target area but intense in the defended areas which covered the immediate approaches. There was intense searchlight activity in small cones and from around the target. The British wireless intelligence service reported 89 sorties by ground-controlled night-fighters, of which 46 were active against the bomber force. One German account of the raid was as follows: 'British and North American air formations carried out several heavy raids against towns in the west and in occupied territory. Considerable destruction was caused in Oberhausen and Mülheim. In the attacks of yesterday and last night, 92 enemy aircraft, including at least 75 heavy bombers, were shot down.' The number actually shot down over Mülheim was 35.

Flying a Stirling bomber that night was Sergeant Handley, who was known in 15 Squadron as 'Tommy'. He reported seeing four Stirlings being destroyed on their bombing-run. They were silhouetted by searchlight cones. Two appeared to collide and the other two either went down to flak hits or by bombs dropped by aircraft from above them. This was always a problem for Stirling bomber crews on Ruhr targets as their ceiling for bombing was normally 12,000 feet, which was at least 6000 to 7000 feet below the height at which Lancasters and Halifaxes flew.

Sergeant Douglas Cameron was on his first operation with 158 Squadron. After successfully bombing the target, his aircraft was coned by searchlights and then came under intense flak fire. His intercom and radio was rendered useless. During the attack, four of the crew baled out, including navigator, Flying Officer Koch who was heard to say: 'We have been hit'. With the two gunners, Sergeants Les Young and Alan Young acting as navigator and flight engineer respectively they managed to get back to the UK and land at Downham Market in Norfolk. For his efforts on this occasion Cameron was recommended for the CGM, but later was awarded the DFM.

Reconnaissance coverage the next day showed very heavy damage and it was estimated that nearly one fifth of the houses in the town were destroyed. One newspaper's headlines the next day read: 'Mülheim. Mutilated.'

Flight Sergeant Jimmy Hughes of 57 Squadron was recommended for the DFM in November 1943. His recommendation included a mention of the raid on Mülheim, when his aircraft was attacked by a Messerschmitt 109. Hughes had been able to return fire and damaged the German fighter. He achieved a similar feat during the Cologne raid of the 8-9 July 1943. He later went on to serve with the PFF in 35 Squadron. Today he is a past President and stalwart supporter of the Pathfinder Association, and his wife Olivia is their Secretary.

The night of 24-25 June. Target — WUPPERTAL

This was the second raid on Wuppertal, and this time the other half of the city, Elberfeld, was attacked by 556 aircraft out of the 650 despatched. In this attack, 1700 tons of high explosives and incendiaries were dropped. Elberfeld fared even worse than the other half of Wuppertal, Barmen, which had been destroyed in the attack of 29-30 May. Enormous fires sprang up in all parts of the town, and there were three very large explosions caused by bursting 'blockbuster' bombs. The up-draught from these bombs lifted the attacking aircraft many hundreds of feet further in the air. Thirteen factories and 137 industrial concerns were severely damaged, and about 89 smaller plants outside the district were partially or wholly demolished. In the official report Elberfeld was labelled as obliterated. Some 80 per cent of the business and residential property of Wuppertal was destroyed.

The attack had started at 1.50a.m. when red TIs were dropped accurately by seven of the nine Mosquitos despatched. The defences in the target area itself were reported as almost negligible, heavy flak was slight and there were few searchlights. But in the Duisburg, Düsseldorf, Cologne and Bonn area, the bombers found heavy predicted, and barrage flak, and up to 50 searchlights operating. Nine aircraft were estimated to have been lost and 87 damaged. Wireless intelligence picked up 98 sorties by night-fighters of which 52 were against the bomber force. The German report stated that British bombers attacked several towns in western Germany, particularly Wuppertal, Elberfeld and Remscheid. Thirty enemy bombers were shot down. In fact it was 33.

One crew who were on their first sortie together decided to fly over and drop their bomb load on the target flares. Their decision took them right into the middle of the Düsseldorf defences when, as the pilot recalls:

> Searchlights sprang up from nowhere, and before I had time to wet my lips, I found myself coned by about 30 searchlights. The flak was terrific and I honestly do not know how we came through it alive. Having evaded the searchlights I began the run-up to the red target markers when, once more, the searchlights caught me, and once again the flak became very uncomfortable. When the bomb aimer asked for 'straight and level' for the bomb release photograph I thought now we have had it, but somehow we managed to drop our bombs and turn out of the target area; all this with the searchlights still on us. The crew were badly shaken and consequently the navigator's homing navigation was not as good as it might have been, as we seemed to do a tour of Germany, and France as well for that matter. Somehow we made the Dutch coast — never has a coastline looked so good. Back at base, fourteen holes were found in the aircraft, and when I mentioned this to a newspaper reporter at our de-briefing, he printed it.

Sergeant Wilfed Towse and his crew of 15 Squadron, flying in Stirling EH890, were attacked on their outward journey over the Dutch coast by a Junkers 88, but his gunners were able to shoot it down. After they had reached the target and bombed it, their aircraft was hit no less than five times by flak which holed three petrol tanks on the starboard side, and one on the port side. One of the petrol tanks on the starboard wing caught fire, and orders were issued to the crew to begin to prepare to abandon the aircraft. This appears to have been misunderstood by the bomb aimer Flight Sergeant Martin, who immediately baled out over the target.

Sergeant Towse put the aircraft into a dive which extinguished the flames. A course was then set for base, the main problem being that there was only enough petrol for 70 minutes flying. At 3.05a.m. the starboard inner engine failed. While crossing the coast at Dunkirk, they were coned by searchlights but somehow they escaped its clutches. At 3.40a.m. and twenty miles out at sea, the starboard outer engine failed and then the port outer engine failed through lack of petrol. Despite this, Towse flew the Stirling on its port inner engine only and with the petrol gauges showing empty. Eventually his only option was to ditch the aircraft in the sea. When he did this, the aircraft sank within ten seconds of hitting the water and Towse found himself upside down and with his feet through the pilot's escape-hatch, and still held by his straps. He somehow managed to release the safety catch and climb out through the hatch, and to add to his problems, he was cut about the head when the side of the cockpit was crushed. He came to the surface close to their dinghy and was pulled on board by the wireless operator. They had come down nineteen and a half miles east of Felixstowe at 4a.m. The waves at the time were between four and six feet high. They were lucky enought to be spotted by a Spitfire at 5a.m. and within an hour and a half, were picked up by a motor-launch. Both Sergeant Towse and Sergeant Norman Pawly, the wireless operator, were awarded immediate DFMs.

For Wing Commander Barrell, the CO of 7 Squadron, this was his 60th operation. He and his crew in their Lancaster bomber were attacked by an enemy fighter and, as a result, their port outer engine caught fire. The order to bale out was given, as Barrell was unable to control the aircraft. The navigator, Flight Lieutenant Hilton, who was on his 33rd operation, got stuck in the escape-hatch but was pushed out by the flight engineer, Pilot Officer Hudson. He, in turn, handed the pilot his chute and then tried to bale out himself. It was only Hudson's third operation on Lancasters and he seemed a little confused as to the correct baling out drill because he baled out head first, or tried to, as his shoulders got caught until he, in turn, was pushed out. By this time, the aircraft was at 7000 feet. The aircraft crashed and exploded about three miles north-west of where Hudson landed. He later heard that two members of the crew had come down in the water and drowned. Three other members of the crew were later reported to be POWs, and another three were reported killed, including the gallant Barrell, who had, like many captains, stayed with his aircraft until it was too late to get out. This only left Hudson, who was able to evade capture and get back to the UK. In total this crew had completed no less than 308 operations between them.

The destruction of another Ruhr town heavily attacked in 1943 — Dortmund. (Mike King)

'For You The War Is Over'. A member of a Halifax crew shot down on 27 March 1943 during a raid on Bremen and now a prisoner being interrogated by a Luftwaffe officer. (Imperial War Museum)

The crew of Wellington HE 980 who were members of the Wellington Veterans' Club. (Imperial War Museum)

Flt Lt Gibson's crew. (Bill Powell)

12 The End Of the Battle

The night of 25-26 June. Target — GELSENKIRCHEN

The town of Gelsenkirchen was situated near the middle of the Ruhr area, 27 miles west of Dortmund. It was a centre for the mining of coal and had two of the largest synthetic oil plants in Germany. It was also the site of a number of iron furnaces, chemical, tin, and steelworks. Much of the raw material feeding the blast-furnaces of the Ruhr industrial towns passed through Gelsenkirchen. It had a population of about 300,000 and could be compared in size with Bradford in Yorkshire.

The operational code-name for the raid was 'Ferox'. Of the 473 aircraft that took off to attack Gelsenkirchen, 424 attacked the target. Zero hour was 1.20a.m. The target was marked by seven of the twelve Mosquitos despatched, four of them with flares using the 'skymarking' method. The first Mosquito was ten minutes late and many main force crews bombed before the first skymarkers had ignited. and many between the gap of the 3rd and 4th flare load igniting.

At Amsterdam and en route to the target a number of searchlights were working in co-operation with heavy flak. In the Ruhr area 63 aircraft were damaged by flak. The barrage was one of the heaviest put up so far in the Battle and the bombers also had to contend with night-fighters all along the route. Some 23 of the recorded night-fighters were operating against the bombers. Of the 30 aircraft that went missing, 18 to 25 were thought to have been shot down by fighters. From the bomber side, four claims were made of shooting down enemy fighters.

The flak was so intense that one of the Lancasters caught in a barrage was blown upside down on two occasions. The pilot of this aircraft recalled that:

> So many things were happening at the same time, that I didn't have time to think. Flak was bursting all around us and then a shell suddenly exploded just beneath us and threw the Lanc on its back. I didn't realize this had happened until a few mintues later. When it exploded, the aircraft went into a dive and there I was fighting like made to regain control. I had lost 5000 feet before I could steady it, and when I looked up, I saw clouds where they should not be. It was then, and only then, that I realized we were flying upside down. I then got the Lanc the right way up but as I did, it happened again. A complete repeat of the first time.

As Sergeant Alfred Ames, flying with 75 Squadron as a flight engineer, moved forward to adjust one of the engine controls on take-off, the aircraft dropped back on to the runway very heavily, throwing Ames in such a way that he suffed a rupture in his left groin. What had happened, in fact, was that the aircraft had been thrown into the air by the tough surface on the runway, and this gave the impression to the crew that they had taken off. In spite of considerable pain and having to hold his side throughout the four-hour flight, Ames did not mention it to the pilot or the rest of the crew until they had landed back at base. He was then taken to hospital, where he underwent an immediate operation. He was later awarded an immediate DFM.

Wing Commander Dudley Burnside of 427 Squadron was in Halifax DK 144 and actually going down the runway, fully bombed-up, when he realized the aircraft had no brake pressure. As he swung off the runway, he saw he was going to hit other parked aircraft, so he opened up the throttles on the outer engines to bring the aircraft around and in doing so, the undercarriage collapsed. The aircraft was later written-off. It had only arrived on the Squadron that morning as a brand new aircraft.

Sergeant Powell of 102 Squadron, remembers their aircraft being caught in a searchlight beam, which was soon followed by five more. However, the pilot managed to get the aircraft clear after taking violent evasive action, escaping with just minor superficial damage. However, a large washer from the nose-cone of a shell had penetrated the floor of the aircraft and came up through Sergeant Powell's seat, smashing the main fuse panel and embedded itself in his 'Gen Bag' in which he carried his torch and various bits and pieces to do with his radio if he needed to do a running repair. Luckily for him, he had left his seat and was standing by the pilot at the time.

On this operation against Gelsenkirchen two buildings of the Vereinigte Stahlwerke were destroyed and five others damaged. Coal mines also suffered badly. The target area was packed with vast coal dumps and batteries of coke ovens vital to the steel industries of Essen. An account of the raid was written by Edward J.Hart of the *Sunday Express*, he was their air reporter at the time. He wrote his story from the RAF station at Binbrook in Lincolnshire.

One of the pilots on this operation, Squadron Leader Charles Martin, DFC, was on his 43rd trip, so knew all about bombing and the Ruhr, and he had no illusions about the strength of the Ruhr defences. He said: 'They are increasing all the time their co-ordination of ground and night-fighter defences. We can no longer just weave in and out of their barrage, speed is the thing now. A solid and continuous block of flak stretches for nearly 50 miles, all the way from Cologne to well beyond Gelsenkirchen.'

With so many operations going on, one would expect the records to show more incidents of bombs exploding while being loaded into the aircraft, but, surprisingly, there were few. On the 3 July 1943, aircraft of 460 Squadron at Binbrook were being bombed-up to go to Cologne, when unexpectedly, an entire bomb load from Lancaster DV 172, comprising one 4000lb bomb, several 500lb high explosive bombs and clusters of 4lb incendiary bombs fell on to the runway. The incendiary bombs immediately caught fire and although the groundcrew tried to throw them clear of the bombs, these bombs were, in fact, being roasted in the middle of the fires. Two groundcrew members jumped from the aircraft, where they had been working and ran for cover. When the fire crews arrived, DV 172 was well alight and all personnel in the area were evacuated and took cover. Very soon the bombs exploded and the nearest Lancaster's, R 5745 and ED 774 also caught fire. In the explosions several huts in the area were destroyed, windows were blown in, and a hangar roof blown off. Both DV 172 and R 5745 were destroyed but ED 774 was saved by Flight Sergeant Kan and the CO of 460 Squadron, Wing Commander Martin, only recently promoted from Squadron Leader, who tackled the blaze from inside the aircraft with hand extinguishers. As soon at it was safe, the duty Defence Watch was assembled in two sections and all debris was cleared from the perimeter of the airfield, making it possible for seventeen aircraft to take-off for Cologne. There were still two 500lb bombs unexploded, but when the bomb disposal unit from RAF Digby arrived at 1.30a.m. they found that the bombs had been removed from the area to enable the aircraft to take off. This had been done on the instructions of Group Captain Hughie Edwards, VC, and although this did not please the disposal boys, it was pointed out to them that the war effort had to go on.

In the court of inquiry it was stated that the 4000lb bomb had not been fused, but in the memories of Ted Loveridge, who was the Corporal in charge of the bomb dump at Binbrook, all bombs were fused in the dump and not at the aircraft, as was the case on some airfields. In his opinion the accident occurred because the jettison button in the aircraft had not been covered, and when two armourers working in the aircraft saw this, they tried to cover it, but in doing so, jettisoned the bombs on to the runway. In addition to the two Lancasters destroyed, seven other aircraft were damaged and not able to take part in that night's operations.

Another similar explosion took place at Snaith in Yorkshire, while aircraft were being bombed-up for a mining operation. When smoke was seen coming from the bomb-bay of one of the aircraft, Sergeant John Richards, who looked like the film actor, David Niven, entered the aircraft and found the fuselage floor above the bomb-bay on fire. He tried to put it out with an extinguisher but failed, so he grabbed the two carrier pigeon boxes and abandoned the aircraft. As he did so, a large, red sheet of flame erupted from the centre of the aircraft, which then buckled and fell on to the centre of the runway ending up in a V-shape. By this time, all aircrew and groundcrew personnel had taken cover. Shortly, there came a huge explosion as the aircraft's fuel supply and bomb load blew up.

On another occasion, this time at Scampton in Lincolnshire, an aircraft of 50 Squadron caught fire and the bombs exploded. Two aircraft of 50 Squadron and one aircraft of 57 Squadron were destroyed. Conditions at the time were foggy and pilots were ordered to move their aircraft away from the scene of the fire. When the next day came and the fog had cleared, aircraft were seen spread at all angles on the airfield.

The night of 9-10 July. Target — GELSENKIRCHEN

On this operation, 422 aircraft were despatched, of which 385 attacked the target. The attack overall was not successful, only eight of the fourteen Mosquitos were able to mark the target owing to failure of their *OBOE* equipment. Forty-seven sorties were recorded by ground-controlled night-fighters, of which 25 were against the bomber stream. The Germans reported eleven enemy bombers shot down. Rain and cloud over the German fighter bases possibly limited their activity particularly on the bomber's route through Holland to the target. In the target area, intense heavy flak was encountered and two aircraft were seen to be shot down. Seventy-nine aircraft were hit by flak. One Junkers 88 was claimed as shot down by a Lancaster of No.5 Group. On the return trip, enemy fighters were active in the Florennes area over Belgium and considerable flak was encountered at Amiens, France.

Flying as mid-upper gunner in Halifax DT 792 was Sergeant Fuller. This Halifax had been named 'Farouk' after the King of Egypt, 10 Squadron having connections with the Middle-East before coming to No.4 Group at Melbourne in Yorkshire. This trip to Gelsenkirchen was 10 Squadron's 100th trip from Melbourne. Sergeant Fuller, remembering this trip, said:

> A heavy barrage of flak gave us a hot reception similar to the Cologne raids, except that the bursting shells were more close. Shrapnel damaged the starboard outer cowling and a piece of jagged steel penetrated the side of the rear turret. From memory the ground crew found pieces embedded in the plating of it on our return. I remember distinctly hearing the loud 'pinging' sound the shrapnel pieces made when hitting 'Farouk'. It was a very unpleasant experience, although it could have been worse, and a great relief was felt when we passed out of this heavily defended area. Searchlights were active but did not trouble us. The bomb load was dropped and the return flight straightforward. This seven-hour operation was longer than our previous raids and although the majority of us landed back at Melbourne, two of the squadron's aircraft landed elsewhere because of fuel shortage. Eight of 10 Squadron's aircraft, including our own, were damaged by flak.

Flight Sergeant Liggett and his crew of 78 Squadron were hit by flak over the target. The bomb doors jammed in the open position as a result of being hit by flak. The port engine caught fire and was feathered. They were then attacked by a Messerschmitt 110, which put the rear turret out of action. In the attack, the rear turret had locked on the starboard quarter and the rear gunner, Sergeant Smith had to be freed from his turret with the help of mid-upper gunner, Sergeant Hughes and the navigator Sergeant Trowbridge. On the return trip and with only five minutes flying time of petrol left, Liggett had been unable to find a suitable landing site in the UK, so once again they crossed the English coast and ditched the aircraft 150 yards off the shore from Seaford, Sussex. The aircraft floated for about fifteen minutes and the crew except the wireless operator and the rear gunner were rescued. The wireless operator had swum ashore when they first ditched and the rear gunner had been washed out to sea, but was later picked up by an ASR launch.

Sergeant Clifford of 50 Squadron also ditched his aircraft four and a half miles off Bexhill-on-Sea, Sussex. He and five of his crew were picked up by high-speed launch 190 of No.28 ASR who were operating out of Newhaven. The flight engineer was killed and the aircraft caught fire on ditching because of leaking petrol. The pilot suffered facial burns. They had been hit by heavy flak over the target area. The pilot had, in fact, given the order to bale out but then retracted it, only it was too late for the mid-upper gunner, who had baled out.

The night of 25-26 July. Target — ESSEN

This was the sixth operation against Essen during the Battle. The crews were expecting Hamburg to be the target, but Air Chief Marshal Harris anticipated enemy fighters to be patrolling the area around Hamburg, it having been attacked for the last two nights. Another reason for switching the attack back to the Ruhr, was that the smoke, which still covered Hamburg from the previous raids, would hamper the marking operation.

For this operation, 705 aircraft were despatched, of which 628 attacked the target. The flak at Essen was unusually light, and the searchlights numerous but ineffective. Some reports stated that the searchlights were operating for the benefit of the fighters rather than the gunners on the ground. Seventy-five ground controlled night-fighter interceptions were heard, of which 42 were against the bombers. The Germans reported 61 aircraft shot down, but in fact, the total was 23. The Germans were including the US Air Force aircraft shot down from the previous daylight raid.

As on the Hamburg raids, 'Window'* was once again used, it was dropped at the rate of one bundle per minute. The ground-marking was carried out by fourteen of the sixteen Mosquitos despatched. The weather en route to Essen was clear with only slight cloud and some ground haze over Essen. The marking by the PFF was very close together and the timing exemplary. After the main force of bombers had done their job, white-greyish smoke clouds were seen billowing up to 22,000 feet, and flames from huge fires were seen 150 miles away on their homeward route.

Sergeant Nick Knilans, an American serving with the RCAF remembers several WAAFS waving them off at Woodhall Spa, Lincolnshire, the home

* A strip of metal foil about 10 inches long dropped in bundles, and dropped at about one every minute or so would represent on a radar screen a number of spurious aircraft and make it very difficult for the enemy to decide which is an aircraft and which is not.

of 619 Squadron. He always reminded his crew not to talk on the intercom unless it was important. Said Knilans: 'I had to impress on them that we were in a serious life or death situation'. Also, to sharpen their survival skills, Knilans would carry out the following manoeuvre. He relates: 'As there was no under-belly turret on the Lancaster, I compensated for this blind spot by tilting the aircraft's wing to port and then starboard. This gave the gunners a look at what was below. When I did this, I expected them to answer my movements, and this way I knew they were awake and alert.' Of the Essen raid, he recalls: 'We were flying near the front of the bomber stream. The twin-engine Wellingtons were at 16,000 feet, the Stirlings at 12,000 feet and the Lancs and Halifaxes at 20,000 feet. We were briefed to fly in three, ten minute segments; several squadrons could be in each segment.' The flak over Essen was heavy and their aircraft was hit several times. The starboard engine began to overheat, so it was feathered before it could catch fire. Also, petrol had been lost from the starboard main tank, but the flight engineer, Ken Ryall, who was only eighteen, knew exactly how to use every drop of petrol in the engines. Eventually, they made it back to base with only three engines working. When the aircraft was examined the next day, the groundcrew found that a shell had gone right through the main petrol tank but had not exploded; it did, however, leave a hole big enough to put your leg through.

Flying with Flight Lieutenant Garvey of 83 Squadron, in Lancaster R 5868, was General Anderson of the US Air Force. On his return, he remarked that the view of the burning city of Essen, was one of the most impressive sights he had ever seen.

Squadron Leader Clive Sinton, a flight commander with 432 Squadron, was on his eighth operation with Bomber Command, having previously served with the RCAF in Coastal Command. He was, in fact, British and served in the Merchant Navy before the war. When the war started, he was in Canada and so joined the RCAF. Sinton and his crew had no trouble crossing the Dutch Coast. Sinton remembered watching the motion of the sea below. Even on the blackest night, it would gleam; the more movement of the sea, the more the starlight would be reflected, and if the sea was broken, as it usually was, the top of the swell showed up as parallel lines. As he got near the Ruhr, he saw 'the "picket-fence" of searchlights, which never failed to churn one's gut'. There were, however, no fighters to be seen. It was a very black night but as he had bad night-vision anyway, this did not bother him.

The box barrage was a favourite ploy of the German flak batteries. When they knew the height, track and speed of the main bomber force, the Germans fired up boxes of exploding shells, knowing that some aircraft would have to fly through them. It was all very unnerving as one could see the brilliance of an explosion against the black night sky and feel the odd thump as one or two of the shells got too close. As Sinton described it: 'It was like a giant giving you a kick up the backside with his seven league boots.' An aircraft would be seen exploding some twenty miles ahead on their port side — orange and yellow colours accompanied by bits of aircraft thrown out sideways. Someone would comment over the intercom: 'Poor bugger, didn't know what hit him. Look out for parachutes.'

All of a sudden there was a bang and Clive knew they had been hit. It was one of the petrol tanks, so he switched tanks and feathered the engine. The main problem was maintaining height having lost the use of an engine. The leaking petrol dropped on the rear gunner's turret perspex screen. After crossing the North Sea, Sinton decided to head the aircraft for the nearest bit of coast, which he did with the help of navigator, Sergeant Sharpe. When flying over East Anglia, they saw an airfield with all its lights on, but suddenly they all went out. Of course at the time, he was quite near one of the Royal Homes, Sandringham. Clive Sinton recalls:

> I had a swift discussion with the crew and, bless their hearts, they said whatever I decided, they would go along with. It was now too low to bale out, so I decided to make for the sea once again and find a spot to ditch. This I did, and although I say it myself and despite having the undercarriage and flaps hanging down, I made the best landing I have ever done. Just before we ditched I felt hands on my shoulders; it was Sergeant Pierce, my wireless operator, he was making sure my harness was tight and in place. We hit the water at about 110 knots, and the nose caved in, trapping one of my legs. So I pulled the zip of my flying-boot down and pulled my leg out. When Sergeant Pierce was in the dark, getting out of the escape-hatch he stood on my face. When we eventually got out, we found that the dinghy had not inflated automatically, and all attempts to do this manually failed. The aircraft sank in seven seconds, so there was nothing left to do but swim for if. Having been in the Navy and played water polo, this did not trouble me, but Sergeant Pierce could not swim, so I gave him my Mae West to keep him afloat. George Sharpe was lagging behind in his efforts to make the shore, so I called to him to catch up. He replied that he was dragging his newly issued 'Irvine Suit' behind him, and did not want to lose it.

They had ditched a mile off Cromer, Norfolk, at 2.30a.m. on the 26 July. Suddenly, while they were still struggling towards the shore, a voice shouted from out of the dark: 'Hang on there boys.' Clive replied: 'What the bloody hell do you think we have been doing for the last hour?' Up loomed a craft which turned out to be the Cromer lifeboat. An observant coast guard had seen the splash when the aircraft hit the water and called out the boat. Soon, hands like shovels were pulling them out of the water, hands which were normally used for picking out fishing nets and lobster pots.

The lifeboat was called *HF Bailey* and its coxswain was Henry Blogg, who had as his number two his nephew, 'Shrimp' Davis. Clive and his crew took off their wet clothes and were given coffee laced with rum. They arrived so quickly at Cromer pier that Clive realized that if he had delayed any further in ditching the aircraft, they would have hit the pier itself. They were taken to the Red Lion hotel and given distressed seaman's clothes, which in Clives's words, 'made us look like clowns.'

Later Clive and his crew were taken to RAF Coltishall, which was the airfield that had turned off its landing lights. They arrived in the middle of a mess party and were all invited in. The next day, the CO of flying Coltishall, flew them back to Skipton, Yorkshire, the base of 432 Squadron, in an Oxford aircraft. For his efforts on the night of 25-26 July, Clive Sinton was awarded an immediate DFC.

The coxswain Henry Blogg was, and still is without doubt, one of the most outstanding coxswains in the history of the lifeboat service. He was born in 1876 and served in the lifeboat service from 1894 to 1948. He was awarded no less than three Royal National Lifeboat Institution gold medals and three silver medals. In 1917 he was awarded the Empire Gallantry Medal, which in 1940 was exhanged for the George Cross. On the 6 August 1941, he rescued 88 seaman from six ships which had gone ashore. For this deed he was awarded the BEM. In 1954 and aged 78, Henry Blogg died in a way he would have chosen — helping to launch a lifeboat. He is buried in North Walsham, Norfolk. When he retired in 1948 as coxswain, his nephew 'Shrimp' Davis took over the helm, a job he held until 1976. He was also awarded the BEM and was a subject for the television programme 'This is Your Life'.

In 1973, Clive Sinton, re-visited Cromer and found three of the crew including 'Shrimp', who had picked him up; his first words to Clive were: 'Come and have a drink.'

The *HF Bailey* was the fourth lifeboat to come to Cromer pier, this was in the year 1935. This was the busiest of all the lifeboats during the war, being launched no less than 128 times, and saving 518 lives. In the afternoon of the 26 July 1943, having picked up Clive and his crew in the morning, they then went out and picked up the crew of a USAAF B-17 bomber. At the end of the war a new lifeboat came to Cromer, and was named the *Millie Walton*, but in 1948, on the retirement of Henry Blogg, it was re-named the *Henry Blogg* Lifeboat as a tribute to his service.

Another crew of 75 Squadron also ditched into the sea but were not so lucky. Four bodies were recovered off the east coast, but the remaining three were never found.

Squadron Leader Hartnell-Beavis and his crew of 10 Squadron, took off from Melbourne at 8p.m. on the 25 July for this raid on Essen and went on to successfully bomb the target. At 1.30a.m. while on their way home, they were attacked by fighters, and as a result, the crew ordered to bale out. Sergeant Raymond Smith, the wireless operator, came down in a wood about five miles from Tilburg in Holland. He was helped by two English-speaking Dutchmen and then set out for Rotterdam. From the 26 July to the 9 October, he was sheltered by helpers at various places in Holland. On the 9 October he set out for Paris via Amsterdam. He left Paris on the 14 October, and travelled to Bordeaux and then Bayonne. When he and some companions got to Dax in southern France, they spent a day in a hotel. Later when they tried to get a train for Irún they were told the train was full of troops, so somehow he and his companions got underneath the train and lay flat on a brake car, clinging on to cross girders with hands and feet. This proved very difficult, especially when the train was moving. After reaching Hendaye near the Spanish border, they got off and ran up the track. They discovered that the Lisbon train which they had intended to catch, had already gone, so this meant spending the day under a train in the goods yard. They finally boarded a train which was bound for San Sebastian in Spain, and arrived there on the 16 October. Having no train tickets, they managed to get out of the station by wearing berets and overalls and walking through the goods entrance. In the main street they stopped a man and asked him the way to the British Consulate. He showed them the way, and here they waited until an official turned up. The next day they were taken to Madrid and from there to Gibraltar, where they arrived on the 25 October. Within two days Raymond Smith was back in the UK.

Major Paul Zorner was one of the pilots flying an enemy fighter on this night of 25-26 July. The Germans had picked up very strong wireless communication activity from the UK and were expecting a large bomber force. Zorner recalls:

> We received the order for operations at 11.20p.m. and I took off at 11.26p.m. for the waiting position at the island of Juist, off the north German coast. The weather was very good without any clouds, and over a 1000 metres we had good visibility. We were at 6600 metres height, and the target flew at 6000 metres on a southern course. As we came near to it at a distance of 500 metres I throttled back my engines, and lowered the landing flaps and went down to 5600 metres. I now saw the bomber at 300 metres on the port side, my radar operator, found the target with his Lichtenstein device. Flying at a height of 5700 metres, we came nearer the bomber. My burst of fire went through the starboard wing of the bomber, which instantly became on fire. The bomber went into a right spin downward and crashed at Ten Boer, near Groningen. The time was 11.54p.m. and the bomber was seen to be on fire. Two minutes later, an explosion was heard on my starboard engine and a small fire started. The aircraft had to be abondoned, so we left by parachute at 12.06a.m. and arrived at our air base the next morning. We heard that during the night, Essen had been bombed.

At 6.10p.m. on the evening of 26 July, during the bomb fusing operations at RAF Graveley, a 1000lb bomb exploded and killed seven men. The bomb dump area was declared unsafe because five 1000lb General Purpose bombs were still lying in the fusing area. It was said that while fusing the bombs, one of the armourers found he had a cross thread on the nose cap, and tried to turn it back. He had in fact armed the bomb and by trying to take it out again caused the explosion. The golden rule was that if you got a cross thread never try and turn it back. Part of the bomb landed on the roofs of the airfield hangars at Graveley and into the tarmac perimeter of the airfield.

On this night, over 2000 tons of bombs were dropped on Essen, equal to the combined total of all the previous raids. Over 90 per cent of the industrial area was demolished and the whole of Krupps was obscured by fire, and it was still burning twelve hours after the attack. Of the 190 workshops, 160 had been damaged or destroyed; many were completely gutted. A whole Pioneer Battalion was despatched to rebuild the factory. Albert Speer, the Armaments Minister, was most concerned and worried. The raid had caused a complete stoppage of production in the factory. On the 28 July, Goebbels stated that 800,000 people were homeless in Essen.

The last raid of the Battle was on Remscheid, a town about the size of St Helens, Lancashire. The code-name for the target was 'Chavender'. Of the 273 aircraft despatched on this raid, 244 attacked the target. One German eye-witness report of the raid stated: 'It was a warm summer night. The telegraph lines spread the word that enemy formations were on their way to the Raum area of Koblenz. There was also talk about Kassel. At about 11.20p.m. the air raid warning was sounded and then the usual droning of bombers overhead followed. Around 12.05a.m. came the so-called *Christ Bäume*. [Target Indicators were called Christmas Trees by the Germans].

The target area had been marked by nine Mosquitos, although one of them had to return owing to an unserviceable Air Speed Indicator (ASI). The timing was good and almost continuous marking achieved. The planned period of bombing of eighteen minutes was extended by ten minutes. The concentrated air raid that followed came from the south-east. After the main force had dropped their bombs, they withdrew towards the west and north-west, so as to try and avoid the heavy anti-aircraft artillery. [The air raid on Remscheid lasted an hour and a half, but for those people who were in the cellars in the centre of the city it must have seemed like an eternity. With noises from hell came high explosives and incendiary bombs. The centre of the attack was directed against the living quarters between Handweiser and the railway line between Remscheid and Solingen. Some of the high explosive bombs had time-delayed fuses that caused them to explode on the morning of 31 July. Anti-aircraft artillery batteries, like the double battery of 88mm guns at Westhausen, and the battery at Sudburg which had Russian 84mm guns with a Skoda system, or the other batteries in the area, could only play a limited defensive role. The RAF were using chaff* which forced the anti-aircraft defence to mainly fire barrage.†

At Remscheid eastern railway station, their 105mm guns were put out of service at the beginning of the attack. Elsewhere, the anti-aircraft cannons were firing continuously for half an hour. One eye-witness at the time said:

* Chaff is a German term for 'Window'.

† The Germans were having to resort to a barrage form of fire, as opposed to selective targets, the presence of 'Window' or 'Chaff' gave the impression of a lot more aircraft being present, than of course there was.

'The men who manned these cannons often glanced towards the centre of the town, which was becoming more and more red with fire. The domestic youth that were manning the guns kept looking towards their burning, native town with anxious eyes, and a feeling of the unknown regarding their relatives. They did their best, but with little success.'

Some six aircraft were claimed to have been shot down over the town. The fighters had at first been ordered to Kassel because the German defences thought there was to be a follow-up of the day raid on Kassel which had taken place the day before. The Allies had, in fact, made this raid with only about 30 aircraft, and its purpose was to draw the night-fighters to Kassel and away from Remscheid.

At 2.45a.m. the 'all clear' was sounded. When the survivors left their cellars and shelters, they were confronted with the destruction of their town. People stood speechless in front of their shattered homes and possessions. A raging fire-storm began to spread and people who believed their houses to be safe from fire were forced to look as giant sparks ignited their property. They tried to bring the fires under control by using every last drop of water there was. In all, 1063 people were killed in this raid and many more wounded. Of the 14,000 houses in Remscheid, at least 11,000 were destroyed or damaged.

The total number of people killed for all the air raids on Remscheid was 1,344. It had been attacked in March 1942 and again in January 1943. The last attack against Remscheid was in November 1944. But it was this raid of July 1943, which was the most destructive. Engineering works which made crankshafts for aircraft, aero-engines and other essential accessories in arms production, were destroyed or damaged. The main railway station and goods depot was almost completely destroyed.

The Stirlings of No.3 Group bombed over a period of twenty minutes and in consequence they received very little protection from the 'Window' dropped by higher flying aircraft. The Stirling had a very limited service ceiling height of about 12,000 feet, whereas the Halifax and Lancasters could fly up to 20,000 feet. They were also over the target area much longer than had been planned, and so flying so low they were soon picked off by the flak gunners below. The 'Window' dropped by the higher flying aircraft had lost its overall effect and protection by the time it had reached the area of the Stirlings. This probably had considerable bearing on the relatively high number of Stirling bombers lost during this raid. Eight of the 75 despatched went missing, which gave a 9.2 per cent loss rate compared with a 3.85 per cent loss rate for the other bombers in the force. On the outward trip, heavy and light flak was encountered in several places in Belgium, particularly Antwerp. The defence in the target area appeared to be weak and ineffective with only a few searchlights and a little heavy and light flak being in operation. The most severe opposition came from Düsseldorf and Cologne, where six aircraft were damaged by flak (two Stirlings and four Lancasters) and three aircraft damaged by fighters. The Halifaxes of No.6 Group were flying in the heaviest concentration of 'Window' and got away without any aircraft being damaged. Of the 130 contacts heard from the German night-fighter control centre, only 45 mentioned British aircraft. Of the fifteen missing aircraft, seven were lost to flak after being coned, six were lost to fighters, and the remaining two to unknown causes.

The Germans reported: 'Enemy air formations last night attacked the town of Remscheid. Heavy destruction and damage by fire was caused. Air defences destroyed 60 aircraft, most of them four-engine enemy bombers.'

*Sgt Joe Edgley (*left*) and the crew of Stirling BK 611 letter U of 15 Squadron which crash-landed in Venlo, Holland.* (Joe Edgley)

Sgt Edgley evaded capture for six weeks and amongst those who helped him were this Dutch farmer and his wife. (Joe Edgley)

Fresnes prison in Paris where Joe Edgley was imprisoned after being finally captured and treated as a spy. (Joe Edgley)

The memorial at Dronten: a propeller of a 12 Sqdn Lancaster flown by Flt Sgt McNicol is the centrepiece. The propeller was reclaimed back from the sea many years after the war. (Bill Pringle)

13 Non-Ruhr Targets

During the period of the Battle of the Ruhr, there were a number of operations against targets other than the Ruhr itself.

On the 8-9 March, 335 aircraft were detailed to attack Nuremberg. The main target was the M.A.N. factory, which made diesel engines for submarines. Because of the longer distance involved, the target had to be marked by the H2S method, and not the *OBOE* method normally used against the Ruhr targets. Another factory attacked was the manufacturer of electrical goods, Siemen Schuckert. Other electrical works, an aluminium and chemical works, a few engineering workshops were also destroyed. Marshalling yards, repair shops and the adjacent railway buildings also received direct hits. The people in Nuremberg were told to repair their own houses, and also to help their neighbours. They were also ordered to help clear up the town centre after the raid.

On the 9-10 March, the target was Munich in southern Germany. On this operation the wind forecast proved to be incorrect and the attack opened late. Despite this the attack proved to be a great success and serious damage was done to the BMW factory, which made aero-engines. This operation also showed the difference between H2S and *OBOE*. In *OBOE*, the element of error was reduced to the minimum, whereas H2S had a number of set-backs, and faults. This was because H2S was not as precise as *OBOE* but *OBOE* had a limited range — as far as the Ruhr was its limit. A lot more accuracy with H2S depended on the operator. Poor serviceability was a big problem: during the first few months only 55% of H2S sets which arrived in the target area were serviceable — teething trouble on a new and delicate instrument. Also on this date, as a diversion, eight Mosquitos attacked targets in the Ruhr.

On the 11-12 March, 314 aircraft were sent on a raid to Stuttgart also in southern Germany. The marking was done by nine Stirlings of 7 Squadron and three Halifaxes of 35 Squadron, all carrying H2S sets, but the three Halifaxes had H2S failure. The problem was found to be a breakdown in the power unit. The early marking was spoilt by the late arrival of the main force. The No.1 Group pilots reported the early bombing as being scattered, but the later attacks being more concentrated. The early attacks were, unfortunately three and a half miles south-west of the target, and the late arrival of the main force was aggravated by the German use of dummy indicators. As a consequence, the small village of Vaihingen outside Stuttgart, suffered considerable damage.

The main cause of losses on this operation were attacks by night-fighters. Flight Lieutenant Norman Mackie, DFC, who was on his 51st operation, and his crew of 83 Squadron, had taken off late owing to two of the crew having unserviceable flying helmets. They went on to bomb the target successfully, but while on their way home and flying over France, they were attacked from below by a Messerschmitt 110 night-fighter. The starboard inner engine was hit and set on fire. As the fighter continued to attack, the damaged engine became engulfed in flames, as did the starboard wing as well, and nothing Norman did would abate the flames, so he gave the dreaded order to bale out. As the navigator, Flight Lieutenant Allan Ogilvie, a Canadian from Newfoundland, passed him, Norman asked Ogilvie to pass his parachute. This he did and helped him on with it. This, today he maintains saved his life. When Norman called the gunners on the intercom, he got no reply so he assumed they had already gone. By this time the aircraft was down to 1500 feet. Eventually, the aircraft crashed, taking with it the two gunners, Flight Sergeant Lynch and Sergeant Chipchase. They were probably killed during the fighter attack.

After Norman had landed safely, he was told by the local French people who helped him, that it was unwise to make for Spain, and to head for Switzerland instead. However, when he reached Switzerland, instead of being sent back to the UK, as was the rule for men who had escaped from prison camp; men who had evaded capture, as he had, were put into prison. Eventually he was released into the custody of the Air Attaché in Berne, Air Commodore Freddie West, VC. Here he worked as his assistant until December 1943, when he was able to travel back through France and Spain to Gibraltar. In 1985 he found out the name of the German pilot who had shot him down. It was Feldwebel Gerhard Rase, who was later shot down himself on the 16-17 April 1943, but had obviously survived. Another member of Norman's crew, Sergeant Ralph Henderson, the flight engineer, who was only on his fourth operation, had also made it back to the UK, as did Allan Ogilvie. Flight Sergeant Humber, and Flight Sergeant Barrett, DFM, both on their 57th operation, were made prisoners of war.

For Wing Commander Guy Gibson, the operation against Stuttgart was to be his last as CO of 106 Squadron. Afterwards he went to 617 Squadron as its CO and to prepare for the Dams raid. By contrast, it was the first operation for Flying Officer Walter Thompson, who had only arrived at 106 Squadron that day. When he met Gibson he was told by him that he was flying that night. Thompson, being a pilot, assumed that it would be with his new crew, but Gibson told him 'no, with me!' It was to be an eventful trip. When crossing the enemy coast on the outward journey, their aircraft was hit by flak, which rendered the starboard engine useless, and forced them down to a height of 12,000 feet. The route to Stuttgart entailed them crossing over Lake Constance in Switzerland; the Swiss, being neutral, just fired a few warning shots. After they had dropped their bombs, they were again hit and lost another engine. This put a tremendous strain on Gibson who had to try and keep the aircraft level, and to do so, he had to keep his leg firmly on the right rudder. At one point, it became such a strain that he asked Thompson to take over for a while at the controls. Later, a safe landing was made at base. Gibson received an immediate award of a bar to his DSO.

During the month of March 1943, there were two raids against the port of St. Nazaire, on the Brittany coast of France. On the 2 April another attack was made on St. Nazaire, in which 55 aircraft attacked the port, and another 47 aircraft attacked the port of Lorient further along the coast.

On the 27-28 March, 396 aircraft were sent on a raid to Berlin which, on the whole, was not successful. The two areas marked by Pathfinders were well short of the city and most of the actual bombing fell between seven and seventeen miles short of the aiming point. Two days later, the city was again attacked, but the wind forecast was inaccurate and caused the marking to be too far south, and the main bomber force to arrive late.

On the 4-5 April, 577 aircraft attacked the German Naval base of Kiel on the Baltic coast. This was the largest raid on Kiel so far in the war. Thick cloud and, once again, strong winds made accurate marking during this operation very difficult. One aircraft and its crew due for this operation on Kiel, did not get any further than the end of their airfield's runway. Sitting in the mid-upper turret of Halifax DT 580 of 51 Squadron, was Sergeant Louis Woolridge. That day, his turret had been installed with four new guns to supplement the four-gun rear turret. As he sat there, he observed white smoke coming from the exhaust manifolds of the four Rolls-Royce engines as the aircraft roared down the runway on its take-off. He then heard Claude Wilson, the pilot, comment that the four engines appeared to be losing take-off power. By now a stream of dense smoke was coming over the wings of their aircraft, and down the runway. It was soon realized that the automatic fire extinguishers had functioned and dampened the ignition sparks of the four engines. Wilson closed the throttles and pulled back the control column of the Halifax. This forced down the tail of the aircraft on to the runway. By this time the aircraft was well past the half-way mark. The wooden fence at the end of the runway was adjacent to the Selby-Doncaster railway line, and also part of the main Edinburgh to London line. As the Halifax with full bomb and fuel loads charged towards the boundary fence, the black smoke of a train was seen approaching from Selby. The aircraft had been followed down the runway by fire-engine and ambulance teams. Wilson, to avoid crashing through the wooden fence, swung the aircraft to port and off the runway on to the grass area where the aircraft shuddered to a halt. Some minuters later, an express train of about thirteen coaches and full of service men and women standing shoulder to shoulder in the corridors, passed the airfield on its way to London. The rest of the bombers then took off for the operation against Kiel.

On the 10-11 April, the target was Frankfurt, code-named 'Sole'. The raid was only a partial success owing to cloud cover which rose between 6000 and 10,000 feet over the target area. The bombing was scattered over a wide area mainly because the crew had difficulty in identifying the technique employed by the Pathfinders. Most of the main force crews said they saw flares on their way in to the target, but not many were seen in the target area itself. Some crew had bombed the preliminary warning flares instead of the target indicator markers.

A number of crews ditched in the sea on their return journey. One Wellington bomber crashed into the sea near Hastings, and one Lancaster crashed into the North Sea 60 miles east of Skegness. A Stirling of 75 Squadron flown by Flight Sergeant Rothschild, was hit by flak while flying over the target. Then after being attacked and chased by fighters they began to run out of petrol and decided to ditch the aircraft in the sea. A wireless message sent out before ditching seems to have worked perfectly as a Spitfire aircraft tracked the crippled Stirling until it ditched four miles south of Shoreham into the English Channel. A Walrus seaplane of Air Sea Rescue arrived almost at the same time as they hit the water. The only hitch in what seemed to be a perfect rescue operation was when the Walrus, having landed on water, collided with the Stirling's emergency dinghy, knocking the crew into the water. They were not harmed, however, and were soon inside the seaplane, though one can imagine some of the choice remarks made as to whose side the crew of the Walrus was on, for example, or: 'Where did he learn to fly?' The whole rescue operation from touchdown to pick-up, only took 40 minutes.

Flying Officer George Lambert and his crew were attacked by a fighter near Luxembourg, resulting in their aircraft being set on fire and them having to bale out. Lambert switched the controls to the automatic pilot known as 'George', and then went to check that all the crew had baled out. As he did so, the aircraft went into a dive and he was thrown into the nose of the aircraft. When he eventually fell through a hole in the aircraft, he discovered he had no ripcord on his parachute, but somehow, as sometimes happens in these situations, his parachute opened. He landed in a tree and in so doing, tore his trousers, and this seemed to worry him more than anything else. In serious situations, the unimportant can often seem to be very important. He kept his trousers together with thorns, renewing them as required. Having decided to set off for Switzerland, he walked mostly at night and slept during the day. On one occasion as he walked through a field, he saw and was seen by a German officer on a horse who bade him good-morning, and proceeded to open a gate with his foot and waited until George had gone through, then closed it behind him. When George got on to the road, he was dismayed to see about 500 German soldiers. The officer on the horse went to the front and the soldiers walked down the road. He once again nodded to George as he rode passed. Going through George's mind was the thought of what would happen if they recognized his RAF uniform. However, it is possible they had never seen one before, as no one took any notice of him.

Eventually he reached Switzerland and surrendered to a solider who was riding along on his bike. The soldier gave George his rifle to hold for him and asked him to sit on the crossbar of his bike and then he pedalled along to the local army camp. The guard there locked George up and then promptly marched the soldier who had brought him in, to the officer-in-charge. The soldier was put on a charge for surrendering his rifle to George. George was kept in custody for a week and then released to the British Legation in Berne. After some while, he decided to try and get back to France, and contact the French resistance. This he did and he was given a forged pass. From France, he headed for Spain, travelling south by train. At one stage, the Nazi SS boarded the train, but George managed to elude them by jumping off the train. He eventually got to Madrid and then Gibraltar, before finally arriving in the UK on the 24 February 1944. Within a month he was back flying. On the 4 July 1944, his aircraft was attacked by fighters. Four of the crew baled out safely. The remaining four men were machine-gunned to death by the Germans as they came down in their parachutes; one of them was George Lambert.

In 1947, George Bouchonett wrote to George Lambert's brother and said that he was the young man who had helped George in France, and because of this, his father had been shot and he himself put in prison. From his time in prison, he was still suffering from tuberculosis.

In April 1943 the station commander at Linton-on-Ouse, Yorkshire, was Group Captain John Rene Whitley, who was a regular officer having joined the RAF in 1926. On this operation against Frankfurt he decided to accompany Flight Lieutenant Hull as his second pilot. On the way to the target they were attacked by a Messerschmitt 110 fighter and the order to bale out was given, not easy at any time and even harder when you have your station commander by your side. Group Captain Whitley had some difficulty in leaving the aircraft when the escape hatch slipped back and temporarily trapped him, and he noticed that one of the hooks on his parachute had come undone. As he tried to re-hook it on, he was thrown out of the aircraft. On his descent he pulled the rip-cord despite his parachute only holding him by one hook, he landed safely near a village about 400 yards from the crashed aircraft.

Whitley had with him a haversack in which he carried civilian clothes. He had attended all the station escape lectures, usually given by someone who had evaded capture or escaped from a POW camp, and taken full note of what they said, so he was prepared for the days ahead. One of the lectures he had attended was given by Flight Lieutenant Harry Burton, the first officer to escape from a POW camp back in 1941. In the days ahead, he was given a lot of help by some French people along his route. On the 14 April, he came in contact with the bomb aimer of his aircraft, Sergeant Davies and the flight engineer, Sergeant Strange. Whitley heard about the funeral of three of the crew in which over 8000 French people turned up, and when the Germans had left, and were thought to be out of earshot, they sang '*La Marseillaise*' and shouted '*Vive L'Angleterre*'. The Germans, however, heard this and in reprisal, cut-off the electric light supplies in the area for the next three months. The German fighter pilot who was said to have shot down their aircraft was at the funeral. He was about 24-years old and had a wooden leg. It is thought to have been oberleutnant Lother Linke, a holder of the Knights Cross, and who flew with NJG1. He was later shot down by a British bomber that was on a raid to Pilsen on the 13-14 May 1943.

Sometime later Whitley arrived in Paris, and from there was taken by train through Le Mans, Angers and Nantes to Bordeaux, where he arrived on the 9 May. Here he was given fresh ID cards and boarded a train for the South of France. When he arrived at St-Jean-de-Luz, he could see in the distance, the Pyrenees, over which he would travel to his freedom. He was welcomed by a man called Florentino, a husky-looking fellow of about 40-years old, and with him was a typical French peasant woman all dressed in black. Florentino took him over the Pyrenees and into Spain. When Whitley arrived in San Sebastián he was met by Mr. M J Creswell, the Second Secretary of the British Embassy in Madrid, who said normally airmen would stay in the Embassy but because of Whitley's rank, he would stay at his house. During his time in Spain he was taken to a bullfight by the Military Secretary, Major Lubbock. On the 21 May he arrived in Gibraltar, and left here by a Dakota aircraft on the 24 May, bound for Hendon near London. He had been away for 45 days.

In 1945, Whitley made a point of returning to Paris and other places to thank the people who had helped him. By the end of the day he was full of Cognac, as everywhere he had gone he had been given a nip of this drink. The family of Mahoudeauxs all came out to greet him, except one son who had been taken to Buchenwald concentration camp. One of his 'helpers' had been shot by the Germans in March 1944, and another had frozen to death in a railway truck. A man called Poiner, who had helped him, had died of starvation and torture in prison. Two others had been executed, and another was in Switzerland recovering from tuberculosis of both lungs. Florentino had been hit by machine-gun fire which had damaged his legs so badly that he walked with a limp for the rest of his life. Group Captain John Whitley was to end his RAF service as Air Marshal Sir John Whitley.

There were two raids on La Spézia, the Italian naval base. The first was on the 13-14 April 1943, when 211 aircraft attacked and severely damaged the docks. On the same date, six Mosquitos attacked Bremen, Hamburg, and Wilhelmshaven. This type of attack, which showed Bomber Command the potential of the Mosquito, was later carried out by the 'Light Night-Striking Force'. The capabilities of the Mosquito was always a problem to the Germans. One of its many uses was that it could carry a 4000lb bomb to the target, a load greater than that carried by the American 'Flying Fortresses'. Five days later, 178 aircraft dropped 460 tons of bombs on La Spézia. On this occasion, it was the town and not the docks that was hit, owing to the haze and smoke making the identification of the target difficult.

After this attack Churchill sent a personal telegram to Stalin, mentioning the raid on La Spézia, and also the raid on Pilsen on the 16-17 April. The target at Pilsen was the Skoda works, where workmen had been transferred from the severely damaged Krupps factory in Essen. He repeated his assurance that the bombing of German cities would continue throughout the summer on an ever-increasing scale. In his reply, Stalin said he was glad to hear this. It is interesting to note that in this personal telegram from Stalin to Churchill dated 19 April 1943, there is a mention of a possible gas war: 'Your information to use gas on our Front [meaning the Eastern Front] is corroborated also by our own information. It goes without saying that I fully support your intention to warn Hitler and his Allies and threaten them with a powerful chemical attack in case they well make a gas attack on our Front. The Soviet troops in their turn will be prepared to resist.'

Sergeant George Calver of 106 Squadron remembers after a raid on La Spézia and getting a direct hit being sent a 'Goodboy' card.

The second attack on Stuttgart on the 14-15 April 1943, involved 462 aircraft and a total of 88 tons of bombs were dropped on the town. Sergeant Carrie and his crew of 76 Squadron were attacked by two Junkers 88s. The bomb aimer, Sergeant Weir, was wounded and later died in hospital. The remainder of the crew suffered flesh wounds. When they landed at Manston in Kent, no less than nineteen holes were counted on their aircraft, DT 698 letter W.

There were two operations during the Ruhr period which were of an exceptional nature. These were against the Baltic seaports of Stettin and Rostock. On the 20-21 April, an attack was made on Stettin (now part of Poland) Germany's main port in the Baltic. The code-name for the attack was 'Sole-Sewin'. From Russian intelligence sources, it was revealed that a large quantity of German fighter and bomber aircraft had been concentrated at Stettin, in preparation for use against Russia along the Eastern Front. The Russians asked the RAF to eliminate this menace to their forces situated between Leningrad and Moscow. No previous attack on Stettin had been successful. Of the 339 aircraft despatched, 326 attacked the target. At the same time, diversionary raids were made on the Heinkel aircraft works at Rostock, but this proved to be unsuccessful owing to the factory being covered by a smoke-screen which had been generated by the attack on Stettin. Instead 69 of the 86 Stirlings despatched, attacked the town, causing a fair amount of damage to the docks. In the Neptunwerft submarine yards, four and a half acres were laid to waste.

The plan of the attack on Stettin was that at the zero hour of 1a.m. H2S-carrying aircraft were to drop red TIs blindly on the aiming point and ten seconds later, on the same heading, bundles of white flares were to be released at four-second intervals. Two and three minutes later, aircraft were to identify the aiming point (visually guided by the red TIs) and to mark it with green TIs. The route into Stettin took the main bomber force over Denmark. The weather conditions were satisfactory and, flying as low as possible, the crews had no difficulty seeing the green TIs. It would appear that the initial markers were placed in the southern part of the town. Flames were soon rising up as high as 12,000 feet, particularly in the dock area. Many explosions were reported from 1.18a.m. onwards. The defences at the target were moderate and generally ineffective, however, on the bomber's route, light flak was reported from most of the Danish towns and from numerous flak-ships in the Baltic. Some 66 aircraft were damaged by heavy flak and 38 damaged by light flak, which was received mostly when flying over Denmark. Of the 31 aircraft whose height at the time of being hit was known, 80 per cent were reported to have been flying at 500 feet or below. In all, 22 aircraft went missing on the Stettin raid and eight aircraft went missing on the raid against Rostock. Of the 30 missing aircraft over half were estimated to have been shot down by light flak and flak-ships.

The Germans reported that one mine bomb, 53 high explosive bombs, 3000 incendiary bombs and 33 phosphorous bombs had been dropped on Stettin. Some 276 fires were reported, with 59 houses destroyed, and three German army and police barracks damaged by fire. Some 21 people were killed, 60 wounded and 32 reported missing. An eye-witness account said the fires were so widespread that the firemen found it impossible to cope. Berlin was asked to send extra fire brigades but this request was refused because a small raid on Berlin by Mosquitos had made the authorities think that a large raid was imminent, and so many houses and buildings of Stettin were just left to burn.

Two days after the attack, 23 emergency feeding centres were opened in Stettin. All the ships of over 2000 tons weight were being diverted from Stettin because of the obstructions in the deep-water channel. Eight days after the attack, lighting in many districts was still dependent on candles and spirit lamps. Water for essential use was being pumped from the River Oder. The eye-witness ended his account by saying: 'What saved Stettin from almost total destruction, was the fact that there was no wind, either on the night of the raid or on the two following days. If there had been, I shudder to think what Stettin would look like now. As it is, it looks as if the centre of the city has been knocked flat. It was a hell of a bang.'

On this operation, Flight Lieutenant Gerald Cooper of 61 Squadron carried as an extra member in his crew, a Public Relations Officer, Flight Lieutenant Sweeney, who recorded the intercom conversation while they were over the target. As they left the shores of the UK, Gerald asked his rear gunner if there were many Allied aircraft around them; he replied in a cockney accent, 'cor lummy skipper they're "fick" as bugs on a dog's back'. One tactic which Gerald always adopted in areas where night-fighters could be expected, was 'stepping down'. After ensuring that all was clear below, he would pull the nose of his aircraft up to almost stalling speed, then push the nose down and lose several thousand feet at maximum speed. He would then hold this position for a while before zooming up to the orginal height. This would confuse the German radar screen of any fighters following them, or upset the aim of any guns that may be tracking them. They reached the target successfully and the PRO, Flight Lieutenant Sweeney began his recording:

> Target straight ahead skipper. Over the lake now on aircraft beamer 146,170, 2 mins 10 secs, you can weave a bit skipper. Flares just to the left. One minute. Keep weaving skipper. Straight and level. Bomb doors open, left, left, twenty steady, steady, twenty-five seconds, steady, bombs away. There goes the 'cookie', lovely, lovely. There goes the incendiaries. Bomb doors closed. New course. Look at those

> fires boys. Lanc on your starboard beam. OK, I see him. Starboard bow now. Coming again, Lanc on the starboard beam, no he's turning off. Keep you eyes skinned gunners for fighters, they're crawling around the target like flies.

John Petrie Andrew and his crew of 35 Squadron, were flying in Halifax W 7779 letter U for Uncle. Andrew narrates: 'I shall never forget that raid on Stettin. The night was very clear and a full moon was out. As we were visual marking, we were in at zero hour and up the front. We were very low when, suddenly, this 20mm gun started "hosing-up" at us from each side, like swords at a military wedding, and we were mostly underneath it. One shell exploded just below me and caught Sergeant "Jock" Berwick in the legs with shrapnel. Flight Lieutenant Jack Armitage was also wounded.' The aircraft's air speed indicator, DR Compass, intercom and bomb sight were all rendered useless, as were the brakes. Despite this they attacked the target successfully. When they landed back at Graveley, they only just managed to stop the aircraft at the end of the runway owing to their brakes not working. When the groundcrew tried to move the aircraft clear, later that day, it became bogged down. When Andrew met 'Jock' Berwick in 1986, he told him he still had bits of shrapnel in his leg but that it had now moved from the lower part of his leg, up to his hip.

The aircraft Louis Woolridge normally flew in was undergoing undercarriage repairs at the time of the Stettin raid. He remembers the aircraft he did fly in, Halifax HR 750 letter W, being fitted for the operation to Stettin with an auxiliary petrol tank in the bomb-bay. This aircraft was quite a veteran of 51 Squadron, having a number of bomb symbols painted in yellow beneath the pilot's window. It also bore the words 'Wanchors Castle' and with a small castle drawn below this. On leaving Snaith, Yorkshire, the home of 51 Squadron, the weather was clear and almost cloudless with brilliant moonlight, and because these were not the normal operating conditions for bombers, perhaps this, it was hoped, would make the Germans think there was not to be a raid that night. They were ordered to fly at a height of 500 feet and climb to 12,000 feet to attack the target and then descend to 500 feet once again. As they were approaching the Danish coast, Lewis, sitting in his mid-upper turret saw the outline of a German U-boat on the water. He reported this to his pilot, Claude Wilson. Its position and compass bearing was recorded in the navigator's log-book, and the wireless operator reported it by coded message to Snaith. Normally, except for regular wireless transmission times, wireless silence was kept, but emergency sightings such as this were permitted to be transmitted. This message would finally end up at the Admiralty in London. On seeing the Halifax at a low height coming towards it, the U-boat had crash-dived. The U-boat did not know that the Halifax had the wrong type of bomb load to attack them, and the gunners could not move their guns enough to fire on it.

When they were half-way across Denmark, the door of a farmhouse opened and a family of four came out waving a white cloth to attract attention. Says Louis: 'I turned the mid-upper turret towards them and rapidly raised it up and down to acknowledge their greetings.' On leaving the German mainland to fly out over the Baltic Sea, they started to climb in preparation for the bombing-run on Stettin. The PFF were hard at work marking the target; two of their Lancasters on the Halifax's starboard beam suddenly became enveloped in black smoke and flames, and fell rapidly out of the sky crashing into the sea below. The Pathfinders had had a bad start being formed but were now showing their worth and why they had been formed. Marking a target clearly for the follow-up main force was crucial if operations were to be successful.

After releasing its bombs the Halifax descended back to 500 feet for the return flight to base. Says Louis: 'Whilst flying low over the German countryside, the flight engineer suddenly appeared beside me in the mid-upper turret and the aircraft ditching-hatch was suddenly swung downwards. It was then that I remembered we had to dispose of a lot of propaganda leaflets, which were written in German and depicted scenes of the Russo-German conflict at Stalingrad.' On the return flight over Germany, they found themselves over an airbase at Anklam, north-west of Stettin, so both gunners opened fire on the hangars and the parked aircraft. Just after this, their aircraft was hit by shells probably from a flak-ship. The external wireless aerial was shot away. When they landed at Snaith at about 6a.m. having flown for some eight and a half hours, they were interrogated by the intelligence officers. They were told that having flown over Esbjerg owing to a navigational error, they were lucky to have survived. The next day, Lewis was approached by the ground staff sergeant who looked after the aircraft, and he said that there was only about 40 rounds of ammunition left in the turret boxes which served the mid-upper turret.

It seems the Germans were expecting a big raid over the northern part of Europe that night. German Signal Intelligence covered the radio traffic of every RAF bomber airfield, night and day. It was the custom of these airfields to test the radio equipment before a raid, and this would give the Germans some indication that a raid was on that night; also, by the number of aircraft being tested, the size of the bomber force could be estimated. They also tracked the RAF meteorological flights, which at the time were over the northern part of Europe. In Denmark, the German Navy flak-gunners were ordered to their guns at 9.28p.m. They were expecting a raid by the Americans not by the RAF. At 9.35p.m. a 'high alert' order came from the flak commander to all anti-aircraft units. American bombers were expected.

According to German reports, the British planes crossed the Danish west coast at Esbjerg, which had the only real harbour on the west coast of Denmark and was well defended by the German Navy flak-gunners, that were thought to be far superior to their opposite numbers in the Army or *Luftwaffe*. The ships in and just outside the harbour, were also armed with light flak guns. The *Flieger* alarm was sounded at 12.07a.m. at which time the first bombers were crossing the Danish coast from west to east. The Germans estimated that about 70 aircraft crossed over Esbjerg on different courses. The searchlights began working and about 30 aircraft were lit up. The Germans claimed five aircraft shot down here, the first being Halifax JB 930 from 10 Squadron and flown by Sergeant Percy Glover. It was shot down by the German Navy (Marine Flak *Abteilung* 204) at 12.30a.m. and crashed at Tjaerborg. The German Admiral in charge of Denmark admitted that three German soldiers were wounded by return machine-gun fire from the attacking aircraft. Glover, who had been wounded and suffered burns, was to spend the next two years as a POW, as did the rest of his crew, all of whom suffered serious injuries.

One bomber, Lancaster ED 620 letter K from 49 Squadron and flown by Sergeant Anderson, was shot down as it crossed the Danish coast near Ringelnatter radar station at 12.35a.m. Three of the crew were killed. One of the crew, Sergeant Boulton, was badly wounded and taken to hospital. He was made a POW and not repatriated to the UK until May 1944. Sergeant Anderson died in hospital. Another two of the crew became POWs. On the 15 July, three months after the raid, Boulton wrote a letter home from the hospital he was in:

> I am still in hospital but getting around on crutches in great style. We were unlucky in getting shot down, our incendiaries got hit by light flak and we were burning like hell. We were flying too low to bale out or jettison the bombs, as we would have blown ourselves up, so we had to make a crash-landing with the bombs aboard. I was hit by machine-gun fire and my leg shattered by a shell when we hit the deck. I was pitched clear and the next thing I knew I was in hospital.

One aircraft and crew of 83 Squadron were attacked by a Junkers 88 which set the aircraft on fire and wounded members of the crew. It was decided to make for Sweden and try a force landing, which they did on a beach five miles sout-west of Malmö. The crew got out of their aircraft and found that the water they had come down on was only knee high, so they waded ashore and were taken to the local Swedish military HQ. One of the wounded, Sergeant Ford, was taken by ambulance to a military hospital in Malmö. The remainder of the aircrew were taken to Stockholm and then to Falun for internment until 16 August, by which time Sergeant Ford had rejoined them. On the 16 August they left once again for Stockholm and from there were flown home to the UK, arriving on the 19 August.

For one aircraft, Lancaster W 4964 of 9 Squadron, this had been its first of 106 operations that it went on to complete. It was known by many for its name of 'Johnny Walker'.

The night of this raid on Stettin was also remembered because it was Hitler's birthday, and the Danes had firmly believed that the RAF were bombing Germany because of this. As a result, it was a great morale builder in Denmark.

On the 1 June 1943, an aircraft of the Photographic Reconnaissance Unit from RAF Benson spotted the reflections of giant and normal size *Würzburgs* (baskets and bowl fires) at the Zeppelin works in Friedrichshafen, southern Germany on the shores of Lake Constance. These *Würzburgs* were essential for the efficiency of the German night-fighter system. The night-fighters accounted for at least 70 per cent of the British bomber losses. There were about 150 German Ground Controlled Interception (GCI) stations and the number was steadily increasing. The idea was to spread the night-fighter defences all over Germany and the Rumanian oilfields; also French and Norwegian ports and the Russian lines of communications. A stock of about 250 reflectors, which were 24 feet in diameter, had been despatched to the Zeppelin works on 24 February 1943. On the 8 June 1943, Air Commodore Sydney Bufton, the deputy head of Bomber Command operations, suggested to Sir Arthur Harris that this factory be destroyed. The Zeppelin factory, however, was only 500 yards long by 350 yards wide, and heavily defended.

The crews were selected from No.5 Group squadrons and the code-name for this attack was 'Bellicose'. The attack was to be controlled by the two leading aircraft flown by Group Captain Slee, in Lancaster ED 702 of 49 Squadron and his deputy, Wing Commander Gomm from 467 Squadron. Group Captain Slee's bomb aimer was Flying Officer Astbury, who later joined 617 Squadron as bomb aimer to Group Captain Leonard Cheshire. The attack was similar in many ways to the Dams raid and where it was found that wireless transmissions were entirely satisfactory in the training in daylight, much interference was found at night with the same radio transmissions (TR1196). But there was no time to change to VHF, as was done for the Dams raid. Because it was thought impossible to continue accurate marking on such a small target as the Zeppelin factory, it was decided that when the target indicator was accurately placed, the maximum number of crews should attack immediately. To achieve this, crews were trained to orbit the target at a distance of four to six miles with not more than two aircraft flying at the same height and to attack immediately on receipt of a special signal given by the leader when a TI was dropped very near or on the target. In the event of the target becoming obscured by smoke, an alternative, indirect method of attack was developed. The crews practised making a bombing-run from a well-defined point, sighting on a second point 2000 yards in front of the target, and delaying the release of their bombs by the time taken for the aircraft to fly from the second point to the target.

The marking was to be done by four Pathfinder aircraft of 97 Squadron. The main force consisted of 60 Lancasters from 9, 49, 50, 57, 61, 106, 44, 207, 457, and 619 Squadrons. Of the 60 aircraft, 59 attacked the primary target. The target was clearly visible on arrival but the defences were heavier than expected. Thirty to 40 searchlights and 36 light guns, plus a number of Junker 88s were seen. Due to Group Captain Slee having engine trouble for a period, the command was handed over to Wing Commander Gomm. Later Slee resumed command and ordered all aircraft to increase height by some 5000 feet. The order was given by Gomm but on the instructions of Slee. The increase in height, however, brought the aircraft into a zone where the wind was stronger and this made it difficult for the PFF to do the marking and to start the attack on time. Nevertheless, the attack went ahead, and there were many hits on hangars and workshops causing explosions and four large fires which could been seen 100 miles away. The last Lancaster of the main force (number 60) had been driven off-track by thunderstorms in France, and lost the main formation after being held in searchlights for three and a half minutes. Its bomb load was jettisoned on an unidentified town. This Lancaster reached Friedrichshafen about half an hour after the attack had ended. As they had already jettisoned their bombs, it is difficult to know why they flew on to the target. At the end of the attack, Slee sent a message to Gomm: 'Port engine useless, am returning on three engines and maintaining height. Good Morning.' It appears that at one stage the fire in the port engine was so fierce that Slee had to jettison his bombs and told the crew to prepare to bale out, but not before they had flown across the lake and into Switzerland. As they were about to bale out, the engine seized and the fire went out. Although the shaft broke, the propeller continued to rotate.

In all, 155 tons of high explosive bombs and twenty tons of incendiary bombs were dropped. Some three acres were devastated in the Zeppelin factory area. No aircraft were lost on this operation, but six were damaged by flak. On completing the operation, all aircraft flew to Algeria, in North Africa, landing at Maison Blanche, a flight of over ten hours. They returned to the UK on the 23-24 June, attacking La Spézia en route, bombing the port and harbour installations.

The PFF aircraft of 97 Squadron, were led by Flight Lieutenant Joseph Henri Jean Sauvage, DFC. While Sauvage and his crew were on their fourth run over the Zeppelin works, their aircraft was hit by heavy flak and suffered serious damage, but they were able to make the journey to North Africa. Four PFF aircraft piloted by Sauvage, Flight Lieutenant Rodley, Pilot Officer Jones and Pilot Officer Munro, did not take part in the La Spézia raid on the return journey to the UK. On the 28 July, Sauvage was recommended for a bar to add to his DFC for the Zeppelin operation. At the time Sauvage had completed 43 operations.

On the 27 June 1943, Air Chief Marshal Harris received a message from Air Chief Marshal Arthur Tedder: 'Thanks for your Lancaster party, they are a fine lot and did a job which was most useful to us at this juncture. Grateful if you would convey to the crews my congratulations on their success and thanks for their help, which this success will be to us.' On the 29 June Harris replied: 'Thanks for your message which has been passed on to the crews, and for the promise of facilities, without which this trip could not have been made. We hope to repeat our visit in the future.' This was in fact the first type of operation which became known as a 'shuttle' trip.

On the 13-14 July in a raid on Aachen, the Deutsche Phillips factory was totally destroyed. During the raid, in which 374 aircraft took part, 900 tons of high explosives and incendiaries were dropped, including many 8000 lb bombs, or 'block busters' as they were known. Two thousand individual buildings were destroyed. The defences were strong and night-fighters were especially active. In addition to the Phillips factory, 27 identified factories were either destroyed or damaged. After this raid industrial production in Aachen almost ceased to exist.

The day before, a raid on Turin had taken place involving 295 Lancasters. Thirteen of these aircraft were lost, one of which was flown by Wing Commander John Nettleton, VC, the commanding officer of 44 Squadron, and who was thought to have been shot down by a night-fighter. He and his crew were never found.

During the period of the Battle of the Ruhr, there were four attacks on the city of Cologne, code-name 'Trout'. They were the heaviest attacks since the 1000 strong bomber raid on May 1942, and since that time, many of the factories and plants had been repaired. Bomber Command had been aware of this and so again made it one of the targets for bombing operations. On the 16-17 June, over 200 aircraft were despatched against Cologne. A German report at the time, stated that the air raid warning had already reported 250 enemy bombers; and that others were waiting to take-off from airfields in England. The weather grew worse and the city was partially covered by clouds at the time of the attack. The bombers were recalled on their way to the target, but the first units were too far ahead and did not get the recall order in time. So about 100 aircraft bombed the target and damage was done to sixteen industrial areas of Cologne.

In the second attack on the 28-29 June, over 600 aircraft dropped 1500 bombs on to targets on the west side of the River Rhine. At least 80 per cent of the central area of Cologne was destroyed. According to police reports, 4377 people were killed and 230,000 were made homeless and evacuated. Over 43 industrial plants were destroyed and 43 heavily damaged. A typical newspaper headline the next day proclaimed: '30,000 Guns and 1000 Night Fighters Defend the Ruhr.'

On this raid Sergeant Fuller of 10 Squadron, had been issued with caffeine tablets to help keep him awake and alert for any fighter attack. Both for him and the crew, it was their maiden flight. The pilot, who had done a few trips as a second pilot, said: 'Don't worry about the flak chaps, it looks a lot worse that it is. Hang on, we'll get through it okay.' While flying over Cologne, Flying Officer Eddie Hearn, a bomb aimer with 50 Squadron remembers their aircraft being damaged by flak and the pilot blinded. Eddie himself had also been wounded in three places, but carried on with the bombing run. Afterwards he guided the pilot through a maze of searchlights and predicted flak, from Cologne to Düsseldorf. On the 4 July 1943, he was recommended for an immediate DFC, and the pilot, Sergeant Wilkie, was recommended for the CGM.

One of the *Luftwaffe* pilots defending the Ruhr at that time was Major Paul Zorner. He had started the war as a transport pilot flying Junkers 52s, the German equivalent of the Dakota aircraft used by the Allies. Hitler's private aircraft was a Junkers 52. In 1941 Zorner transferred to a night-fighter training school, and in 1942 he joined NJG 2 at Gilze Rijen airfield. In the Spring of 1943 and at the start of the Battle of the Ruhr, he was a Captain with NJG 3 at Vechta, which was between Bremen and Osnabrück. On the

12 June he was transferred to St. Trond and on the 13 June to Leeuwarden, Holland. On the 24 June he remembers:

> I flew the first operation without any encounters. On the 29th, I was ordered to take off at 1.10a.m. and flew on a north-west course and against the bomber stream. I was then told by my set operator in the aircraft that we had lost one target; but soon picked up another with the aid of our Lichtenstein equipment in the aircraft, and located a Wellington bomber. From behind, I opened fire from 100 metres and hit the right wing of the bomber. With its wing on fire, the bomber went down and crashed at 2.20a.m. fifteen kilometres south-east of Antwerp.

The third attack on Cologne came on the 3-4 July, when 653 aircraft were despatched of which 581 attacked the target, dropping 1700 tons of high explosive bombs on the east bank of the River Rhine, hitting the industrial area that had escaped damage from the bomber raid of May 1942. Some nineteen industrial plants were destroyed and thirteen heavily damaged. The Germans reported 588 people killed on this raid, 106 ground-controlled night-fighters were recorded operating, of which 53 were in action against the bombers. Paul Zorner was one of these night-fighter pilots and once again he located a Wellington bomber, which he shot down at the recorded time of 1.41a.m.

There were a number of aircraft which crashed on return or came back with wounded aircrew aboard. Pilot Officer 'Paddy' Gingless's aircraft was hit by machine gun fire from another Lancaster and had to crash-land in Gravesend. Sergeant John Baker's aircraft crashed into cottages at Arnhurst in Kent. At the time he was making for West Malling but ran out of petrol in the fog. Three of the crew were killed, including Baker. Two airmen, Flight Sergeant Arthur Boulay and Sergeant Elmer Dungey of 408 Squadron, had their aircraft shot down but managed to get away unhurt, being helped by a woman called Hortense Daman, who was later arrested by the Gestapo and taken to Ravensbruck concentration camp. While there she was injected with gangrene in her legs. After the war she had to have skin grafts and still has the scars today and walks with a limp. Boulay and Dungey made it back to the UK via Gibraltar.

The final attack on Cologne during the Battle was on the 8-9 July, when a much reduced force of 288 aircraft were sent, of which 257 attacked the target. The marshalling yards in the north of the city were attacked and disabled after 1000 tons of bombs were dropped on the area. The Germans reported the city being without gas and electricity, and water was only available after tremendous difficulties had been surmounted. The city of Cologne was a burnt-out shell, and only the cathedral had escaped damage. Once again Paul Zorner had been in action; he relates: 'I attacked a British bomber but my fire was returned by the rear gunner and it escaped into cloud. When I attacked another bomber, having seen its bluish exhaust flames, I gave a long burst into the exhausts and I saw it explode and later crash.'

A report made by the Cabinet Joint Intelligence sub-committee, dated 22 July 1943, stated that the aim of the strategic bombing was to destroy the economic and industrial structure of Germany and to undermine the endurance and capacity of their population to work.

In the latter part of July there were three attacks on Hamburg. In all, 213 bomber raids were mounted against Hamburg during the war, but the raid on the night of 27-28 July 1943, is the one most people remember. It became known as the 'fire-storm raid' when the winds whipped up the fires that swept through the town. Only the day before Goebbels had mentioned that General Weiss had taken the heavy anti-aircraft guns away from Hamburg, and sent them to Italy. The raids on Hamburg were the first in which 'Window' was used to wreck the German radar system, and with great success one must add. It had for some time been considered in its use but there was always a fear that the Germans, once knowing about it, would use it in reprisal attacks on the UK.

OBOE — HOW IT WORKS

Two *OBOE* ground stations are required to control each *OBOE* aircraft over the target. One station known as the 'cat', transmits signals to the pilot of the aircraft to enable him to fly on an arc of a circle passing through a point directly over the target. The second ground station known as the 'mouse', enables the controller to calculate the speed of the aircraft along the track and informs the navigator when to release his bombs. The two stations are situated some miles apart so that the angle between the lines joining the ground stations to the track, is preferably not less than 30 degrees.

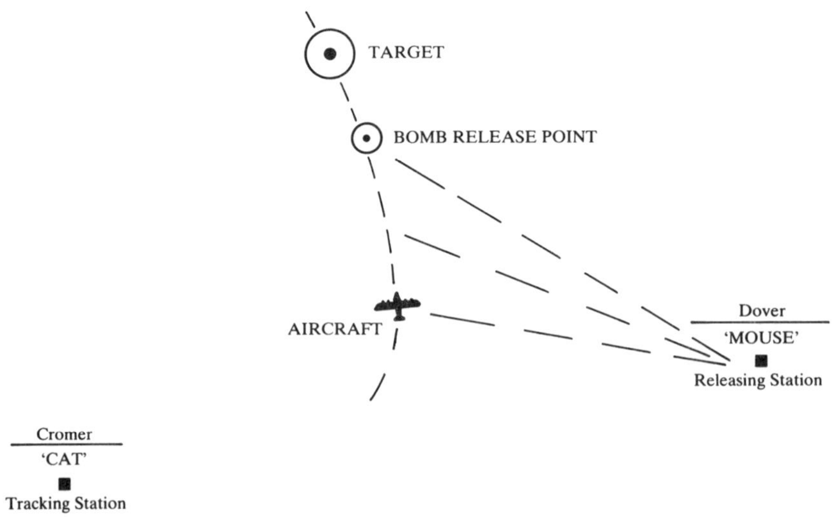

Another target during the Air Battle of the Ruhr was Krefeld which was virtually destroyed. (Mike King)

And another Ruhr target Gelsenkirchen as seen in 1945. (Mike King)

The stalwart and dependable Stirling bomber in this case R 9189 K — King.

P/O Terry and his crew of 7 Sqdn. His Stirling crashed at Luxembourg on the night of 10/11 April 1943, during the Battle of the Ruhr and he and his crew were all killed. A memorial was erected on the site of the crash. (7 Squadron)

14 Mining Operations

The Admiralty claimed in World War II, that for every mine dropped, the RAF sank on an average, 50 tons of shipping.

The requirement in mining operations was to drop mines in the enemy shipping lanes. The airborne magnetic sea mine was designed for use against surface craft and submarines and, as its name implied, was activated by an alteration in the magnetic field surrounding the mine. It had a steel cylindrical shell, about eighteen inches in diameter and approximately ten feet in length. A parachute attached at one end, opened automatically when the mine was released. When it struck the water, the parachute became detached by means of an inertia device. The parachute itself was weighted and slowly sank in the water. The total weight of the mine was 1500lb which included an explosive charge of about 740lb encased in its front section. It was primed and a detonator inserted before it was loaded into the aircraft, which would be done on such stations as Binbrook in the bomb dump and by Corporal Ted Loveridge and his party. The firing circuit could not operate until the mine had been immersed in the water for some time, and had reached a depth of twelve feet. To achieve this, a soluble plug made of salt, was incorporated in a switch in the electrical circuits. After a while, the plug would dissolve and the pressure of the water would operate the switch and complete the circuit, making the mine 'live' to the first magnetic influence. If this soluble salt plug was no included in the circuit, the mine would become 'live' at its moment of release. The movement of the aircraft or the movement in the mine itself as it fell, could also set it off. It was usual to drop the mines about a quarter of a mile apart, and not to drop them below a height of 200 feet or above a height of 6000 feet. The maximum speed for the drop was 200m.p.h.

Having found the arranged Pin-Point* the bomb aimer would direct the aircraft directly over it with the aid of the bomb sight, and with the stop watch started. A steady course and air speed was essential and the first mine released by the bomb aimer at the end of the timed run. Unless the aircraft was directly over the 'pin-point' itself at the commencement of the run-up, it was quite possible to introduce an additional error of as much as half a mile or more.

When dropping mines, the main problems encountered were flak-ships or light flak from the shore, and also searchlights either onshore or at sea.

* A start point to make a bombing run.

In strongly defended areas, a 'glide' approach from 3000 or 4000 feet down to 800 feet proved effective in deluding the defences, otherwise a level run may be made.

Another method of dropping mines as well as the 'pin-point' one, was the 'Gee' method, in which a short-timed run was made from a 'Gee' fix. This method was used frequently when dropping mines near the Frisian Islands. The wind speed and direction had to be taken into account, unless the mines could be dropped miles away from the selected area.

During the period of the Battle of the Ruhr, from March to June 1943, a number of outstanding mining operations took place. In all, some 1485 mining sorties were carried out and 4191 mines dropped over an area covering 1,367,135 miles. (1170 square miles).

On the 13-14 March 1943, 68 aircraft, comprising Wellingtons and Lancasters, dropped mines off the Brittany coast near Lorient, code-name 'Artichoke' and in the waters of the Kattegat, between Denmark and Sweden, code-name 'Silverthorn'. On this operation three aircraft were lost. On the 23-24 March, 45 aircraft dropped mines near the Frisian Islands, code-name 'Nectarines' and Texel, off the Dutch coast, code-name 'Lettuce'. Only one aircraft was lost. On the 6-7 April, 47 aircraft laid mines off the Biscay ports. Two aircraft were lost. On the same night, 46 mines were dropped off Texel, Brittany, and the Biscay ports. Two aircraft were also lost on this operation.

The operation on the night of 27-28 April, involved a significantly larger force of 160 aircraft, comprising Halifaxes, Lancasters, Wellingtons and Stirlings. This was by far the largest force ever sent on a mining operation during World War II. Of the 160 aircraft, 123 reached their target area and dropped a record number of 458 mines. The target areas were the Frisian Islands, and further south along the Dutch coast, and the Bay of Biscay. Only one aircraft, a Lancaster of No.1 Group, failed to return. Of the 39 aircraft despatched by No.4 Group, 32 managed to drop their mines.

The next night an even larger force of 207 aircraft were despatched to the Gt Belt code-name 'Quince' and 'Broccoli'; Little Belt (Denmark area) code-name 'Carrotts' and 'Endives'; Langelands Belt (Denmark area) code-name 'Quince'; Kiel Bay, code-name 'Wallflowers', 'Quince' and 'Radishes'; Fehmarn Channel, code-name 'Radishes'; Travemunde, code-name 'Hollyhock'; Warnemunde, code-name 'Jasmine'; Cadet Channel, West Baltic, code-name 'Sweetpeas'; Swinemunde, code-name 'Geraniums'; Bornholm, code-name 'Pollock'; and Danzig Bay, code-name 'Privet'. The losses suffered during these attacks were higher than the night before. Of the 167 aircraft which found their target, 22 were lost, the highest number of aircraft lost on mining operations up to this date. Eight of these losses were from No.3 Group. In all, 593 mines were dropped, which was the highest number of mines dropped so far in a mining operation. Out of the 68 aircraft despatched by No.4 Group, 56 were successful.

On the 29 May 1943, a memo arrived at Bomber Command HQ from the naval Staff Officer of No.1 Group. It stated:

> The Gardening of 100 Squadron in the Baltic on the 28-29 April had excellent results. One of the vessels sunk was of 1500 tons. The details of the second one sunk are not yet to hand, 100 Squadron were the sole representatives in this area. There is also a possibility that the liner *Gneisenau*, was beached after striking a mine dropped by one aircraft of 100 Squadron, Pilot Officer McHardy flying in ED 553, who was the only aircraft to drop his 'veg' in the area of the liner.

On 21-22 May 1943, of the 104 aircraft sent, 87 dropped their mines near the Frisian Islands; in the estuary of the River Gironde, France, code-name 'Deodar'; and off La Pallice code-name 'Cinnamon'. On the 29-30 May, 34 aircraft dropped mines near the Frisian Islands; the Brittany ports and the River Gironde again.

15 The Summing Up

The purpose of the RAF's bomber offensive against Germany was to smash the enemy's war effort by destroying the main German industrial towns, which could be defined as those with 50,000 or more inhabitants. By the end of 1943 Bomber Command had attacked 38 such towns, of which a great number were in the Ruhr. Excluding the suburbs, more than 30 per cent of the built-up area of these towns, amounting to 139 square miles, was attacked. Of this total, 38 square miles (or 28 per cent) had been devastated by the end of 1943 and most of this area, 34 square miles (or 25 per cent) was laid waste during the Battle of the Ruhr between March and July 1943. During the Battle, there were 43 attacks on targets in the Ruhr, which amounted to 18,506 sorties and 34,000 tons of bombs being dropped.

The Ruhr was the seat of the German heavy industries, mainly coal mining, coke ovens, iron and steel works, and related engineering industries. Almost all the great steel works had received such damage as to reduce their output appreciably for many weeks. The Germans had to make desperate and unsuccessful attempts to replace the lost output of the Ruhr, which included bringing in blast furnaces and steel works of occupied territories. More than 50 collieries, targets which exposed little of their importance above ground, were known to have been hit.

There were many examples of the effects that the bombing of the Ruhr had on its industries. Several thousand Daimler-Benz engines, which lacked only their crankshafts, had to be placed in store and by mid-August the shortage of available engines was so acute, that operational fighter units had aircraft grounded owing to lack of replacements. The production of a new type of flak was prevented for several months owing to damage to an important machine-tool workshop in Düsseldorf. Having been hit a number of times, the works was finally abandoned. When it was merged with a firm in Leipzig, this too was bombed on the 3-4 December 1943. Krupps and other Ruhr plants were unable to maintain deliveries of steel plates for the hulls and conning-towers of U-boats which were under construction.

The railway and canal systems became congested due to the cumulative effects of numerous incidents and the piling up of huge stocks of Swedish iron ore on the quays of Emden on the German North Sea coast. Between 1939 and March 1943 no less than 761 locomotives had been produced, but in March 1943, all production stopped and was never re-started. Production of ammunition fuses for guns stopped in March 1943.

Previously 200,000 per month had been produced. The production of large shells, which had been running at 400 per month, stopped in July 1943. Guns, gun tubes, and liner production dropped from its 50 to 75 per month, to half. Some of the worst problems were in Essen, where there was a shortage of labour caused by the destruction of so much housing. It was reported in June 1943, that 100,000 people had no roofs over their heads and this was one of the reasons why the resumption of activities at Krupp's was out of the question.

All this was directly attributed to the Bomber Command attacks during the ten months from March to December 1943. The Germans had lost 1,000,000 man-years in this period of the 29 Ruhr towns being attacked. The results of the Bomber Command attacks over ten months were equivalent to a loss of at least four months output by every factory worker in 29 of the largest industrial cities in Germany including Berlin. In all, 19 cities in Germany were virtually destroyed, and of these, eleven were in the Ruhr area. The number not so seriously damaged was also 19, and damaged 9. In Essen, for example, 1030 acres out of a possible 2630 acres, were devastated. Apart from the actual damage to its industries there were several indirect effects, such as time lost due to workers being in air raid shelters, and the lowering of individual efficiency through nervousness and fatigue. Other effects included the disruption of gas, water and electricity supplies; and the difficulties in obtaining raw material because of damage to the transport systems. Essen's industrial production in 1943 was about 30 per cent less than what it was in 1942. The production of the Krupps works on average, during the last two years of the war, was less than half of the 1942 production, and the condition of Essen at the time of its occupation by the Allies in 1945, was such that production could not have been re-started for some considerable time.

In 1945, production records found in the Ruhr mines told the story of the Allied bombing. Normally producing 100,000,000 tons of coal a year, it reached an all-time low just prior to the Allied thrust into Germany. Coal mines, synthetic oil plants and industrial works all showed evidence of being closed down for more than a year due to the bombing. Severe damage was inflicted on 28,000,000 square feet of industrial buildings and 126,000,000 square feet on industrial buildings in the Ruhr area. Because of the crippling damage to the factories, 794,600 man-hours or work was lost in the Ruhr area. Between March 1943 and April 1945, 11,336 sorties were made on the Krupps complex; and 186 full-scale air raids, 36,420 tons of incendiary and high explosive bombs were dropped. Goebbels wrote in his diary that: 'Essen was the city hit hardest by English air raids.'

On the 11 April 1945, when American troops arrived in Essen, they found the factories totally destroyed. In the centre of the city, a 1000lb bomb had toppled the old Cannon King (statue of Alfred Krupps) off its mountings. All the Krupps directors were eventually charged as War Criminals, the main charge being the use of slave labour in their factories. All but one were found guilty and given sentences of between two and twelve years in prison.

At the end of the war the head of the main committee for the iron-producing industry in the Speer Ministry, Dr Rohland stated: 'The mass attacks in the Spring of 1943 came as a complete surprise. This led to the formation of the Ruhr Staff by Albert Speer and to the mobilization of available forces to prevent the collapse which threatened.' In summing up, Dr Rohland declared: 'The actual loss of production achieved was in no case proportional to the destruction.' Speer said: 'The first serious threat to production came after the attack on the dams in May 1943, when the pumping stations were flooded and choked with mud and the water supply to the mining and blast furnaces was stopped.' He went on to say that if the Sorpe dam had been destroyed instead of the Eder dam, production in the Ruhr would have suffered much more. The repairs to the Mohne dam were rushed through in time to catch the Autumn rains. The attack on the dams had given the Germans a big scare. Dr Schrieber, the head of the armaments supply office in the Speer Ministry said the extensive damage inflicted on workers' settlements near Krupps was making it very difficult to keep the people together. The same was true of Cologne and other towns in the Ruhr. The most severely devastated town in the Ruhr was Remscheid, with 83 per cent of its built-up area being destroyed. Wuppertal came next, with 74 per cent being destroyed. In Dortmund, 35 per cent of its built-up area was damaged in two raids, and a few days after the second attack, it was flooded by the water from the breached Mohne dam. Speer stated that if another six German cities had been devastated, he would not have been able to maintain armaments production.

The cost to Bomber Command during the Battle of the Ruhr, was 640 aircraft missing, 2126 aircraft damaged and 5000 aircrew casualties, suffered as a result of 18,506 sorties carried out. On Essen alone, 2070 sorties were carried out at a cost of 92 aircraft missing.

Whenever Tom Parsons sees films on the television which portray the German forces as semi-idiots, he gets annoyed. 'They were not', is his reponse. Recalling his memories of that period, Tom says: 'In retrospect, I think that perhaps the searchlights were even more frightening than the guns on occasion. At least the guns could not be seen. The searchlights were constant, whereas the shells were not, and if they got you, you were completely naked in the sky, and in the Ruhr there were a hell of a lot of searchlights. The Ruhr was very much the same for each target, the only consolation one had, was that there were upward of about 300 to 500 aircraft in the sky and you could not be given special treatment by the gunners.'

Frank Hugo remembers: 'The bravado and boasting in the de-briefing but, later in the dark, the tears being shed into one's pillow. Being very scared and frightened, but even more of showing it, and not being able to do the job properly.'

When Don Bennett, the head of the Pathfinders heard of the losses suffered from their operations, he would sometimes shed tears. He said: 'No man should be branded a coward for not being able to go on in such terrible circumstances.' He was, of course, talking about the very few aircrew who could not go on, many having done a number of operations but had reached the end of their tether. Bennett also felt they would be a menace to the rest of the crew if they carried on. There were some men who experienced LMF (Lack of Moral Fibre) and others who lost the confidence of their commanding officer. As a result, some men would be examined by the medical officer and declared medically unfit to fly.

Air Chief Marshal Harris paid tribute to his men, saying: 'There are no words that can do justice to the aircrew who fought under my command in the RAF. There is no parallel in warfare to such courage and determination which at times was so great that scarcely one man in three could expect to survive his tour of 30 operations. For the RAF crews in general, it must be truly said that no more highly trained body of men has ever gone out to war.' The success was due to the bomber crews who bravely broke through formidable defences time and time again to reach their targets.

When many years after the war a former bomber pilot Group Captain Hamish Mahaddie DSO, DFC, AFC met a famous former German fighter pilot and ace General Galland, Mahaddie at the time was involved in the making of the film 'The Battle of Britain'. When asked by Galland what a former 'Furniture Remover' meaning bomber pilot, was doing in the making of a film about fighters, the reposte was short and sharp: 'Yes, I was a furniture remover during the war, and in the course of this I was able to remove much furniture from one side of the *strasse* to the other.'

When the war ended, the groundcrew personnel, including the WAAFS, were taken on flights over Germany. The operation was known as a 'Cook's' tour. They saw the once mighty Krupps armament plant as a twisted and grotesque wreck. It brought home to the groundcrews how much they should remember with a deep sense of gratitude, and how much they and everyone in the UK, owed those aircrews who had not lived to see the results of their efforts.

In 1987, former air gunner, Jack Catford was awarded a disability pension because he had lost some of his hearing due to firing his guns in the confinement of the gun turret of a Lancaster. The complaint was named as 'Lancaster ear'.

The last word must come from another ex-air gunner, Don Brennan of 10 Squadron: 'I survived German skies, even the Ruhr Valley, with 2000 heavy ack-ack guns defending Krupps works at Essen. At this time, I always made God a lot of promises about not drinking and chasing girls, especially when what seemed like thousands of searchlights would catch us in their beams and we would then be sprayed with predicted flak.'

Acknowledgements

Pathfinder Association
Pathfinder Association (Australia)
Air Gunners Association
Bomber Command Association
Air Historical Branch (MOD)
Public Record Office
Commonwealth War Graves Commission
The Royal National Lifeboat Institution
Cromer Lifeboat Secretary
Gp Capt Stan Slater DSO OBE DFC
Mary Horden (WAAF)
Vera Baker (WAAF)
Noreen King (WAAF)
Gp Capt Dudley H Burnside OBE DSO DFC
A L Fuller
Wg Cdr 'Goldie' Goldstraw DFC
G Archer
F W Fennell
Flt Lt K Newby
David Hodgson
Freddie Brown
Steve Bethell
Joe Clarke DFM
Wg Cdr Clive Sinton DFC
T E Osborn
F W Powell
Ted Loveridge
Sqn Ldr T E Overend DFM
Nick Knilans DSO DFC
Wg Cdr A H Button
K H Ryrie
F Hugo
H D Wood DFM
R Plunckett
H G McLean
H D Coverly
A Cordon

Flt Lt D C Tritton
L F Bradfield
E G Pierce
Wg Cdr Walter Thompson DSO DFC
Eddie Edmonds DFC
Alex S Smith
P C Walder DFM
L Wooldridge DFC
Flt Lt A J Scrivenor DFC
A F C Smith
D V Smith
E Hearn DFC
K J Sockett
L Y Easby
W Baker
P Panichelli
Jack Western JP
R N Lindsey
T L Thackray DFM
D Rowe
E F Hicks CGM
W Overbury
L Blanchard
M Evans
G C Dunn
Air Marshal Sir John Whitley KCB CB DSO AFC
G F Calvert
John Petrie-Andrew DFC DFM
Ralph Barker
Alf Price
Gp Capt Gerald Cooper OBE DFC AFC
S T Wingham
A W Edgley
D B Whittaker
C Dickinson
Vincent Elmer
Gerry Zwanenberg MBE
Carston Petersen
Major Paul Zorner
Alexander Beek and family
Steve Kendall, BBC Radio Kent
Charlie Chester, BBC Soap Box
Major R D A McEachern RCAF
Peter Sharpe for his generous help with the casualty lists
RAF Museum, Hendon

Sources

Public Records Office
Air 14
Air 27
Air 24
Air 8
Air 2 code 30
Stadt Archives, Dortmund
Lancaster to Berlin, Walter Thompson
Letters From A Bomber Pilot, David Hodgson
Bomber Command War Diaries, Martin Middlebrook/Chris Everitt
Epics of Aviation Archaeology, Bruce Robertson
The Great Raids Essen 5 March 1943, Air Cdre John Searby DSO DFC
Inside The Third Reich, Albert Speer
The House of Krupps, Peter Batty
Lancaster Target, Jack Currie
No Moon Tonight, Don Charlwood

Bomber Command Night Operations
March — July 1943
Aircraft Losses

March 1943	
Lancasters	53
Halifaxes	42
Stirlings	24
Wellingtons	41
Mosquitos	1
Total	161

April 1943	
Lancasters	86
Halifaxes	68
Stirlings	43
Wellingtons	45
Mosquitos	2
Total	244

May 1943	
Lancasters	64
Halifaxes	77
Stirlings	41
Wellingtons	47
Mosquitos	2
Total	231

June 1943	
Lancasters	111
Halifaxes	82
Stirlings	44
Wellingtons	39
Whitleys	1
Total	277

July 1943	
Lancasters	69
Halifaxes	65
Stirlings	30
Wellingtons	20
Mosquitos	2
Total	186

Breakdown		
	374	Lancasters
	334	Halifaxes
	182	Stirlings
	182	Wellingtons
	1	Whitley
	7	Mosquitos

Overall Total 1099

Aircrew Losses on Ruhr Targets Only

March — July 1943

Royal Air Force	2122
Royal Canadian Air Force	590
Royal Australian Air Force	150
Royal New Zealand Air Force	102
South African Air Force	2
Polish	21
Danish	1
Fijian	1
West Indian	1
Overall Total Killed	**2990**
Prisoners of War	766
Evaded Capture	36
Died Later	2

Aircraft Missing On All Targets

March — July 1943

Ruhr	640
Non-Ruhr	396
Mining	63
Overall Total	1099
Total Operations	114
Aircraft crashed in the UK returning from operations	11
Aircraft despatched	29,022
Bomb Tonnage Dropped	67,079
Mine Tonnage Dropped	6,277
Bomb Tonnage Dropped on Germany	60,825

Aircraft Missing On The Ruhr

March — July 1943

No 1 Group	— 104	
No 3 Group	— 105	
No 4 Group	— 167	
No 5 Group	— 84	
No 6 Group	— 115	
No 8 Group	— 65	
Overall Total	— 640	
Breakdown	— 195	Lancasters
	— 207	Halifaxes
	— 129	Wellingtons
	— 107	Stirlings
	— 2	Mosquitos
Total number of operations	28	

Chain of Commands

APPENDIX 1
Bomber Command Groups
4 March 1943

No. 1 Group Bawtry, Yorkshire

Squadron	Station	Aircraft type
12	Wickenby	Lancaster
100	Grimsby	Lancaster
101	Holme	Lancaster
103	Elsham Wolds	Lancaster
460 (RAAF)	Breighton	Lancaster
166	Kirmington	Wellington
199	Ingham	Wellington
300 (Pol)	Hemswell	Wellington
301 (Pol)	Hemswell	Wellington
305 (Pol)	Hemswell	Wellington

No. 3 Group Exning near Newmarket, Suffolk

Squadron	Station	Aircraft type
15	Bourn	Stirling
75	Newmarket	Stirling
90	Ridgewell	Stirling
149	Lakenheath	Stirling
214	Chedburgh	Stirling
218	Downham Market	Stirling
115	East Wretham	Lancaster & Wellington
138 (Special)	Tempsford	Halifax
161 (Special)	Tempsford	Halifax
192 (Special)	Gransden Lodge	Halifax, Wellington, Mosquito

No. 4 Group Heslington Hall, Yorkshire

Squadron	Station	Aircraft type
10	Melbourne	Halifax
51	Snaith	Halifax
76	Linton-on-Ouse	Halifax
77	Elvington	Halifax
78	Linton-on-Ouse	Halifax
102	Pocklington	Halifax
158	Rufforth	Halifax
196	Leconfield	Wellington
429 (RCAF)	East Moor	Wellington
431 (RCAF)	Burn	Wellington
466 (RAAF)	Leconfield	Wellington

No. 5 Group St. Vincents near Grantham, Lincolnshire

Squadron	Station	Aircraft type
9	Waddington	Lancaster
44 (Rhod)	Waddington	Lancaster
49	Fiskerton	Lancaster
50	Skellingthorpe	Lancaster
57	Scampton	Lancaster
61	Syerston	Lancaster
97	Woodhall Spa	Lancaster
106	Syerston	Lancaster
207	Langar	Lancaster
467 (RAAF)	Bottesford	Lancaster

No. 6 Group (RCAF) Allerton Park, Yorkshire

Squadron	Station	Aircraft type
405 (RCAF)	Topcliffe	Halifax
408 (RCAF)	Leeming	Halifax
419 (RCAF)	Middleton St. George	Halifax
420 (RCAF)	Middleton St. George	Wellington
424 (RCAF)	Topcliffe	Wellington
425 (RCAF)	Dishforth	Wellington
426 (RCAF)	Dishforth	Wellington
427 (RCAF)	Croft	Wellington
428 (RCAF)	Dalton	Wellington

No. 8 Group Wyton, Huntingdonshire

Squadron	Station	Aircraft type
7 (PFF)	Oakington	Stirling
35 (PFF)	Graveley	Halifax
83 (PFF)	Wyton	Lancaster
156 (PFF)	Warboys	Lancaster
109	Wyton	Mosquito

APPENDIX 2

The Battle of the Ruhr Missing Aircraft and Aircrew 5 March – 31 July 1943

SQUADRON AND AIRCRAFT	CREW
5 – 11 March 1943	
49 Sqdn: Lancaster ED 431-M Probably shot down by Ltn. Denzel, west of Texel	Sgt. JM Thorn Killed Sgt. DG Fairlie Killed Flt. Sgt. JH Prior Killed Flt. Sgt. N Bolton Killed Sgt. DS Bratt Killed Can Sgt. AE Horne Killed Sgt. FLH Vines Killed
76 Sqdn: Halifax BB 282-R Shot down by Major Helmut Lent, crashed Staphorst, Holland	Flt. Sgt. CA Milan Killed Can Flt. Sgt. EJ Fry Killed Flt. Sgt. CG Pitt Killed Flt. Sgt. HW Edwards Killed Flt. Sgt. HC Cope Killed Flt. Sgt. OJ Trainer Killed Can Flt. Sgt. RB Van Buren Killed
78 Sqdn: Halifax HR 687-G Shot down by Major Helmut Lent	Flt. Sgt. J Thompson Killed Sgt. KW Mercer POW Inj. Sgt. AC Loveland POW Inj. Sgt. AC Layshon POW Inj. Sgt. A Blackwell Killed. Parachute did not open Sgt. OV Proctor POW Sgt. EL Williams Killed Can Sgt. DR Cheswell POW
83 Sqdn: Lancaster W 4847-V Exploded over Ijsselmeer	Aust Flt. Sgt. HA Partridge Killed Can Sgt. RD Fulton Killed. Washed up 2.5.43 Scharhorn FO LW Sprackling Killed Sgt. J. Freshwater Killed Sgt. H Fell Killed Sgt. AD Dennis Killed Sgt. JL Organ Killed. Washed up 6.5.43 Hinddoopen
90 Sqdn: Stirling R 9271-Q Crashed München Gladbach	PO WA Fowlie Killed Sgt. M Renaut POW Stalag 344. Later WO Sgt. WM Werkendan POW Stalag 344. Later Flt. Sgt. Sgt. J Eccles POW Stalag 344. Later WO Can Flt. Sgt. JB Courtney Killed Sgt. EF Garnett POW Stalag 344. Later Flt. Sgt.
106 Sqdn: Lancaster W 4918-D Crashed north of Düsseldorf	Can Flt. Lt. WJ Picken DFC Killed Sgt. JPL Wilson Killed Sgt. L Hudson Killed Sgt. JE Bonson Killed Can Sgt. CE Dellar Killed Sgt. CJ Powell Killed Sgt. LA Leadbitter Killed

SQUADRON AND AIRCRAFT	CREW
156 Sqdn: Lancaster LM 304-J Possibly shot down by Ltn. Linke	Sqn. Ldr. SG Hookway DFC Killed Flt. Sgt. FW Hart DFM Killed FO E Luff Killed Sgt. EB Alsop Killed FO RD Turk Killed Sgt. WH Clark Killed Sgt. D Heap DFM Killed
214 Sqdn: Stirling BK 662-K Crashed in the sea, Texel area	Sgt. HW Baldock Killed Sgt. F Kimber Killed Sgt. E Wright Killed Sgt. WH Trotter Killed. Washed up 25.5.43 Texel PO TH Etienne Killed Sgt. W Taylor Killed Can Sgt. AB Amirault Killed
218 Sqdn: Stirling R 9333-Y Crashed Essen	PO GA Ratcliffe Killed Aust Flt. Sgt. KR Heming Killed Sgt. WL Waddington Killed Sgt. DH Melville Killed Sgt. JF Charlton Killed Sgt. WT Hurl Killed Sgt. J Turner Killed
300 (Polish) Sqdn: Wellington BK 150-Q Crashed München Gladbach. Possibly shot down by Fw Vinke	FO K Romiszyn POW Sqn. Ldr. J Janowski Killed Sgt. H Wozniak POW Sgt. Z Abramik POW Sgt. C Zaleski POW
419 (RCAF) Sqdn: Halifax DT 646-S Shot down near Elst, Holland	Sgt. L Bakewell POW Stalag 344. Later PO Can Flt. Sgt. DD Scowen POW Stalag 344. Later PO Can Flt. Sgt. JE Marvel POW Can Sgt. JA Bennett POW Stalag 344. Later WO1 Sgt. AC Turner Inj. Escaped Can Sgt. WJ Clark POW Stalag 344. Later WO2 Flt. Sgt. JR Coupar Killed
420 (RCAF) Sqdn: Wellington HE 280-V	Can PO R Graham Killed PO WG Lee Killed Can PO JK MacDonald Killed Can PO DE Bennett Killed Can Sgt. HTA Lawson Killed Can Flt. Sgt. D Culver Killed
426 (RCAF) Sqdn: Wellington BK 401-Q	Can PO CR Trask Killed PO CE Chapman Killed Can Sgt. W Davies Killed Can Sgt. NF Paterson Killed Can Sgt. RE Williams Killed Can Sgt. G Whalen Killed
466 (RAAF) Sqdn: Wellington HZ 270-Q Crashed Essen	Sgt. AC Yielder Killed Sgt. RD Baker Killed Sgt. CJ Smith Killed Sgt. JW Gould Killed Sgt. J Linacre Killed

Total 74 Killed, 19 POWs, 1 Evaded.

SQUADRON AND AIRCRAFT	CREW
12 – 13 March 1943	
7 Sqdn: Stirling BK 592-P Shot down by night-fighter	Flt. Sgt. DE Street Killed Can Flt. Sgt. RAW Sharpe Killed Can Flt. Sgt. D Neale Killed Sgt. TE Hastings Killed Sgt. WM Meiklejohn Killed Sgt. DC Wilson Killed Flt. Sgt. WS Berry Killed
10 Sqdn: Halifax DT 778-N Crashed at Elberfeld	PO J Dickinson Killed Sgt. JH Harris Killed Sgt. FW Stanners Killed Sgt. HE Hendon Killed Sgt. JE Smith Killed Sgt. FP Crawford Killed Sgt. LJ Gast Killed
10 Sqdn: Halifax HR 692-R Crashed Horst, Holland	Sgt. L Barnes Killed PO RJ Paul Killed Sgt. KA Milles Killed Sgt. LE Thomas Killed Can Sgt. WLG Thompson Killed Sgt. J Free Killed Sgt. GA Hyatt Killed
50 Sqdn: Lancaster ED 449-T Shot down by a fighter. Crashed Bergen, Holland	Can Sgt. F Ward Killed Sgt. F Stephens Killed Flt. Sgt. A Allan Killed Sgt. R Heslop Killed Sgt. R Wilson Killed Sgt. RM Jenkins Killed Sgt. VR Kissick Killed
76 Sqdn: Halifax DT 751-C Shot down by Oblt. von Bonin near America, Holland	Sgt. P Nevines POW Sgt. JB Locke POW Sgt. WJ Wright POW Sgt. PL Ratcliffe POW Inj. Sgt. FJ Stapleton POW Sgt. AC Sharpe Killed in combat Sgt. RG Poland died of TB 19.1.44 when a POW
78 Sqdn: Halifax DT 774-E Crashed Groesbeek, Holland	Can Sgt. FA Morean Killed Sgt. H Bentley Killed Sgt. WH Cosnell Killed Sgt. WJ McLelland Killed Sgt. LG Dyer Killed Sgt. GE Benson Killed Sgt. BM Singleton Killed
83 Sqdn: Lancaster W 4928-S Crashed Düsseldorf	Sqn. Ldr. DAJ McClure DFC Killed Can Flt. Lt. OR Waterbury DFC Killed Sgt. J. McFarlane Killed PO DG Lovell Killed Flt. Sgt. PJ Musk DFM Killed PO LE Warren Killed Flt. Lt. AF McQueen DFC Killed
97 Sqdn: Lancaster R 5607-X Crashed north of Essen	Can WO DC Plaunt Killed Can PO AJ Smith Killed Sgt. TL Williams Killed Can Flt. Sgt. JAJ Viau Killed Flt. Sgt. WC Burr Killed Sgt. GW Dillon Killed Sgt. AWE Taylor Killed

SQUADRON AND AIRCRAFT	CREW
100 Sqdn: Lancaster ED 544-Q Crashed Düsseldorf	Sgt. RM Peake Killed Sgt. H Jowitt Killed Sgt. E Hodgson Killed Sgt. WE Chamberlain Killed PO DI Arthur Killed Sgt. AR Roberts Killed Sgt. RFR Sides Killed
101 Sqdn: Lancaster W 4862-E Crashed Düsseldorf	PO JR Kee Killed Sgt. W Hynd Killed Sgt. AD Slade Killed Sgt. WF Greasley Killed Sgt. SG Smith Killed Sgt. E Shaw Killed Sgt. EA Stead Killed
102 Sqdn: Halifax JB 836-T	FO ADA Barnes Killed FO EH Beeton Killed Sgt. AL Thurlow Killed Sgt. VN Elkins Killed Sgt. WP Quinliven Killed Sgt. JS Lowdell Killed
102 Sqdn: Halifax DT 799-? Shot down by flak 20km from Essen	Sgt. HCA Newland Killed Sgt. DJ Druett Killed Sgt. MHC Crow Killed Sgt. AE Beaven Killed Sgt. CS Jones POW Stalag 344. Later Flt. Sgt. Sgt. JD Haigh Killed
102 Sqdn: Halifax DT 739-P Hit by flak crashed Hydyn, near Essen	Sgt. EWL Charlebois Killed Sgt. EA Hughes Killed Sgt. BA Horne POW Sgt. WS Hedges POW Inj. Stalag 344. Later WO Sgt. HF Powers POW Stalag 344. Later Flt. Sgt. Sgt. HR Kemp POW Stalag 344. Sgt. AD Williams POW Stalag 344. Later Flt. Sgt.
103 Sqdn: Lancaster ED 419-X Crashed Germeinde/Medhop Rehen	FO HW Dugard Killed PO PG Harris Killed Sgt. EC Fermanian Killed Sgt. RA Gerrard Killed Sgt. WR Jones Killed Sgt. W Andrews Killed Sgt. PE Trew Killed
106 Sqdn: Lancaster R 5749-G Crashed Düsseldorf	Aust PO AL McDonald Killed Sgt. RGC Owen Killed Sgt. KRJ Young Died on the 13th March Sgt. HSF Bishell Killed Flt. Sgt. EB Clampitt Killed Sgt. BJ Eckett Killed
115 Sqdn: Wellington BJ 756-Q Ditched Ijsselmeer	Sgt. LP Fallon Killed Sgt. CJJW Lamb Killed Sgt. WE Akrill Killed Sgt. LG Collings Killed Sgt. C Moffatt Killed

SQUADRON AND AIRCRAFT	CREW
149 Sqdn: Stirling EF 330-P Shot down by Oblt. Sigmund Crashed Berghbeek south of Doetinchem, Holland	Flt. Sgt. FA Pearson Killed PO LHR Binning Killed Sgt. WH Clayton Killed Can WO2 GW Miller Killed Can Sgt. J Misseldine Killed Sgt. V Page Killed FO GW Sellers Killed Flt. Sgt. PH Skinner Killed
199 Sqdn: Wellington HZ 263 Lost at sea	Flt. Lt. WJ King Killed Aust Sgt. CR Townsend Killed Sgt. DA Nunn Killed Sgt. CF White Killed Can Sgt. RI Edwards Killed
199 Sqdn: Wellington HE 519-X Shot down at Camperdon by an ME 110	Sgt. DJ Clifford Killed FO CM Kitson POW Stalag L3. Later Flt. Lt. Sgt. LM Jones Killed Can Sgt. JG Richardson Killed Sgt. R Lambert Killed
207 Sqdn: Lancaster ED 604-A Shot down at Bothop	FO HE Doble DFC Killed FO S Clitheroe DFC Killed Sgt. A Garden Killed PO IAH Linklater DFM Killed Sgt. BL Litoloff Killed Flt. Sgt. RS Carr DFM Killed Flt. Sgt. TJ Walker Killed
420 Sqdn: Wellington HE 690-U Crashed Hellevoetsluis, Holland	Can Sgt. GH Cooke POW Stalag 344. Later WO2 Sgt. J Morris POW Stalag 344. Later Flt. Sgt. Sgt. RG Mercer POW Stalag 344. Later Flt. Sgt. Can Sgt. TS McKinnon POW Stalag L6. Later WO2 Sgt. AR Dawson Hit in the head by flak and killed
424 Sqdn: Wellington BK 348-J Crashed Uden, Holland	Can PO RG Caldwell Killed FO GJ Cory Killed Flt. Sgt. WP Topping Killed Sgt. AP Larson Killed Sgt. LA Parker Killed
425 Sqdn: Wellington BK 340-T Shot down by Fw Vinke north-west of Hoorn at Hoogwoud, Holland	Can Sgt. JGGC Lamontagne POW Can Flt. Sgt. AW Brown POW Inj. Can. Flt. Sgt. JRA Goulet POW Stalag L6. Later WO1 RCAF Can. Flt. Sgt. JAV Gauthier POW Stalag 6. Later WO2 Can Flt. Sgt. MJAJ Aumond POW Inj.

Total 112 Killed, 22 POWs, 1 Died later

26 – 27 March 1943

SQUADRON AND AIRCRAFT	CREW
78 Sqdn: Halifax W 7931-J Crashed Gaanderen, Holland	Flt. Sgt. JM Tait Killed Sgt. A Wilson Killed NZ Sgt. JA Wilson Killed WO S Hauxwell POW Can Sgt. G Johnstone POW PO RW Keen POW Inj. Sgt. FE Lemon POW Sgt. RR Holeatt POW

SQUADRON AND AIRCRAFT	CREW
109 Sqdn: Mosquito DK 318-B Lost at sea, the first *OBOE* Mosquito lost during the Battle. SOS north of Foreland	Flt. Lt. LJ Ackland DFC Killed Can PO FS Strouts DFC Killed
426 Sqdn: Wellington X 3696-T Lost at sea	Sgt. E Hall Killed Sgt. JJ Reade Killed Sgt. CD Reed Killed Sgt. F Simpson Killed Sgt. W Stevenson Killed Sgt. C Darlington POW
429 Sqdn: Wellington MS 487-C Shot down by flak Crashed Leyden, Holland	FO G Fox Inj. Sgt. GH Murray Evaded Sgt. AA Skelly POW PO PS Bastin Killed Sgt. J.M. Murray Died a POW
431 Sqdn: Wellington HE 503	Flt. Lt. GHT Eades Killed Flt. Lt. MK Gardner Killed Can Flt. Lt. AM Hill Killed Can WO JM Rogal Killed Can Sgt. BV Ducker Killed
460 Sqdn: Lancaster ED 354 Ditched Ijsselmeer	Flt. Sgt. RE Wilson Killed Sgt. FV Harrison Killed Sgt. DJ Cooper Killed Sgt. HD Brown Killed Sgt. PJ Haseman Killed Sgt. NA Lever Killed PO CD Bramham Killed
Total 23 Killed, 9 POWs, 1 Evaded	

29 – 30 March 1943

SQUADRON AND AIRCRAFT	CREW
166 Sqdn: Wellington X 3965-L Crashed Groesbeek, Holland	Sgt. OE Collins Killed Sgt. JG Howard Killed FO L Young Killed Sgt. JG Hubard Killed Aust Sgt. JB Bayliss Killed Aust Flt. Sgt. SN Curtis Killed
166 Sqdn: Wellington He 545-H Shot down by night-fighter flown by Obst. Werner Streib Schaarsbergen	Sgt. JRA Hodgson Killed Sgt. SR Farley Killed Can PO FE Dupré Killed Sgt. D Keenan Killed Can Sgt. RA Weese Killed
196 Sqdn: Wellington HE 548	Sgt. A Lucas Killed Sgt. D Andrew Killed Sgt. AWE Wilson Killed WO HG Allen Killed FO KF Smart Killed
196 Sqdn: Wellington HE 385-M On a house Zwiepsebrock 7-Lochen, Laren-Borchem, Holland	FO ER Culff Killed Sgt. TA Dew Killed Can FO LD McAllister Killed Sgt. ACA Veeck Killed Sgt. HR Wilmore Killed

SQUADRON AND AIRCRAFT	CREW
420 Sqdn: Wellington X 3814 Crashed Düsseldorf	Can Sgt. RL Brandow Killed Can Flt. Sgt. HC Sleep Killed Can Sgt. LG Jones Killed Sgt. CW Cockaday Killed Can Flt. Sgt. J.M. Green Killed
420 Sqdn: Wellington MS 484 Exploded near Boxmeir Crashed Noord-Brabant	Can PO BA Grant Killed Can Sgt. R Dyson Killed WO AG Skiggs POW Sgt. PE Baron Killed Can Sgt. SV Brandshaw Killed
426 Sqdn: Wellington BJ 762-O Crashed near Sondelerleyen	Can Flt. Sgt. RE Todd Killed Sgt. J Taylor POW Can Sgt. JA Bailey Killed Can Sgt. H Martin POW Can Sgt. JF Grubb Killed. Found with parachute on
427 Sqdn: Wellington HE 744	Can Sgt. DF McFadden Killed Can FO LTE Sweet Killed Can Sgt. CA Boyd Killed Sgt. AR Dove Killed Can Sgt. WM Bassett Killed
428 Sqdn: Wellington BJ 920-R Crashed Gelsenkirchen	Can Sgt. JL Cartier Killed Can Flt. Sgt. PB Gustavsen Killed Can FO JF Spencer Killed Sgt. HS Rhodes Died a POW Can Sgt. D King POW
428 Sqdn: Wellington HE 175	NZ Sgt. JB Maryn Killed Flt. Sgt. LW Hayward Killed Sgt. NS Farr Killed NZ Sgt. JC Donaldson Killed Sgt. K Benjamin Killed
429 Sqdn: Wellington BK 540- Crashed in the sea near Esbjerg, Denmark	Sgt. HDG Carty Killed FO PB Crosswell Killed Sgt. WF Whiteland Killed Sgt. RE Scott Killed Flt. Sgt. EK Hart Killed Can Flt. Sgt. DL Bain Killed
429 Sqdn: Wellington BJ 920-	Sgt. KA Burini Killed Sgt. WGJ Asplin Killed Sgt. JW Kerr Killed Sgt. WE Jones Killed Sgt. R Dolbean Killed
431 Sqdn: Wellington HE 182-A	Sgt EJ Aspden Killed Sgt. JM Kimber Killed Can WO PF Yellin Killed Sgt. R Davies Killed Sgt. DD Jones POW Inj.
Total 61 Killed, 6 POWs	

3 – 4 April 1943

9 Sqdn: Lancaster ED 694 Shot down by Oblt.von Bonin Eindhoven, Holland	PO WH Swire Killed Sgt. W Watts Killed Sgt. GR Gilbert Killed Sgt. RD Francis Killed Flt. Sgt. RR Feeley Killed Sgt. GH Evans Killed Sgt. EW Cook Killed

SQUADRON AND AIRCRAFT	CREW
9 Sqdn: Lancaster ED 479	Sqn. Ldr. GWJ Jarret Killed PO G Smith Killed FO AG Seymour Killed Sgt. H Precious Killed Sgt. J Francis Killed Sgt. J Miles Killed FO GR Dale Killed
51 Sqdn: Halifax DT 738	Sgt. J Rawcliffe Killed Sgt. RK Guy Killed Flt. Sgt. J Richards Killed Sgt. JV Branscombe Killed Sgt. WG Richardson Killed Sgt. DC Ralston Killed Sgt. A Howarth Killed
76 Sqdn: Halifax W 7805-M Hervest-Dorsten	Sgt. JK Howarth Killed Sgt. WC Pitt Killed FO PW Digby Mentioned in Despatches Killed Sgt. FG Williams Killed Flt. Sgt. JW Blakey POW Stalag L6. Later Flt. Sgt. Flt. Sgt. GA Egan POW Stalag L6. Later Flt. Sgt. Sgt. HH Richards POW
78 Sqdn: Halifax JB 845 Crashed Brabant, Belgium	Flt. Lt. THO Richardson Killed Sgt. TH Webb Killed FO LRC Shadwell Killed Sgt. J McCormick Killed Sgt. RJ Kernick Killed FO RCA Allberry Killed Can Sgt. RO Dunlop Killed
78 Sqdn: Halifax W 7937 Engine failure. Aircraft blew up	FO TN Foster Killed Sgt. GE Sendall POW Can PO JH Jamieston POW Sgt. EA Drury POW Stalag 6 Flt. Sgt. WF Hodgson POW Sgt. C Wayte POW Stalag 6 Sgt. NV Thomson POW
78 Sqdn: Halifax DT 780 Crashed München Gladbach	PO G Riach Killed Sqn. Ldr. BJ Bourchier POW Sgt. EC Lacey POW Inj. WO W Ingles POW Stalag 3 Sgt. DH Howard POW Stalag 6 Sgt. AM Parker Killed Flt. Sgt. A Wright POW Stalag 3 Flt. Sgt. LL Stas POW Stalag 6
83 Sqdn: Lancaster LM 302-R	FO RB Hope DFC Killed Can WO LN McArthur Killed Sgt. CL Billington Killed Sgt. RG Pegg Killed Flt. Sgt. JS Keay Killed Sgt. D Brennan Killed Sgt. W Billington Killed
83 Sqdn: Lancaster R 5626-T Crashed Winterswijk, Holland	Sqn. Ldr. FT Flower Killed FO DA Southon Killed Sgt. D McEwen Killed Flt. Sgt. L Fieldhouse Killed Flt. Sgt. EL Shandley Killed Can WO2 CM Coghill Killed Flt. Sgt. FW Routledge DFM Killed

SQUADRON AND AIRCRAFT	CREW
83 Sqdn: Lancaster ED 334-H Crashed near Winterswijk	PO CD Calvert DFM Killed Sgt. R Bee Killed PO G Mackay Killed Sgt. R O'Brien Killed PO JH Ridd Killed Sgt. LR Tomlinson Killed Sgt. JC Aston Killed
101 Sqdn: Lancaster ED 736-W Crashed Wische, east-north-east of Bocholt	FO RN Johnson Killed Sgt. GW Jones Killed Sgt. IW Llewellyn Killed Sgt. F.J. Hackett Killed Sgt. RC Horton Killed Sgt. HA Ramsay Killed Sgt. RL Hodgson Killed
106 Sqdn: Lancaster ED 542 Rear turret blown away four miles north of Duisberg	Sgt. TJ Ridd Killed FO AC Palmer Killed FO JW Simpson Killed Sgt. RC Webb Killed Sgt. A Burson Killed Sgt. RS Sabell Killed Sgt. E Williams Killed
156 Sqdn: Lancaster W 4894-T Shot down by Lt. Lent over North Sea	Aust Flt. Sgt. RH Byass Killed Sgt. GR Minns Killed Sgt. DL Robertson Killed Sgt. SE Crooks Killed. Washed up 7.5.43 Osterland Aust Sgt. RS Trigwell Killed Aust PO GJ Black Killed
158 Sqdn: Halifax DT 635-F	Flt. Lt. JD Cole Killed PO CG Dawson Killed Sgt. R Gowing Killed PO WA Robinson Killed PO RC Stemp Killed Sgt. A Ward Killed Sgt. BJ Warr Killed
158 Sqdn: Halifax DT 795-M Shot down by night-fighter near Amersfoort, Apeldoorn, Holland	Can PO FH Blake Killed Sgt. JC Jones Killed Sgt. WD Hawkins Killed Sgt. DH Eldridge Killed Sgt. GS Walters Killed Sgt. R Webber Killed Sgt. TV Trollope Killed
405 Sqdn: Halifax DT 723-F Shot down by night-fighter off Rotterdam All Canadian crew	Flt. Lt. Lago POW Stalag L3 Can Flt. Lt. JH Colwell POW Stalag L3 WO WS Beatty Killed Can FO WH Hoddinott POW Stalag L3 Can WO HC Waugh POW Stalag L6 Sgt. AB Grabois POW Can Sgt. WW Phipps POW Stalag L6 Flt. Sgt. KO Perry 2nd Pilot. Died a POW 23.8.43
405 Sqdn: Halifax DT 808 Shot down by night-fighter Holland All Canadian crew	WO2 WJ McAlpine Killed WO2 JD White Killed Flt. Lt. FE Luxford Killed WO2 JW Halikowski Killed Flt. Sgt. E Brady POW Flt. Lt. WL Murphy POW Stalag L3 Sgt. HJ McQueen Killed

SQUADRON AND AIRCRAFT	CREW
408 Sqdn: Halifax HR 713-F Crashed near Opheusden- Kesteren	Flt. Lt. RHP Gamble Killed FO ER Ray Killed Sgt. A.J. Hawkins Killed Can WO DL Jarrett Killed US/Can Flt. Sgt. RW Barker Killed Aust PO KS McColl Killed PO NC Black POW US/Can Sgt. RR Edmond POW
408: Sqdn: Halifax JB 866-T Crashed Uden	Can PO EA Sirett Nine ops. Killed Can Flt. Sgt. MG Church Killed Can Flt. Sgt. RGA Fletcher Killed Can FO JD McBridge Killed Can Sgt. GD Boyer Killed Can Sgt. FR Burke Killed Sgt. KO Brice Killed
419 Sqdn: Halifax DT 617-R Crashed Olst, Holland Hit a farm, which was burned	PO PD Boyd Killed PO GW Lawry Killed Can Sgt. GB Langley Killed Can Sgt. SN Hall Killed PO HT MacDonald Killed Can Sgt. GW Agar Killed
467 Sqdn: Lancaster ED 524-? OC 'B' Flight Crashed Düsseldorf	Aust Sqn. Ldr. AM Paape DFC Killed FO H North Killed Sgt. DJ Robinson Killed Sgt. LT Fulcher Killed FO T Dring DFC Killed FO JM Stewart AFM Killed Sgt. W Johnson Killed

Total 124 Killed, 27 POWs

8 – 9 April 1943

SQUADRON AND AIRCRAFT	CREW
7 Sqdn: Stirling R 9199-F	Can FO LJ Stewart Killed PO GMML De Meillac Killed Can FO AM Jackson Killed Sgt. RS Hamilton Fox Killed Sgt. V Walters Killed Flt. Sgt. GC Gale Killed Sgt. R Wilson Killed Sgt. GM Boardman Killed
15 Sqdn: Stirling EF 359-B Crashed Meerbeck	PO AJ Gurr Killed Sgt. WS Bragg Killed Sgt. JS Kimber Killed Sgt. FG Lambert Killed Sgt. P Lutivyche Killed Sgt. I Williams Killed. Washed up Rhein 31.5.43 Sgt. J Hall Killed
44 Sqdn: Lancaster ED 351	Flt. Sgt. IC Haines Killed Sgt. S Richardson Killed Sgt. RA Asbury Killed Agt. RG Prince Killed Sgt. FG Ward Killed Can Sgt. E Strandberg Killed Sgt. LJ Yeo Killed

SQUADRON AND AIRCRAFT	CREW
49 Sqdn: Lancaster ED 590	FO DJN Southern DFM Killed FO JB Lapping Killed Sgt. GS Pring Killed Sgt. CJ Tiley Killed FO AL Munro Killed Sgt. H Chatterton Killed Aust PO JL Rollins Killed
76 Sqdn: Halifax W 1236-G	FO MAS Elliott Killed FO HH Rogers DFM Killed PO RR Johnston Killed FO AM Houston Killed Flt. Sgt. J Appleton Killed Sgt. RJ Matthews Killed Sgt. JD Armstrong Killed Sgt. CK Wagstaff Killed
77 Sqdn: Halifax JB 847 Shot down by night-fighter St-Quentin, France	Aust Flt. Lt. JWN Balley Killed Sgt. TS McStay Killed PO Wilson-Rowland POW Flt. Sgt. PA Greene Killed Sgt. W Woodley Killed Sgt. Hedicker Killed Sgt. T Cossland Killed
100 Sqdn: Lancaster ED 568-T	Sqn. Ldr. JA McKinnon Killed Sgt. SFO Chappell Killed Sgt. CJ Grimshaw Killed Sgt. H Jenkinson Killed Sgt. MH Knowles Killed Sgt. RJB Montigue Killed Sgt. RS Sweetlove Killed
106 Sqdn: Lancaster W 4156	PO JL Irvine Killed Sgt. FA Smith Killed Sgt. LJ Tate Killed Sgt. S Cordery Killed Sgt. WG Harvey Killed Sgt. LJ Hemus Killed Aust Flt. Sgt. FWG Limbrick Killed
156 Sqdn: Lancaster ED 622-Q	Aust Flt. Sgt. RG Younger Killed Sgt. NG Stopford Killed Sgt. AJ Jackson Killed Aust PO N Ferguson Killed Aust Flt. Sgt. RH Flett Killed Aust Flt. Sgt. JPM Grace Killed Aust Sgt. SM White Killed
166 Sqdn: Wellington BK361	NZ Sgt. GS Barclay POW PO BH Marion POW Sgt. RW Hart POW Sgt. A Conrad POW Sgt. R Limage POW
166 Sqdn: Wellington HE 658 Crashed due to 'icing' at Essen	PO DHW Morgan Killed Can PO JE Hardy Killed Sgt. W Myersclough Killed PO PP Stevens Killed PO CC Lee Killed
199 Sqdn: Wellington HE 495	Sgt. KA Pinchin Killed PO LC Wheeler Killed Can PO LR Townsend Killed Can Sgt. JH Paguin Killed Sgt. JW Green Killed. Washed up 11.5.43

SQUADRON AND AIRCRAFT	CREW
218 Sqdn: Stirling BF 502-P	PO DAS Tomkins Killed Sgt. TR Davidson Killed Sgt. DIN Eggleton Killed Sgt. DCI Guest Killed Sgt. A Ridge Killed Sgt. J Forrest Killed Sgt. JR Tait Killed
300 Sqdn: Wellington HE 148-T Crashed in North Sea	PO Tonnicki Killed Sgt. S Sluarski Killed. Washed up 10.5.43 PO J Ruek Killed. Washed up 10.5.43 Pol Sgt. T Kniazychi Killed Pol Sgt. W Marcquk Killed Sgt. S Stephen Killed. Washed up 10.4.43
419 Sqdn: Halifax BB 327	Can Sgt. JH Morris Killed Sgt. KH Godbold Killed Can FO AR Hickey Killed Sgt. RJ Amos Killed Can Sgt. PJ Ireland Killed Can Flt Sgt. DC Way Killed Can Sgt. LE Turner Killed
420 Sqdn: Wellington MS 479-	Can PO WA Walkinshaw Killed Can WO DF Evans Killed Can PO KW MacDonald Killed Can WO F Benni Killed Can WO RG Rispin Killed PO JL Rollins Killed
425 Sqdn: Wellington HE 592-Q	Can WO2 JF Smith Killed Can FO RG Cook Killed Can Flt. Sgt. CW Burke Killed Can PO OEE Schulty Killed Sgt. PA Smith Killed
428 Sqdn: Wellington DF 635 Shot down by night-fighter Düsseldorf	PO R Buckham POW Inj. Stalag L3 Can FO NW Rodin POW Stalag L3 PO GC Fletcher POW Sgt. JD Fraser POW Sgt. T Whitehead POW
460 Sqdn: Lancaster W 4785-J Crashed Düsseldorf	Aust Sgt. JH Ball Killed Sgt. CEJ Frampton Killed Sgt. WC Langley Killed Sgt. DG Mordecai Killed Flt. Sgt. AA Garvey Killed Sgt. GG Dobson Killed Aust Sgt. AA Garven Killed
466 Sqdn: Wellington HE155 Crashed Hoof Blerick, near Venlo	PO SM Wood Killed PO AC Kneeshaw Killed Sgt. AB Pennycord Killed Can WO LR Crowe Killed Sgt. JG Chalmers Killed

Total 122 Killed, 6 POWs

SQUADRON AND AIRCRAFT	CREW
9 – 10 April 1943	
9 Sqdn: Lancaster ED 806-L Crashed Uden	PO AF Paramore Killed Sgt. T Hughes Killed FO E Hesketh Killed Sgt. AM Coulthard Killed Sgt. RD Benning Killed Sgt. DH Mactier Killed Sgt. RD Wood Killed
9 Sqdn: Lancaster ED 566-L	Sgt. AR Hobbs Killed Can WO HL Heuther Killed Sgt. SJ Argent Killed Sgt. DN Bysouth Killed WO WJ Reid Killed Sgt. RH Thomas Killed Sgt. GA Taylor Killed NZ WO AM White Killed
9 Sqdn: Lancaster ED 502-V Crashed near Souda, Holland	Sgt WA Barker Killed FO N Bird Killed PO GJ Gibbings Killed Sgt WR Jakeway Killed FO H Robertson Killed Sgt. NP Tutt Killed
44 Sqdn: Lancaster R 5898 Crashed Uden	PO W Smith Killed FO JH Salt Killed Sgt. LJ Nash Killed Sgt. S Dixon Killed Can Sgt. JW Wardlaw POW Stalag L6. Later WO1 Sgt. B Waite POW Sgt. JT Broughton POW Stalag L6. Later Flt. Sgt. Sgt. AN Cowe Killed
101 Sqdn: ED 608-T	PO EM Nelson POW Sgt. EV Newstead POW Flt. Sgt. RBA Pender POW Flt. Sgt. RA Parnell POW Flt. Sgt. CW Shields POW Flt. Sgt. JR Riley Killed Sgt. TA Bird Killed
101 Sqdn: ED 618-X Crashed Doornsspijk	Can WO2 JD Steele Killed Flt. Sgt. MJ Bennett Killed Sgt. D Gould Killed Flt. Sgt. S Grundy DFM Killed Sgt. J Hence Killed Sgt. WDG O'Brien Killed Aust FO NJ Ritchie Killed
207 Sqdn: ED 554-Q	Can Sgt. HA Healey Killed Sgt. AR Lewis Killed Sgt. R Bishop Killed Sgt. DE Whittaker Killed Sgt. WL Whitehouse Killed Sgt. REA Dampier Killed Flt. Sgt. CW Kheynhaus Killed
460 Sqdn: ED 521-B	Aust PO DI MacDonald Killed Flt. Sgt. WF Jones Killed Sgt. M Hoofe Killed Aust Flt. Sgt. WF Alsopp Killed Aust Flt. Sgt. J Forrest Killed Aust Flt. Sgt. JH Dodgshun Killed Aust Sgt. AK Meadows Killed
Total 49 Killed, 5 POWs	

SQUADRON AND AIRCRAFT	CREW
16 – 17 April 1943	
15 Sqdn: Stirling BK 691-F	Flt. Lt. D Haylock Killed Sgt. JS Blackburn Killed Sgt. H Fortune Killed Sgt HC Fiddes Killed Sgt. TL Bromley Killed Sgt. JW Greenwood Killed Sgt. NA Hobden Killed
15 Sqdn: Stirling BK 474-H	Flt. Sgt. J.L. Shields Killed FO KM Pilhe Killed FO LB Perring Killed Sgt. J Gould Killed Sgt. LA James Killed Can Sgt. BJ Bessette Killed Sgt. DJA Hyde Killed Sgt. J Lacy Killed
75 Sqdn: Stirling W 7469-T	NZ Flt. Sgt. KF Debenham Killed Can Flt. Sgt. R.J. Barnes Killed Sgt. WMT Watts Killed Sgt. P.B. Pearson Killed Sgt. D Wainwright POW Sgt. JL Marlow POW Sgt. JJ Davis POW
75 Sqdn: Stirling BF 451-Z	NZ PO KHG Greaves Killed Can Sgt. JO Way Killed Sgt. DTG Shergold Killed Sgt. RF Wangstall Killed Sgt. RC Pierson Killed Sgt. LC Cameron Killed NZ Sgt. RC Stone Killed Sgt. LL Everden Killed
78 Sqdn: Halifax JB 870-F Crashed Roye, River Somme, France	Sgt. Illingworth Killed Sgt. CG West Killed PO HD Dixon Killed Sgt. EG Thomas Killed Sgt. R Woodhall Killed Sgt. SW Patton Killed Sgt. DA Warkins Killed
90 Sqdn: Stirling BK 725-M Crash-landed Commenschon after being hit by flak	PO PD White POW Inj. Sgt. WE Phillips Evaded PO SF Everiss Evaded Sgt. DG Ross Evaded Sgt. EG Gaisford Evaded Sgt. JB Ford Evaded NZ Sgt. W Fitzgerald Evaded Sgt. A Smith Evaded
158 Sqdn: Halifax HR 779-Z Hit by night-fighter over Saarbrücken Crash-landed	FO D Bertera Evaded Sgt. JW Barker Evaded Sgt. WJ Jenkins Evaded Sgt. A Ruge POW Sgt. JW Lawrence Evaded Sgt. E Durant POW Sgt. FR Berkeley POW

SQUADRON AND AIRCRAFT	CREW
196 Sqdn: Wellington HE 387-Z Crashed France	PO IMP Morgan Killed Flt. Sgt. R Hill Killed PO AWA Trevethen Killed Sgt. N Bruce Killed Sgt. L Pickford Killed
214 Sqdn: Stirling BK 653- Attacked by night-fighters south of St-Quentin	Can Flt. Sgt. DE Jones Evaded Sgt. JA Smith Evaded Sgt. RW Adams Evaded Sgt. CG Walton POW Sgt. J Hall Evaded Sgt. WG Groves Evaded Sgt. EM Lee Killed Sgt. GB Gall POW
218 Sqdn: Stirling BF 514-X Crashed Ardennes	PO DF Howlett Killed PO VS Bird Killed Sgt. W Hamilton Evaded Can Sgt DE Roberts Killed Sgt. LW Canningt Evaded Sgt. FJ Knight Killed Can Sgt. EJ Longstaff Killed
420 Sqdn: Wellington HE 682 Crashed St.Trond	Can Sgt. LN Horaham Killed Can Sgt. JE Essacs Killed Can Sgt. LK Clark Killed Sgt. HSP Radford Killed Can Sgt. KTP Allan POW
425 Sqdn: Wellington HE 475-E Crashed Saarbrücken	Can Sgt. PL Brijdd POW Sgt. W Harris POW Aust WO WF Redding POW Aust PO H Gray Killed Can Sgt JM Leblanc Killed
426 Sqdn: Wellington HE 591	Sgt. L Thompson Killed Can Sgt. JC Kennedy Killed PO RG Wood Killed Sgt. J Parkinson Killed Can Flt. Sgt. EA Whalen Killed
427 Sqdn: Wellington HE 547-D	Can Sgt. S Tomyn Killed Sgt. GW Hall POW Sgt. AF Johnson POW Sgt. AT Symond POW Can Sgt. W Ostaficuilk POW
429 Sqdn: Wellington BK 162-B Hit by light flak at Rheims	Sqn. Ldr. FA Homes Killed Sgt. Milne Escaped PO J McMaster Killed Can Sgt. DS Ritchie Killed Flt. Sgt. G Gill Killed Can Flt. Lt. GA Lunn Killed
431 Sqdn: Wellington HE 379-Z	Sgt. H Sutterby POW Can PO WE Paton POW Can Sgt. RD Rudd POW Sgt. P Cartwright POW Sgt. MR Hadland Killed
466 Sqdn: Wellington HE 501-J	Aust Flt. Sgt. CF Tozer Killed Can Flt. Sgt. GK Young Killed Sgt. HE Jones Killed Sgt. RK White Killed Sgt. G Errington Killed

Total 67 Killed, 22 POWs, 18 Evaded.

SQUADRON AND AIRCRAFT	CREW
26 – 27 April 1943	
15 Sqdn: Stirling BK657-C Shot down by a fighter Portengen, Holland	PO R Watson POW Sgt. W Dyson Killed NZ Sgt. G Mora Killed Sgt. H Phillips Killed Sgt. G Whittaker Killed Can Sgt. W Bearnes Killed Sgt. S Spencer POW
51 Sqdn: Halifax HR787	Flt. Sgt. CM Brigden Killed Sgt. N Thompson Killed. 2nd Pilot Sgt. WD Griffiths Killed Sgt. GC Peters Killed Sgt. W Holding Killed Sgt. RGH Lees Killed Aust Sgt. BFK Green Killed Aust Sgt. WV Chittock Killed
51 Sqdn: Halifax HR 778	Sgt. G Fisher Killed Sgt. BH James Killed Sgt. JS Boyce Killed Sgt. WH Stacey Killed Sgt. S Hawkins Killed Sgt. JL Readman Killed Sgt. ALW Pond Killed FO BP Jay Killed
76 Sqdn: Halifax DG 423-H Shot down by FW Vinke Crashed in Amsterdam, landed on the Carlton Hotel	NZ Sgt. DC McNab Killed Sgt. J Clegg Killed FO ND Fleming Killed Sgt. FN Slingsby Killed Can Sgt. CC Strain Killed Sgt. J Wood Killed Sgt. BF Keable Killed
77 Sqdn: Halifax DT 796-P	Aust WO JD Pye Killed FO RC Stewart POW, Murdered after the Great Escape from Stalag 3 PO D Atter POW Stalag 3. Later Flt. Lt. Flt. Sgt. GE Barfoot POW Stalag L1. Later WO Sgt. EJ Fassell POW Stalag 6. Later Flt. Sgt. Sgt. PG Gibbs POW Stalag 6. Later Flt. Sgt. Sgt. JR Wells POW
90 Sqdn: Stirling BF 383-T Crashed Ijsslmeer	FO IF McKensie Killed Sgt. RF Cocking Killed Sgt. PA Walker Killed Sgt. J Wilson Killed Sgt. VG Leak Killed Sgt. JR Boyes Killed Sgt. RE Hardingham Killed. Washed up Ijsselmeer 13.5.43
102 Sqdn: Halifax JB 918- Shot down by Uffz. Kraft Crashed Texel	Can WO2 JG Grainger Killed. Washed up Vlieland 11.6.43 Sgt. FG Harris Killed Sgt. WA Wills Killed Sgt. H Beek Killed Sgt. W Foley Killed Sgt. K Oatridge Killed. Washed up Numindegab 26.6.43
115 Sqdn: Lancaster DS 609-M	Can PO HB Minnis DFC Killed Can Sgt. WC Snook Killed Sgt. WA Timms Killed Sgt. LG Webster Killed Sgt. N Law DFM Killed Can PO EAN Foster DFC Killed Can Sgt. LE Thorpe Killed

SQUADRON AND AIRCRAFT	CREW
156 Sqdn: Lancaster W 4140-K	Can Sgt. DH Waugh Killed PO LE Lindsey Killed Sgt. RE Funnell Killed Sgt. CN Bonar Killed Sgt. SC Brown Killed Sgt. VP Ashcroft Killed Aust Flt. Sgt. LHF Watters Killed
158 Sqdn: Halifax HR 737-U Crashed target area	Can FO CW Gebhard Killed Flt. Sgt. RH Barnes Killed Sgt. EWJ Bennett Killed Sgt. FC Brownlow Killed Sgt. EG Goodfellow Killed Can PO AE Taylor Killed Sgt HL Baines Killed
196 Sqdn: Wellington HE 168-X Shot down Poederoijn/ Gorinchem, The Netherlands	Sgt GF Fletcher Killed PO EG Francis Killed Sgt. ETD Hardee Killed Sgt. FT Pratt Killed Sgt. JA Hawkins Killed
207: Sqdn: Lancaster W 4171-J Crashed Antwerp	Sgt. IB Jones Killed Sgt. FW Davies Killed Can Sgt J Gillespie Killed Sgt. GJ Glare Killed Sgt. WA Hollett Killed Sgt. BPM Hyland Killed Sgt. BB Jones Killed
405 Sqdn: Halifax JB 920-F	Can PO DE Crockatt Killed Can PO CB Dixon Killed Can PO JR Marriott Killed Can Sgt. IA Penner Killed Can WO S Sleeth Killed Can WO TL Bentley Killed Flt. Sgt. SL Stordy Killed PO FE O'Hare Killed
420 Sqdn: Wellington HE 693 Shot down Osterhout, Holland	Can Flt. Sgt. EL Newburg Killed Can Sgt. R Mucklow Killed Can Flt. Sgt. FJ Duffy Killed Can Sgt. OK Glasscock Killed Sgt. KB Cooke Killed
428 Sqdn: Wellington HZ 365-U Shot down by flak and night-fighter, Dulmen	Can Flt. Sgt. LR Coutts Killed Can Flt. Sgt. JA Smith Killed Sgt. PM Snow POW Sgt. RW Stockton Killed Can WO HL Hencke Killed
429 Sqdn: Wellington HE 737 Shot down over Bergen, Holland by Oblt. Linke	Sqn Ldr. JL Cairns POW Stalag 3 Can Flt. Lt. CMS Awad Killed FO RH Larkins Killed Sgt. KE Rabbelt Killed Flt. Sgt. RT Lang POW Inj. Stalag L3 Can FO SMN Pozer POW Inj. Stalag L3
429 Sqdn: Wellington HE 382 Shot down by Lt. Grimm	Can WO Hannam Killed Sgt. GK Thompson Killed Sgt. MP Brown Killed Can Flt. Sgt. FH Purchase Killed Sgt. FG Litchford Killed Can Sgt FS Lane Killed

Total 102 Killed, 12 POWs

SQUADRON AND AIRCRAFT	CREW
30 April – 1 May	
7 Sqdn: Stirling R 9263-D Crashed Akkerwoide, Holland Shot down by Lt. Grimm or Oblt. Bredereck	Can PO EC Hallding Killed Sgt. AE Emms Killed Can WO2 L Nutik Killed Sgt. NA Peachey Killed Can Flt. Sgt. H Sorbel Killed PO G Wragge Killed Sgt. FA Painter POW Inj.
9 Sqdn: Lancaster ED 838-R	PO GA Nunez Killed Sgt. DR Barber Killed Sgt. J Bayliss Killed Sgt. A Beard Killed Sgt. RA Knapman Killed Sgt. CH Collins Killed Sgt. EF Doolittle Killed
12 Sqdn: Lancaster W 4925-N Crashed Winterswijk	Flt. Lt. JW Potts Killed Sgt. W Woodland Killed Aust Flt. Sgt. FB Gillan Killed Flt. Sgt. K Hall DFM Killed Sgt. R Martin Killed Sgt. L Gill Killed Sgt. JS Harris Killed Flt. Sgt. D Sheldon Killed
44 Sqdn: Lancaster ED 783-R Crashed Dalfsen	PO LJ Ellis Killed Sgt. RL LePage Killed Can FO WA Rollings Killed Sgt. JB Brown Killed Sgt. HC Ellis Killed Sgt. R Williams Killed Sgt. SS McClellan Killed
51 Sqdn: Halifax HR 733	Sgt DR Wilson Killed Sgt. HA Briggs Killed Sgt. CH Longley Killed Flt. Sgt. HP Spencer Killed WO WRA Hewitt Killed Sgt. L Allen POW Sgt. JW Peacock POW
57 Sqdn: Lancaster ED 706 Crashed Ijsselmeer	Sgt. WJ Glotham Killed Sgt. W Nugent Killed Sgt. MJ Grace Killed Sgt. J Hodgson Killed Sgt. CD Todd Killed Sgt. AV Ansell Killed Sgt. JR Mansley Killed
76 Sqdn: Halifax DK 171-J Crashed Essen	Sgt. BW Thomas Killed Sgt. F Norris POW Stalag L6. Later Flt. Sgt. Sgt. EH Wood Killed Sgt. FJ Chandler Killed Sgt. GE Testal POW Stalag L6. Later Flt. Sgt. Sgt. A Hawley Killed Sgt. RE Hemsworth POW Stalag L6. Later Flt. Sgt.
77 Sqdn: Halifax JB 783-N Crashed Spelderholt Hit a hill	Sgt. AR Camburn Killed Sgt. RE Hawkins Killed Sgt. KHC Hendry Killed Sgt. TT Jardine Killed Sgt. NA Fearnyhaugh POW Can Sgt. L Dubetz Killed Sgt. A Butlin Killed

SQUADRON AND AIRCRAFT	CREW
77 Sqdn: Halifax JB 803-G Crashed Muiden	Sgt. G Watson Killed Sgt. R Shepherd Killed Can Flt. Sgt. TD Scarff Killed Can FO AE Parsons Killed Sgt. L Hannam Killed Sgt. JD Crawford Killed Sgt. WR Louth Killed
77 Sqdn: Halifax JB 846-L	Sqn. Ldr. FC Bertram Killed Sgt. CW Warne Killed Sgt. CH Herbert Killed Sgt. K Ambler Killed Sgt. JPH Brownlee Killed Sgt. JD Olding Killed Sgt. WC Bostock Killed
106 Sqdn: Lancaster ED 451	Sgt. S Abel Killed PO VA Nono Killed PO S Plaskett Killed Sgt. CM Harrower Killed Sgt. D Brown Killed Sgt. AL Barber Killed Can Sgt. JG Alderson Killed
405 Sqdn: Halifax DT 741-P Crashed Lent All Canadian crew	Can Flt. Lt. HP Atkinson Killed FO WAG Hardy Killed FO RM Reilley POW Sgt. GL MacAllum POW Sgt. NH Weiler POW Flt. Sgt. FR O'Neil POW Sgt. GK Collopy POW FO EP Nurse POW 2nd Pilot
467 Sqdn: Lancaster ED 771 Crashed Harderwijk	FO RD Craigie POW Sgt. W Fair POW PO JG Phillips POW FO RAH Capton Killed Sgt. JA Peat Killed Sgt. GH Edwards Killed Sgt. JA Proctor Killed
Total 82 Killed, 16 POWs	

4 – 5 May 1943

SQUADRON AND AIRCRAFT	CREW
7 Sqdn: Stirling BK 773 Shot down by Major Lent Ijsselmeer	Can PO W Holden Killed Sgt. AJ Phillips Killed Sgt. TW Hunt Killed Sgt. J Avery POW Sgt. RW Connel Killed Sgt. JBJ Hook Killed Sgt. PEC Flood Killed
15 Sqdn: Stirling BK 658-K Crashed in Oldambt	NZ Sgt. WM McLeod POW Sgt. AH Law POW Sgt. AEJ Eaton POW Inj. Sgt. E Willis POW Sgt. E Routh POW Sgt. H Floweday POW Inj. Sgt. P NcNulty Killed in combat

SQUADRON AND AIRCRAFT	CREW
15 Sqdn: Stirling BK 782-X Crashed Houten-Schalkwijk	PO TE Imberson Killed PO WL Lambie Killed Sgt. GA Rodway Killed Sgt. HG Brown Killed Sgt. PF Hanberger Killed Sgt. HG Mugridge Killed Sgt. G Rutherford Killed
15 Sqdn: Stirling EF 345-M Crashed West of Bocholt	NZ PO JH Stowell Killed Sgt. TS Malcolm POW PO D Spooner Killed Sgt. T Banyer Killed Sgt. LH Pattison Killed Sgt. F Stevens Killed Sgt. PR Sharman Killed Sgt. W Jennings Killed
57 Sqdn: Lancaster ED 390	Sgt. VD Farmer Killed Sgt. LAW Sanders Killed PO T Armstrong Killed Flt. Sgt. JT Taylor Killed Sgt. MA James Killed Sgt. LH Learney Killed Sgt. N Long Killed
76 Sqdn: Halifax DK 134-Y Crashed Kilder	PO JIM Bell POW Sgt. AE Bumstead POW Sgt. HM Farington POW Sgt. HJ Hamlyn POW Sgt. DJ Marshall POW Sgt. A Forster POW Can Flt. Sgt. DB Brown POW Sgt. B Thompson POW
78 Sqdn: Halifax JB 973	Flt. Sgt. A Burns Killed Sgt. H Gamble POW FO JB Thompson POW Sgt. JR Heslop POW. Repatriated May 1944 Sgt. FG Hockin POW Sgt. W Ashley POW Sgt. HC Tyler POW
78 Sqdn: Halifax JB 903-S	Sgt. A Heppard POW Sgt. VCG Moody Killed Sgt. R Baydell POW Sgt. PE Mellish Killed Sgt. DN Brown Killed Sgt. F Moore Killed Sgt. C Lawis POW
78 Sqdn: Halifax JB 915 Hit by night-fighter from below, South of Epe, Holland	Sqn. Ldr. JH Chapple POW Can PO BA Campbell POW FO HJ Kim POW Sgt. E Blackwell POW Sgt. R Hillary POW Sgt. B Legg Killed in combat FO EW Barnes POW
83 Sqdn: Lancaster R 5629-J Crashed Dortmund	Sgt. JR Elliott Killed Can FO OM Cornish Killed Wg/Cdr. JR Gillman Killed Sgt. FA Griffith Killed Sgt. F Johnson Killed Sgt. FJ Cleasby Killed Sgt. DH Rock Killed FO PR Smith Killed

SQUADRON AND AIRCRAFT	CREW
90 Sqdn: Stirling BK 814 Crashed Dortmund	Sgt FC Maxwell Killed
101 Sqdn: Lancaster W 4888-P Shot down by night-fighter flown by Major Lent Workum, Friesland	FO NJ Stanford Killed PO RD Patterson POW Inj. Sgt. AJL Lyon Killed Can FO WT Lewis Killed Sgt. AH Clark Killed Can Flt. Sgt. GWF Reynolds Killed Sgt. JM Hatfield Killed
101 Sqdn: Lancaster W 4784-E	Sgt. W Nicholson Killed PO HK Wainier Killed Sgt. G Eastwood Killed Sgt. BW Squires Killed Sgt. G Brick Killed Sgt. DW Rowley Killed PO N Ainsworth Killed
102 Sqdn: Halifax JB 869-H Crashed München Gladbach	Sgt. WBJ Happold Killed Sgt. JH Barratt POW PO J Baxter Killed Sgt. J Brownlie POW Sgt. GS Bowles Killed Sgt. DR McGregor Killed Sgt. HJ Jones POW
102 Sqdn: Halifax W 7820-V	FO J Bowen POW Sgt. D Galbraith POW Sgt. JH Loveless POW Sgt. GL Parry POW Sgt. HR Mock POW Sgt. JJ Prinsloo POW Sgt. SJ Tregunno POW
102 Sqdn: Halifax HR 667	Sqn. Ldr. JB Flowerden Killed PO DE Grant Killed PO HGR Chiverton Killed Sgt. JGS Dutton Killed Can Flt. Sgt. PE Tiller Killed Sgt. G Rose Killed Sgt. KH Buck Killed
149 Sqdn: Stirling EF 343 Shot down by night-fighter Flown by Major Lent west of Heeg	Flt. Lt. WE Davey Killed FO TC Timney Killed Aust Flt. Sgt. EH Finch Killed Flt. Sgt. RF Whitaker Killed Sgt. DR Higgs Killed Sgt. CWE Leach Killed Sgt. JJ O'Neil Killed Sgt. GJC Hall Killed
156 Sqdn: Lancaster ED 837 Hit by flak over target	Flt. Lt. AG Lang DFC POW NZ Flt. Lt. FM Gray Killed NZ Flt. Sgt. DG Riddings Killed Sgt. JL Clark DFM POW Inj. Sgt. NH Wood Killed Flt. Sgt. EN Kenn Killed
166 Sqdn: Wellington HE 244 Crashed Wertendau	Sgt. AI Stark Killed Sgt. D High Killed Can Sgt. HJ Salisbury Killed Sgt. JA Beedim Killed Can Sgt. TJP Lapontain Killed

SQUADRON AND AIRCRAFT	CREW
166 Sqdn: Wellington HE 923	Can Sgt. AP Uditsky Killed Can Sgt. JF Machsinchuk Killed Can Sgt. EN Moore Killed Sgt. TAS Buchanan Killed Can Sgt. GE Armstrong Killed
196 Sqdn: Wellington HE 162 Crashed Gelsenkirchen	Sgt. J Stanforth Killed Sgt. HB Graham Killed Sgt. RW Lynn Killed Sgt. GW James Killed Sgt. BE Taylor Killed
218 Sqdn: Stirling BF 505 Hit by flak	Can Flt. Lt. WL Turner Killed Sgt. FN Robinson Killed Sgt. JL While POW Flt. Sgt. JMJ Smith POW PO PS Beck POW Inj. Sgt. WN Forth Killed Sgt. HW Sawkins Killed Flt. Sgt. GA Hinslewood Killed
405 Sqdn: Halifax JB 904 Crashed at Quendof/Gra/Oschaft Grapschapt Bentheim	Can PO JW Lennex Killed Sgt. AJ Knight POW PO JJB Graham POW Sgt. FV Roberts POW Sgt. AA Aplan POW Can Sgt. JL Prieur POW Inj. Sgt. B Moody Killed in combat
408 Sqdn: Halifax JB 898-Q Attacked from below by night-fighter flown by Oblt. Lothar Linke, Akkrum	Can Flt. Sgt. RO Blackhall Killed PO CB Norton POW Sgt. GI Semper Killed Flt. Sgt. KE Godfrey POW Inj. Parachute split PO FH Scythes POW Can Sgt. KE Emmons Killed Can Sgt. CL Horn POW Inj. Can Sgt AJ Sutton Killed
408 Sqdn: Halifax HR 658-V	Can Flt. Sgt. GA Johannessen Killed Can Flt. Sgt. WA Grant Killed Can Flt. Sgt. ME Metcalfe Killed Can Sgt. DG Hault POW Can Sgt. CW Ellard Killed Can Sgt. RV Clitheroe POW Can Flt. Sgt. JC Archer Killed
419 Sqdn: Halifax W 7817 Attacked from below by night-fighter	Can FO GJ Vaillancourt PO D Grimshaw POW Sgt. NM Douglas POW Can Sgt. AJ Morrison POW Can Sgt. A James POW Can WO JL Peck POW Can Flt. Sgt. FT Stanlis Killed in combat
419 Sqdn: Halifax DT 794	Can FO GW Elliott Killed FO EE Kennedy Killed FO HM Metcalfe Killed Sgt. G Sandfield Killed Can Sgt. GD Menzies Killed Can Flt. Sgt. JW McIntosh Killed Can Flt. Sgt. JA Farrel Killed

SQUADRON AND AIRCRAFT	CREW
428 Sqdn: Wellington HE 864-S Crashed City of Swolle	Can Sgt. DW Johnson Killed Can Sgt. JL Boyd POW Can Sgt. J Prosnyck Killed Can Sgt. DE Thompson POW Can Sgt. JJ Levaseur POW Can Flt. Sgt. FT Stanley Killed
428 Sqdn: Wellington HE 727	Can WO RB Moulton Killed Sgt. GC Carter POW Can Sgt. J White Killed Sgt. HH Hoddicott POW Can Sgt. JEA Thibaudeau Killed
460 Sqdn: Lancaster W 4818	Aust Flt. Sgt. DN Jackel Killed Aust PO SM Nuss Killed Aust Flt. Sgt. EJ Candish Killed Aust Flt. Sgt. A Hilton Killed Aust Sgt. WJ Turpin Killed Aust Flt. Sgt. JL Barry Killed Aust Flt. Sgt. W Williams Killed
466 Sqdn: Wellington HE 530 Shot down by night-fighter	Aust Sgt. LF James POW Aust Sgt. RE Dolby POW Aust Sgt. RG Lutton POW Aust Sgt JR Baxter POW Aust Sgt. FG Latham Killed in combat

Total 129 Killed, 69 POWs

Crashed in the UK on return

10 Sqdn: Halifax JD 105-K Crashed into high ground Hood Grange Sutton Bank near Topcliffe, Yorkshire. Sgt. Cox became ill after leaving the target. Pilot reduced height to help him and hit high ground, he also had engine trouble.	Sgt. RH Geddes Inj. Sgt. AB Hill Killed 2nd Pilot Sgt. T Cox Killed Sgt. HS Taylor Killed Sgt. HH Way Killed Sgt. GF Ward Killed Sgt. W Dunbar Inj. Sgt. K Hart Inj.
35 Sqdn: Halifax DT 489-Y Hit high ground when short of fuel in bad visibility. Crashed half mile north of Forland X Rds, Cambridge in reduced visibility	Flt. Sgt. JA Cobb Killed Sgt. S Russell Killed FO SL Coles Killed Sgt. JD Colling Killed Sgt. H Fisher Killed Sgt. FI Leech Killed Sgt. JH Robertson Inj.
35 Sqdn: Halifax W 7887-E Crew baled out near Warthton Northants, aircraft short of fuel. And starboard outer engine failed, aircraft crashed at Culverston. All crew uninjured.	Sgt. JJ Williams Pilot
97 Sqdn: Lancaster ED 880-N Crashed at Waterbeach, having overshot and collided with a Stirling in dispersal	Sgt. A Reilly Killed Sgt. R Gibson Inj. Sgt. H MacFarlane Inj. FO RJ Hopps Inj. Sgt. H Horne Inj. Sgt. RL Griffiths Inj. Sgt. F Fisher Inj.

SQUADRON AND AIRCRAFT	CREW
101 Sqdn: Lancaster ED 608-T Crashed at Holtham north of North Cove, Yorks. On beam approach at the time	Flt. Sgt. G Hough Killed Sgt. HC Hooper Killed FO FW Gates DSO Killed Flt. Sgt. CL Outhouse Inj. Sgt. PA Ratcliffe Inj. FO SH Bearson Inj. Sgt. WDG Merlin Inj.
101 Sqdn: Lancaster W 4863-G Struck trees and then crashed at Scorton in bad visibility	Sgt. JR Browning Killed Sgt. J Stretton Killed Sgt. R Allison Killed Sgt. E Davies Killed Sgt. LC Hogben Inj. Sgt. SL Granville Inj. Flt. Sgt. RJ Rays Inj.
156 Sqdn: Lancaster ED 715 Directed to Honiley on return, but short of petrol so crew baled out at Chalerois, East Anglia. Rest of crew okay	Sqn. Ldr. BL Duigan DFC Flt. Lt. JA Rogers Inj. Sgt. R Drysdale Inj.
405 Sqdn: Lancaster JB 897-T Collided with a tree attempting to force land at Graveley in fog and out of petrol Weiser went on to complete his Tour Total 19 Killed on return.	Can FO W Weiser FO GB Ellwood Inj. PO RE Baker Inj. Sgt. FD Mayon Inj. Flt. Sgt. L. Coburn Inj. FO HC Banks Inj. Sgt. T Geary Inj.
12 – 13 May 1943	
12 Sqdn: Lancaster ED 476	NZ Sgt. I H Alexander Killed Can Sgt. RD Fraser Killed Sgt. ED Harrison Killed Sgt. JA Stephen Killed Sgt. E Rowe POW Sgt. R Bell Killed Flt. Sgt. DH Williams Killed
35 Sqdn: Halifax DT 801-A Crashed Haavs, Bergen, Aaalen Germany	Can Flt. Lt. J Sale Evaded PO RG Sawyer Killed FO GE Heard POW Sgt. SA Moores POW Sgt. DJ Richards Killed Can Sgt. RO Elton POW Sgt. CW Rowley POW Inj.
50 Sqdn: Lancaster W 4762- Crashed in North Sea	PO FH Huntley DFM Killed PO CW Clarke Killed FO GD Priestly Killed Can PO HM Ivatt Killed Sgt. A Stott Killed Sgt. FC Grening Killed Sgt. M Bates Killed
51 Sqdn: Halifax DT 645 Harlingen	Sgt. DC Smith Killed Sgt. EW Thompson Killed Sgt. R Bunting Killed Sgt. CC King Killed Sgt. EF Kinerman Killed Can Sgt. MH Nesbitt Killed Sgt. WJ Merigan Killed

SQUADRON AND AIRCRAFT	CREW
51 Sqdn: Halifax HR 786	PO W Locksmith Killed Sgt. R Tunstall Killed FO AV Hendry Killed Sgt. HA Roberts Killed Sgt. J Noble Killed Sgt. CNY Cogdell Killed PO SOM Massip-de-Turnville Killed
51 Sqdn: Halifax JB 806	PO GOM Massip de Turnville Killed Aust Sgt. B Brown POW Sgt. WB Henderson POW Sgt. JD Rae POW Sgt. KA Goodchild Killed Sgt. ALS Knight POW Sgt. W North-Lewis POW Sgt. PLMC de Bourbon POW Inj.
51 Sqdn: Halifax DT 685	Flt. Sgt. NE Jones Killed Sgt. KS Hobkirk Killed Sgt. EG Brown Killed Sgt. L Wakenshaw POW Sgt. PCW Rich Killed Sgt. H Goddard Killed Sgt. PT Blake Killed
57 Sqdn: Lancaster ED 329	FO VA Wilson Killed PO JD Wallace Killed Sgt. PG Kehl POW Sgt. CL Gerding Killed Sgt. S Loughlin Killed Sgt. A Steel Killed Sgt. RB Loverseed Killed
57 Sqdn: Lancaster ED 778 Shot down by night-fighter Netterden	Flt. Sgt. GB Clark POW FO HC MacReid Killed Sgt. TJ Gregory Killed Can WO2 HA Sheehan Killed Sgt. N Rees POW Can WO2 MG Levis Killed in combat Can WO2 AL Home Killed in combat
61 Sqdn: Lancaster W4269 Crashed Amsterdam	Sgt. P Alderton Killed Sgt. E Sloan Killed Can PO JVO Wood Killed Can Sgt. WJ Reid Killed Sgt. S Lupton Killed Sgt. CD Whitehall Killed Sgt. J Thomas Killed
77 Sqdn: Halifax DT 632-	Can Flt. Sgt. T Moran Killed Sgt. DA Stimpson Killed PO KA Clark Killed Sgt. RG Miles Killed Sgt. JD Mahoney Killed Sgt. W Pasquali Killed Sgt. J Murray Killed
83 Sqdn: Lancaster W 4955-R Flak and night-fighter over Holland crashed south of Laren Aircraft on its 53rd operation	Aust Flt. Lt. LA Rickenson DFC Killed Aust Flt. Lt. HDM Ransom DFC POW Flt. Sgt. JR Cairns Killed Aust PO WL Gibbs Killed Flt. Sgt. DB Bourns Killed Flt. Sgt. SA Hathaway Killed Flt. Sgt. H Plant Killed

SQUADRON AND AIRCRAFT	CREW
90 Sqdn: Stirling BF 523 Aircraft recovered by the Dutch Air Force at Ijsselmeer in 1967	Can Sgt. W Money POW Sgt. BA Bacon Killed Sgt. W Murray Killed Sgt. EW Eke Killed. Washed up 26.5.43 Sgt. RMS Shaw Killed Sgt. AJ Buxton Killed. Washed up 27.5.43 Sgt. C Green Killed
90 Sqdn: Stirling BK 661 Shot down by night-fighter over North Sea	Can PO Harrison Killed Sgt. DH Gedak Killed Sgt. AV Edwards Killed Sgt. L Urry Killed Sgt. S James Killed Sgt. S Owen Killed Sgt. TG Matthews Killed
102 Sqdn: Halifax JB 799	Can Flt. Sgt. MO Moffatt Killed Can FO JD Erzinger Killed Sgt. DF Moon Killed Sgt. CH Hurle Killed Can Sgt C Gowen Killed PO G Davies Killed Sgt. WJ Holman Killed
149 Sqdn: Stirling EF 357 Crashed Castle Bergh Circled for fifteen mins to avoid crashing on the city of Rotterdam	Sgt. EG Bass Killed Sgt. KG Roots Killed PO RF Kingham Killed Sgt. JC Newell POW Sgt. FG Salter Killed Sgt. RD Evans Killed Sgt. DB Sach Killed
156 Sqdn: Lancaster ED 837	Sgt. WM Wendow Killed Flt. Sgt. ES McKenzie Killed Flt. Sgt. NR Mason Killed Sgt. C Askham Killed Aust Sgt. RG Wynn Killed Aust Flt. Sgt. AC Johnston Killed Sgt. GA Williams Killed
156 Sqdn: Lancaster ED 857 Crashed Düsseldorf	Flt. Lt. R Verdon-Roe DFC Killed PO F Giles DFM Killed Flt. Sgt. EW Banks DFM Killed Flt. Sgt. TJ Pritchard DFM Killed Sgt. JC Stewart Killed PO HF Jolley Killed Sgt. KC Harmon Killed
196 Sqdn: Wellington HE 398	Flt. Sgt. J Greenfield Killed Flt. Sgt. R Burridge Killed Sgt. W O'Neil Killed Sgt. KF Bell Killed Sgt. E Eddington Killed
199 Sqdn: Wellington HE 702 Crashed west of Ijmuiden	Sgt. L Waldorf Killed Sgt. R Hughes Killed Sgt. JG Wilson Killed FO RHD Cook Killed Sgt. T Wharmby Killed
207 Sqdn: Lancaster W 4938 Crashed Düsseldorf	FO DWH Evans Killed Sgt. S Ogden Killed Sgt. TH Skelton Killed Sgt. RE Meyer Killed Sgt. SL Goodwin Killed PO FA Alp Killed Sgt. SLR Whitehead Killed

SQUADRON AND AIRCRAFT	CREW
207 Sqdn: Lancaster ED 418	PO WD Hawkes Killed Sgt. AW Whiteoak Killed Sgt. GR Nipper Killed Can Sgt. WA Mohair POW Sgt. ES Tompkins Killed Sgt. HR Dick Killed Flt Lt. AD Coldicott DFM Killed Sgt. J Smith Killed
214 Sqdn: Stirling BF 381 Crashed Düsseldorf	PO H Broadbent Killed PO H Catch Killed Sgt. N Douglas Killed Sgt. WFW Hardo Killed Sgt. SF Dean Killed Sgt. JA Brown Killed Sgt. W Duthie Killed
218 Sqdn: Stirling BK 705 Shot down by night-fighter over North Sea	PO RJ Bryans Killed Sgt. JR Thompson Killed Sgt. J Davies Killed Sgt. J Pitten Killed Sgt. FB Holmes Killed Sgt. KG Money Killed
300 Sqdn: Wellington HE 295-P	Pol Sqn. Ldr. S Werner Killed Pol FO R Tabazynski Killed Sgt. H Sqymanwing Killed Sgt. HW Lercel Killed Flt. Sgt. M Galas Killed
419 Sqdn: Halifax JB 791-X Crashed München Gladbach	Can WO GA McMillan Killed Can Flt. Sgt. WJ Klein POW FO Everer POW Sgt. WHD Alison Killed Can WO WJ Howell POW Can PO AR Wallace POW Can WO HG Bees POW
419 Sqdn: Halifax JB 861	Can WO J Palmer Killed Sgt. H Walsh Killed FO T Brown Killed Can WO R Weedy Killed Can Sgt. WA Simonett Killed Can Flt. Sgt. REC Ratelle Killed Sgt. AJ Searing Killed
426 Sqdn: Wellington HE 157 Shot down by night-fighter Noordschaus in Klundert Aircraft parts recovered 1970	Can WO KF Fighter Killed Can FO G McMillan Killed Can Flt. Sgt. DC Maxwell Killed Sgt. EW Betts Killed Can FO HR Drake Killed
426 Sqdn: Wellington HE 905-V Hit by heavy flak north-east of Spa	Can Sgt. IRA Runciman POW Can FO DG Fraser Killed Can FO G Miller POW Can PO D Laskey DFC POW Sgt. DH Lennock POW Can Flt. Sgt. VW Forland Evaded
428 Sqdn: Wellington HE 656 Crashed near Dieppe	Can Sgt. WE Mann Killed Can PO WW O'Brien Killed Can Sgt. PG Kelly Killed Can PO LA Dingley Killed Can Sgt. E Lundy Killed

SQUADRON AND AIRCRAFT	CREW
428 Sqdn: Wellington HE 321-Z	Can Sgt. AE Hatch Killed Can FO RL Baumgarten Killed Can Sgt. DR Horwood Killed Sgt. W Leven Killed Can Sgt. CC Hildreth Killed
429 Sqdn: Wellington HE 913	Sgt. AF Halstead Killed PO PJ Dunger Killed PO SA Willoughby Killed Sgt. C Taylor Killed Can Sgt. DO Broughton Killed
429 Sqdn: Wellington HE 423	PO BA Geale Killed Can PO HA Tenins Killed Can Flt. Sgt. SJ Voze Killed Sgt. J Liggot Killed Can Sgt. TR Grimmins Killed
431 Sqdn: Wellington HE 440 Crashed Winterswijk	Sgt. GRY Wood Killed Sgt. EL Gummer Killed Sgt. IE Nobley Killed Sgt. A Cresswell Killed Sgt. TH Smith Killed

Total 189 Killed, 29 POWs, 2 Evaded

13 – 14 May 1943

SQUADRON AND AIRCRAFT	CREW
9 Sqdn: ED 589 Shot down by Fw Vinke near Hisshum	Sgt. GH Saxton Killed Can Sgt. WR McDonald Killed Sgt. RM Morris Killed Sgt. J Reddish Killed Sgt. DC Ferris Killed Sgt. JC Owen Killed Sgt. J Buntin Killed
10 Sqdn: Halifax DT 732-X Crashed Ijsselmeer near Amsterdam	Aust PO JF Mills Killed Sgt. JS McAdam Killed Sgt. JW Avent Killed Sgt. A Jones Killed Sgt. JC Howrie Killed Sgt. C Maltby Killed Sgt. EJC Howard Killed
12 Sqdn: Lancaster W 4366 Crashed Scherlebeek	Aust Sgt. FW Morgan Killed Sgt. GL Fountain POW Sgt. KJ Walker POW Sgt. T Mahinnis POW Sgt. K Foote Killed Sgt. JR Richards Killed Can Sgt. GT Spice POW
15 Sqdn: Stirling BK 204-Z	Flt. Lt. LJ Bowyer Killed PO DC Smith POW Inj. Can FO WGM Oliver POW Sgt. JB Craggs POW Sgt. TP Hawrahan POW Sgt. HC Cooper POW Sgt. EC Warner DFM POW Sgt. CE Keck POW

SQUADRON AND AIRCRAFT	CREW
51 Sqdn: Halifax HR 790-A Reetum-in-Vierden	PO GWH Byres POW FO RH Stark POW Inj. Sgt. DJ Eames POW Flt. Sgt. RT Howell POW Sgt. G Steer Killed Sgt. C Stringer Killed Sgt. JAC Jacobs Killed
51 Sqdn: Halifax DT 526 Hit by flak and FW 190 over Bochum	Flt. Lt. RD Johnstone POW FO RG Wing POW FO MG Gibbs POW FO GI Donkersley POW Sgt. FM Tipton Killed Sgt. DR Fyfield Killed Flt. Lt. P Parnham Killed
77 Sqdn: Halifax JB892-E Shot down by Hpt.Luge Sheenerzand	Flt. Lt. DP Priddephatt Killed Sgt. JIP Morgan Killed Sgt. LW Bolton Killed Sgt. GS Walton Killed Sgt. MJ Brookes Killed Sgt. AW McKillop Killed Sgt. RA Halestrap Killed
78 Sqdn: Halifax JB 873-J Crashed south-east of Louven Belgium	Sgt. GH Dane Killed Sgt. JH Boddy Killed Sgt. RG Goddard Evaded Sgt. L Adams POW Sgt. JS People POW Sgt. ACP Mimmitt POW Sgt. FW Webb POW Sgt. A Beaton POW
78 Sqdn: Halifax DT 777	Sgt. GE Clay POW Sgt. JF O'Reilly POW Sgt. LD Marriott POW Sgt. EA Coates POW Sgt. L Jakes Killed Sgt. WJH Perry POW Sgt. CF Leverett POW Inj.
78 Sqdn: JB 924-M Crashed Wijnaldum	Can Flt. Sgt. RE Bragg Killed Sgt. E Pritchard Killed baling out Can Sgt. JM Farrell Killed Sgt. HE Gell POW Broken leg Sgt. RTD Matches Killed Sgt. R Grey Killed Can Sgt. AA Kew Killed Sgt. D Baxter Killed
83 Sqdn: Lancaster W 4981-F Shot down by night-fighter Ijsselmeer	Sgt. AS Renshaw Killed Sgt. JE Lecomber Killed Sgt. HR Williamson Killed Sgt. GW Gould POW Sgt. FA Worsnop Killed Sgt. JMCG Hargreaves Killed Sgt. JR Stones Killed
102 Sqdn: Halifax JB 964-G Shot down by night-fighter near Cologne	Sgt. V Hatchard Killed FO FA James POW Sgt. S Brown Killed Sgt. J Leedham Killed Sgt. W Lee Killed Can Sgt. JA Coughlin POW Sgt. JSW Dowles Killed

SQUADRON AND AIRCRAFT	CREW
106 Sqdn: Lancaster R 5611	Sgt. EJ Howell Killed Can Flt. Sgt. WH Hill Killed Sgt. EGR Beacham Killed Sgt. RW Littelfair Killed Sgt. D Grey Killed Sgt. LA Dunmore Killed Flt. Sgt. RD Johnstone POW Can Flt. Sgt. DS Mitchell Killed
149 Sqdn: Stirling BF 479	FO LC Martin Killed Can Sgt. RC Ferguson POW Sgt. NH Frank Killed FO GR Royde DFC Killed Sgt. EH French POW Sgt. JE Butt Killed Can Flt. Sgt. HPJ Fudge Killed Sgt. HAJ Berry Killed
149 Sqdn: Stirling BK 726 Crashed München Gladbach	Can Sgt. HE Forsyth Killed Can Sgt. DF McDonald Killed Can Sgt. JB Guepin Killed Sgt. DE Sharpe Killed Sgt. JJ Ryan Killed Sgt. LP Barnett Killed Sgt. W McCall Killed
166 Sqdn: Wellington HZ 280-Q Hit by flak Ditched Ijsselmeer	Can FO W Wahl Killed Can Sgt. SA Davis POW Can PO HW Newby POW Can Sgt. WN Partridge Killed Can Sgt. JA Wright POW Inj.
214 Sqdn: Stirling R 9242 Shot down by night-fighter Dutch frontier, Oranje Nassau Three Dutch killed	Sgt RM Gibbney Killed PO AR Minton POW Sgt. FD Stannard Killed Sgt. RF Sullick POW Sgt. L Sutcliffe POW Inj. Sgt. L Leake Killed Sgt. SR Tinkler Killed
405 Sqdn: Halifax JB 966-Q Shot down by night-fighter Balkbridge	Can FO HB Beattie Killed FO JA Hawtin POW Sgt. SB Hawley Killed. Parachute hung up on the tail Sgt. JB Gibson POW Sgt. KW Clarke POW Can Sgt. R Ferguson POW Can Sgt. RE Hart Killed in combat
408 Sqdn: Halifax JB 931-O Shot down by night-fighter Hooldplaat	Sqn Ldr. HBRL Campbell Died of exhaustion and drowning FO AW Thompson POW PO MHJ Hamill POW Sgt. AC Ross POW Inj. Can Sgt. JMCLR Harris Drowned Aust PO AE Horne Killed in combat Can Sgt. LA Stinson Killed
419 Sqdn: Halifax DT 672 Crashed München Gladbach	Sgt. G Adams Killed Can PO E Bruto Killed Can Sgt. WH Bowden Killed Sgt. E Kurring Killed Sgt. FS Neal Killed Can Sgt. CD McEwen Killed Sgt. OJ Haalson Killed

SQUADRON AND AIRCRAFT	CREW
419 Sqdn: Halifax JD 113 Shot down by night-fighter flown by Hpt. Lutje Daalen	Can Sgt. WH Buckwell Killed Can FO RW Lowry POW Can Sgt. WM Reid POW Can Sgt. WJN Duggan POW Stalag 4B Can Sgt. FW Walkerdine Killed Can Flt. Sgt. AA Hurtean Killed Can Flt. Sgt. WL Bovaird Killed
426 Sqdn: Wellington HE 697	Can Sgt. JA Thompson Killed Can Sgt. AF Hopley Killed Can Sgt. PO Ethier Killed Sgt. N Hindspith Killed Can Sgt. TF How Killed
426 Sqdn: Wellington HE 243	Can Sgt. JB Pettigrew Killed Can PO RE Wagner Killed Sgt. WE Delaney Killed Sgt. SE Herbert Killed Sgt. ED Divelly Killed
429 Sqdn: Wellington LN 439-N Crashed München Gladbach	Can Sgt. FR Windilbark Killed Can Sgt. WJ Reid Killed in action Can Sgt. AE Atkinson Killed Can Sgt. NR McKinley POW Inj. Sgt. DI Harvard Killed
431 Sqdn: Wellington HE 183	Sqdn. Ldr. TB Marshall Killed on 32nd operation FO Gooderham Killed FO D Coales Killed Sgt. AE Quaife Killed Can FO DJ McMillen Killed Age 19
466 Sqdn: Wellington MS 473	NZ PO T Sampson Killed Sgt. CW Jones POW Aust Flt. Sgt. JF Cahill POW Flt. Sgt. KK Murphy POW Sgt. JT Lester POW
467 Sqdn: Lancaster ED 545	Aust Sgt. KE Mahoney Killed PO EFH Heard Killed Sgt. MB Squire Killed Sgt. WG Berry Killed Sgt. BG Hickling Killed Can Sgt. BL Haley Killed Sgt. WH Cox Killed
Total 125 Killed, 66 POWs, 1 Evaded	

Crashed in the UK on return

218 Sqdn: Stirling BF 480-I Crashed into the ops block at Downham Market. Sgt. H Lancaster and Sgt. AR Denzey of Sgt. JB Smith's crew, aircraft BF 413-T, were killed. Sgt. W Stewart of Carney's crew injured. Sgt. Lancaster's first operation	Sgt. WC Carney Pilot
466 Sqdn: Wellington HZ 530 Crashed into hills at Towthorpe Wold Farm near Sledmere, Yorks	Aust Sgt. CW Trinder Killed Sgt. H Russell Killed NZ Sgt. DAM Davidson Killed Sgt. DA Traill Killed Sgt. EGL Giggs Killed
Total 7 Killed on return	

SQUADRON AND AIRCRAFT	CREW
23 – 24 May 1943	
10 Sqdn: Halifax DT 789 Hit by night-fighter Crashed in North Sea	Sgt. J Rees Killed. Body recovered from sea 8.7.43 Sgt. SC Rose Killed Sgt. SJ Gaywood Killed Sgt. D Birkhead Killed Sgt. WE Oliver Killed Sgt. EG David Killed Sgt. FW Farrell Killed
10 Sqdn: Halifax HR 696 Crashed Düsseldorf	PO JB Denton Killed Sgt. ID Inglis Killed Sgt. PG Nimmond Killed PO DHT Adams Killed Flt. Sgt. M Harrison Killed Sgt. AE Wallis Killed Sgt. GH Lawson Killed
10 Sqdn: Halifax W 1217 Crashed Ijsselmeer	Flt. Sgt. CJJ Hine Killed. Washed up 11.6.43 PO JWT King Killed Sgt. HG Ashton Killed. Washed up 8.6.43 Sgt. EC Church Killed. Washed up 7.10.43 Sgt. A Hall Killed. Washed up 4.6.43 Can Sgt. GD Nisbeth Killed. Washed up 8.6.43 Sgt. RFF Baggaby Killed
12 Sqdn: Lancaster W 4861-M	FO WN Mounsey Killed PO WB Whitaker Killed Sgt. A Dews POW Sgt. RG Miller Killed Sgt. WB Jarrett POW Sgt. KG Legg Killed Sgt. H Pierpoint Killed
15 Sqdn: Stirling BF 482-Q Hit by flak at Dortmund	Can Sgt. WQ Johnson Killed Flt. Sgt. CF Ryall POW Can FO HN Lyons Killed Sgt. MJJ Flaherty Killed Sgt. SD Hirst POW Sgt. HGC Waite Killed Sgt. NR Elford POW Can Sgt. RO Leonard POW
35 Sqdn: Halifax DT 488 Crashed Wanne-Eickel Germany	Aust FO AM Harvey Killed Sgt. A Groom Killed PO EAN Evans Killed Sgt. JR Johnson Killed Can Sgt. RG Pritchard Killed Sgt. WR Fairey POW Inj. Sgt. SR Shields Killed
35 Sqdn: Halifax W 7825 Crashed Düsseldorf	Sgt. E Garner Killed Sgt. RH Oats Killed Flt. Sgt. MO Fuller Killed Sgt. TCE Simmonds Killed Sgt. LD Bryant Killed Sgt. J Hogg Killed
44 Sqdn: Lancaster ED 723	PO JL Drysdale Killed FO WA Marsden Killed Sgt. HWE Hyett Killed Sgt. S Jones Killed Sgt. JF Lester Killed Sgt. AS Bushill Killed Can PO FA Doherty Killed

SQUADRON AND AIRCRAFT	CREW
49 Sqdn: Lancaster ED 813 Crashed Düsseldorf	PO IW Thomas POW PO EC Dutchie POW PO R Christy Killed Sgt. F Grant POW PO TGH Lewis Killed Sgt. GR Evans Killed Sgt. RH Ansell Killed
51 Sqdn: Halifax HR 836	FO JE Rigby Killed Can Flt. Sgt. HG Freeman Killed FO TH Green Killed Sgt. AE Rochester Killed Sgt. AMH Black Killed Sgt. HJ Gibbs Killed Can Sgt. ME Zaplie Killed
51 Sqdn: Halifax HR 844	Sgt. RR Masscasll POW Inj. Sgt. D Shepherd POW Sgt. FJ Clancy POW Lost a leg. Repatriated Sgt. CD Wilcox-Jones POW Inj. Sgt. C Rands POW Can Sgt. GFD Newman POW Sgt. W Fry POW
51 Sqdn: Halifax HR 835 Crashed Düsseldorf	Sgt. LA Wright Killed FO J Cockson Killed Sgt. J Milton POW Sgt. JL Edwards Killed Sgt. C Newman Killed Sgt. J Jones Killed Can Flt. Sgt. W Brown Killed
51 Sqdn: Halifax HR 842	Sgt. JWG Park Killed Sgt. JJ Maher POW Sgt. WJ Osborn POW Sgt. LH Burnett POW Sgt. O Kirk POW Sgt. A Simpson POW Inj. Sgt. L Willaghby POW
57 Sqdn: Lancaster ED 970 Crashed North Sea	Sgt. AR Leslie Killed PO JR Morton Killed Sgt. P Hemingway Killed Sgt. AK Henderson Killed Sgt. HF Kleiner Killed. Washed up 10.8.43 Sgt. WJ Bennett Killed. Washed up 24.6.43 Sgt. PO Daly Killed. Washed up 25.6.43
57 Sqdn: Lancaster ED 707 Crashed Haren, Den Helder The Netherlands	Can FO EK Chivers Killed Sgt. P Parkin Killed Sgt. TA Jervis Killed. Washed up 21.6.43 Sgt. DA Robb Killed Sgt. TR Bayles Killed Sgt. WH Bestwick Killed Sgt. WB Rawnsley Killed
77 Sqdn: Halifax JB 837	Sgt. JH Waterson Killed Sgt. JW Richardson Killed Sgt. J Kershaw Killed Sgt. WRL Codd Killed Can Sgt. FR Laurence Killed Can Sgt. DW MacFarlane Killed

SQUADRON AND AIRCRAFT	CREW
75 Sqdn: Stirling BK 783-Q Crashed Bees, Holland	NZ Sgt. SM Tietjens Killed NZ Sgt. GW Turnbull Killed Sgt. R Bell Killed Sgt. SJ Wayman Killed NZ Sgt. FJL Joblin Killed Sgt. DG Storey Killed Sgt. LR Vale POW
76 Sqdn: Halifax DK 172-L Shot down by night-fighter Dortmund	Flt. Sgt. ES Bawden Killed Sth Africa Lt. PER Wader POW Sgt. LWS Thick POW Sgt. T Musgrove POW Sgt. JW Smith POW Sgt. T Knowles POW Sgt. C Greenhaigh Killed Sgt. TL Hitchcock Killed
76 Sqdn: Halifax DK 169-M Shot down by night-fighter Raalte Broekland	Sgt. CH Cousins POW PO AWL Pruce POW Sgt. JF Hughes POW Sgt. AG Dale POW Sgt. J Parr POW PO JW Coleman Killed Can Sgt. HA Crouse Killed
78 Sqdn: Halifax W7926 Shot down by night-fighter Dutch coast	Sgt. BWT Horn POW Sgt. G Irving POW Sgt. WA Allely POW Sgt. DR Wilcox POW Sgt. RF Cummins POW Sgt. F Church POW Sgt. GJ Stevens POW
78 Sqdn: Halifax JD 122 Crashed Wierden	Sgt. GE Schubert Killed Sgt. DC Oliver Killed PO AB Ornie Killed Sgt. PJ Wood Killed Sgt. R Goodyear Killed Sgt. J Redman Killed Sgt. A Goldplust Killed
78 Sqdn: Halifax JD 160 Crashed München Gladbach	Sgt. GH Finniswood POW PO H Bear POW PO R Donman POW Sgt. GJ Wallace POW Sgt. EE Harries POW Can Sgt. WJ Manserby POW Sgt. FM Caffey Killed by flak on parachute descent
101 Sqdn: Lancaster W 4919-A Crashed Bergen, Holland	Aust Flt. Sgt. JHT Hayes Killed Sgt. PG Eames Killed Sgt. J Park Killed Sgt. JWC Evans Killed Sgt. WR Cook Killed Can Sgt. OH Gibson Killed Can Sgt. LG Smith Killed
102 Sqdn: Halifax JD 112 Shot down by Major Leuchs near Lake Oude, Gouw in the Polder, Holland	Flt. Sgt. AM Sargent POW Sgt. AG Campbell Killed FO JR Bullock POW Sgt. M Galloway POW Sgt. CR Webb POW Sgt. HD Newberry Killed Sgt. JC Smith Killed

SQUADRON AND AIRCRAFT	CREW
102 Sqdn: Halifax W 1217	Sgt. CJJ Hine Killed FO JWD King Killed. Washed up 21.6.43 Sgt. HG Ashton Killed Sgt. EC Church Killed. Washed up 7.10.43 Sgt. A Hall Killed. Washed up 3.6.43 Sgt. GD Nisbet Killed. Washed up 7.6.43 Sgt. RFF Baggaby Killed. Washed up 5.6.43
158 Sqdn: Halifax HR 781-F Shot down by night-fighter	Sgt. N Gillies Killed Sgt. RE Hall Killed Sgt. TSJ Crawley POW Sgt. J Roberts POW Sgt. JF Hinds Killed Sgt. F Warburton Killed Sgt. RME Harmon POW Inj.
166 Sqdn: Wellington HE 655 Crashed Woensel	Sgt. CWH Westwood Killed Sgt. A Benson Killed Sgt. HW Fields Killed Sgt. WP Baxter Killed Sgt. TW Shadgett Killed
166 Sqdn: Wellington HE 290	Sgt. ES Morris Killed Sgt. HB Thompson Killed Sgt. FRG Falloway Killed Sgt. RF Williamson Killed Sgt. JR Stewart Killed
166 Sqdn: Wellington HE 486	FO AE Stewart Killed Flt. Lt. JG Eldridge DFC Killed Sgt. JH Griffiths Killed Sgt. GB Jobes Killed Sgt. J Saunders Killed
199 Sqdn: Wellington HZ 582	Sgt. HW Austin Killed. Shot while escaping 19.6.43 Aust Sgt DR Keevers POW Inj. Sgt. JPE Last POW Sgt. A Herbert Killed Can Sgt. RM Costello Killed
214 Sqdn: Stirling BF 528 Crashed München Gladbach	NZ Sgt. JK Wilkins Killed Sgt. WS Clifton-Mogg POW Inj. Sgt. L Freeman Killed Sgt. A Mason POW Sgt. BA Kennedy POW Sgt. WA Leslie POW Sgt. ET Hutching POW
214 Sqdn: Stirling MZ 261 Crashed Dortmund	Sgt. J Egan Killed PO PH Liddle Killed Sgt. D Alford Killed Sgt. L Martin Killed Sgt. F North Killed Sgt. V Archer Killed Sgt. J Dodd Killed
214 Sqdn: Stirling BF 478 Crashed Engelsnaaplaat	Can Sgt. JW Evans Killed Sgt. Z Goldfinger Killed Sgt. H Ward Killed Sgt. VN Walker Killed Sgt. ED Ager Killed Sgt. LC Child Killed Sgt. RV Street Killed

SQUADRON AND AIRCRAFT	CREW
218 Sqdn: Stirling BK 706 Crashed Dortmund	FO J Phillips Killed Sgt. GS Wishart Killed Sgt WG Kirby Killed Sgt. DAF Lavelly Killed Sgt. MLG Drabble Killed Can Sgt. GB Leadbeater Killed Sgt. CE Bryant Killed
300 Sqdn: Wellington HZ 374-K Crashed Düsseldorf	Pol FO A Piatkowask Killed Pol FO W Jankowski Killed Pol PO H Lewicki Killed Pol Sgt. L Pataycgyk POW Pol Sgt. E Kulikauski Killed
405 Sqdn: Halifax JB 896	Can Sgt. J Martin Killed Can PO FP Harrison Killed PO M Gluck Killed Can WO2 G Bancesdel Killed Sgt. G McGlory Killed Can Sgt. RO Crae Killed Can Sgt. RW Jennings Killed
408 Sqdn: Halifax JB 841-K Crashed Dortmund	Can FO JM Colvin Killed Can Flt. TR Livermore Killed Can PO H Uretgky Killed Sgt. F Thompson Killed Can Sgt. J Hooper Killed Can Sgt. DS Slobatsky Killed Can Sgt. EH Alderson Killed
419 Sqdn: Halifax JB 862-U Crashed München Gladbach	Can WO2 AS Green Killed PO D Gartery Killed Sgt. AJ Brockway Killed Sgt. RA Harrison Killed Can Sgt. FA Dunn POW Can Sgt. JF Prieut Killed Can Sgt. GR Yowling Killed
426 Sqdn: Wellington HE 281	Can Sgt. LG Sutherland Killed Sgt. W Dunkerley Killed Sgt. G Jepson Killed Can Sgt. KH Masterson Killed Can Flt. Sgt. AL Rivest Killed
460 Sqdn: Lancaster W 4986	Aust Flt. Sgt. GL Stevens POW Aust Flt. Sgt. DL Stubbs POW Aust Flt. Sgt. AJ Harris POW Inj. Sgt. ELH Jones POW Aust Flt. Sgt. TS Easton POW Aust Flt. Sgt. PH Sara POW Sgt. JE Waldron POW
460 Sqdn: Lancaster W4984-J Crashed Schoonebeek	Aust Flt. Sgt. BMT Davis Killed Aust Sgt. KD Dyce Killed Aust Flt. Sgt. L Goldthorpe POW Aust Flt. Sgt. JSV Biffen Killed Sgt. E Rowlands Killed Aust Flt. Sgt. CS Wright Killed Can Sgt. FW Ralph Killed

Total 202 Killed, 61 POWs

SQUADRON AND AIRCRAFT	CREW
25–26 May 1943	
7 Sqdn: Stirling EF 361 Shot down	Can PO EG Berthiaume Killed Sgt. AA Brotherton Killed Sgt. W Denham Killed Sgt. WJ Hills RCAF Killed Sgt. E Broadhead Killed Sgt. N Lagna Killed Sgt. AL Fisher Killed
9 Sqdn: Lancaster ED 934 Shot down Flushing	FO HW Woodhouse Killed Sgt. JB Corbett Killed Sgt. HJ Warren Killed Sgt. W Smith Killed Sgt. LJ Daker Killed Sgt. AG Coffin Killed Sgt. EL Matthews Killed
12 Sqdn: Lancaster ED 967	Flt. Sgt. R Steele Killed FO CB Hooper Killed Sgt. DW Greevy Survived Sgt. ET Powell Killed Sgt. PO Prouse RAAF Killed Sgt. SAJ Bailey Killed Flt. Sgt. LC Schroeder Killed
15 Sqdn: Stirling BF 534	FO IS Thomson RCAF Killed Flt. Sgt. CT Smith RCAF Killed PO RE Newman Killed Sgt. HJ Morris Killed Sgt. DP O'Riordon Killed Sgt. TC L Orchard Killed Sgt. LR Smith Killed
15 Sqdn: Stirling BK 611-U	Sgt. JO Wilson RAAF Killed PO BE Cooper POW Sgt. P Arnott Killed Sgt. SJ Morted POW Sgt. PW Pittard Killed Sgt. EF Seabolt POW Sgt. W Edgley POW
35 Sqdn: Halifax W 7825-P Shot down Venlo	Flt. Sgt. RT Hall POW, later W/O Sgt. E Garner Killed Sgt. RH Oats Killed Flt. Sgt. MO Fuller Killed Sgt. J Hogg Killed Sgt. LD Bryant Killed Sgt. CE Simmons Killed
51 Sqdn: Halifax HR 853 Shot down	Sgt. WP Davies Killed Sgt. CA Richardson Killed Sgt. JC McPhedron Killed Sgt. S Busby Killed Sgt. WJ Chambers Killed Sgt. A Brown Killed Sgt. AC Warden RCAF Killed
75 Sqdn: Stirling BK 602 Crashed in the sea	Sgt. TW Barton RNZAF Survived Sgt. DD Coates RNZAF Killed Sgt. JMP Riordon RNZAF Killed Sgt. JCL Whiteman Killed. Washed up at Ostend, buried at Ostend Sgt. A McQuater Killed Sgt. S Redpath Killed Sgt. FA Willsher Killed

SQUADRON AND AIRCRAFT	CREW
77 Sqdn: Halifax W 7813 Shot down Heverlee, Belgium	Sgt. LW Rees Killed Sgt. H Roots Killed Sgt. HW Moore Killed Sgt. J McLeod Killed Sgt. EV Pass Killed Sgt. J Gilchrist RCAF Killed Sgt. CH Shepwood RCAF Killed
77 Sqdn: Halifax JB 837	Sgt. R Lewis Killed Sgt. JH Walerston Survived Sgt. JW Richardson Killed Sgt. J Kershaw Killed Sgt. WRL Codd Killed Sgt. JE Laurence RCAF Killed Sgt. DW MacFarlane Killed
90 Sqdn: Stirling EH 876	Can PO GW Young DFC Killed Sgt. MGK East RCAF Killed NZ Flt. Sgt. CL Saundercock Killed Flt. Sgt. JL Poulter Killed Sgt. R. Wadsworth Killed Sgt. WH Bryant Killed PO CF O'Connell Killed Sgt. EC Pollon RCAF Killed
100 Sqdn: Lancaster W 4998 Crashed Nymagen, Holland	Aust Sgt. ATW Moore Killed Sgt. DC Stone Killed F/O SWJ Coventry POW Flt. Sgt. JC Wood Killed Sgt. JS Wilkins POW NZ Sgt. LC Maunsell Killed Sgt. M Geogh Killed
100 Sqdn: Lancaster LM 320 Crashed Nymagen, Holland	Sqn Ldr. PR Turgell Killed Can PO HN Pelts Killed PO G Russell Killed PO JM Marnock Killed Sgt. IA Wynn Killed PO D Harkey Killed Sgt. J Hudson Killed
101 Sqdn: Lancaster ED 660-J Crashed Uden, Holland	Sgt. VJS Findale Killed Sgt. ATM Wright Killed Sgt. DL Beresford Killed Sgt. BC Ainsworth Killed Sgt. E Shackleton Killed Sgt. AS Thomson RCAF Killed Sgt. CW Bates Killed
149 Sqdn: Stirling BK 710 Crashed in the sea	Sgt. JH Uden Killed FO WEL Morse Killed PO HS Winchester Killed Sgt. FA Williams Killed Sgt. CG Hadden Killed Sgt. HS Scott Killed Sgt. CJ Percival Killed. Body recovered from the sea by a patrol boat at Heligoland 20.6.43
166 Sqdn: Wellington HE 235	Sgt. R Butterbee POW Can Flt. Sgt. FA Sproule Killed Sgt. AJ Railton Killed Sgt. JT Francis Killed Sgt. K McIntosh POW

SQUADRON AND AIRCRAFT	CREW
166 Sqdn: Wellington HE 699	Sgt. R Lowe Killed Sgt. GJ Mitchner Killed Sgt. GJ Watkins Killed Sgt. S Barron Killed Sgt. L Chisnell Killed
199 Sqdn: Wellington HF 488 Attacked by a fighter	FO D Makin Killed FO FS Reade POW PO RT Douglas Killed Sgt. WH Thomson Killed Sgt. TM Scott Killed
207 Sqdn: Lancaster ED 600	FO PC Bradley-Drayton Killed Sgt. GL Bottomley Killed Sgt. DA Generer Killed Sgt. IEG Hall Killed Sgt. TWT Stoddart Killed Sgt. KJ Frost Killed Sgt. EH Barker Killed
207 Sqdn: Lancaster W 5001-J Shot down	Wg/Cdr. CT Parselle POW FO WC Reynolds Killed PO GE Hapson Killed Sgt. REH Hood-Morris POW Sgt. SAJ Cook Killed Sgt. Falkingham Killed Sgt. AW White Killed Sgt. WF Hayllar Killed
214 Sqdn: Stirling BK 659	Aust Sgt. RA Kerr Killed Sgt. AM Jubb Killed PO R Paisley Killed Sgt. RS Blake Killed Sgt. F Pooley Killed Sgt. GT Davies Killed Sgt. D Littlewood Killed
218 Sqdn: Stirling EH 887 Shot down	Sgt. NS Collins Killed Sgt. FW Bennett POW NZ PO CF Blanchard Killed Sgt. JP Rougham Killed Sgt. WJ Ledbury Killed Sgt. AW Fincham Killed Sgt. JC Lamond Killed Sgt. DC Maynard Killed
426 Sqdn: Wellington HE 590 Crashed Brussels	Can Flt. Sgt. S Pennington Killed Can Sgt. RE Falman Killed Can PO JK Watson Killed Can Sgt. NC Swan Killed Sgt. E Thomas Killed Can Sgt. DL Beatty Killed
428 Sqdn: Wellington HZ 476 Crashed Louvain, Belgium	Can Sgt. WG Pepper Killed Can Flt. Sgt. FG Baker Killed Can Flt. Sgt. NJ Waters Killed Sgt. KG Higgs Killed Can Sgt. WE Douglas Killed Can PO RG Madge Killed

SQUADRON AND AIRCRAFT	CREW
431 Sqdn: Wellington HE 990-Z	Sgt. TRT Barclay POW Sgt. K Dix POW PO RP Davies Killed Can Sgt. DE Campbell Killed Can Sgt. R Zeidel Killed Can Sgt. LPR Dalleper Killed Can Sgt. AJ MacLachlan Killed
431 Sqdn: Wellington HE 392	Sqn Ldr. WE Mulford Killed Can FO CA McDougall Killed Can Sgt. JG Breen Killed, later WO2 Sgt. JR Bell Killed Can Sgt. E Rheanme Killed
431 Sqdn: Wellington HE 184	Sgt. WD Eaglesham Killed PO LC Long Killed Flt. Sgt. HT McClausland Survived Sgt. JH Burrow Killed Sgt. BH Stephenson Killed
432 Sqdn: Wellington HE 729	Can Flt. Lt. LA Bougreouis Killed Can Sgt. JAM Philpott Killed Can PO GA McClintock Killed Can Sgt. HD Warner Killed Can Sgt. SD McCrae Survived
460 Sqdn: Lancaster W 4960	Aust Sgt. R Christie Killed Aust Sgt. J Heath Killed Sgt. JH Horwood Killed Sgt. RL Lewis Killed Sgt. RS Kerwin Killed Aust PO BW Bennett Killed Sgt. PJ Hogan Killed
466 Sqdn: Wellington HE 154	Aust Sgt. FWR Green Killed Aust Sgt. KE Fletcher Killed Sgt. AS Jones Killed Aust Sgt. ED Milliken Killed Aust Sgt. JF Mell Killed
466 Sqdn: Wellington HE 150	FO F Mackkeldon Killed FO S Roxborough Killed Sgt. TC Herbert Killed Sgt. EM Gold Killed Sgt. AG Rawlins Killed Aust Sgt. E Maroney Killed
467 Sqdn: Lancaster W 4983 Crashed Calais, France	Sqn Ldr. DC McKenzie Killed Sqn Ldr. BS Ambrose Killed PO DC Bovis Killed Sgt. AD Moore Killed Aust FO L Pietsch Killed Sgt. JF McCluskey Killed Flt. Lt. LR Betts Killed Aust Sgt. Donohue Killed
467 Sqdn: Lancaster ED 304	Aust Flt. Sgt. BF Willmott Killed Flt. Sgt. TW Hall Killed Sgt. KT White Killed Sgt. WN Crass Killed Aust Sgt. WJ Frazer Killed Sgt. A MacDonald Killed Sgt. W Calvert Killed

SQUADRON AND AIRCRAFT	CREW
619 Sqdn: Lancaster ED 978	Flt. Lt. CO Taylor Evaded Sgt. R Evans POW FO SE Harris POW Repatriated 2.2.45 Sgt. DE Inggo POW Can Sgt. WC Anderson POW Sgt. JW Henderson POW Can Sgt. DE Chisholm POW
Total 189 Killed, 56 POWs, 3 Evaded	

27 – 28 May 1943

SQUADRON AND AIRCRAFT	CREW
10 Sqdn: Halifax JB 960	WO HV Price Killed Sgt. R Leyland Killed PO E Parry Killed Sgt. WE Williams Killed FO ER Curtis Killed Sgt. EG Halston Killed Sgt. WE Waggett Killed
10 Sqdn: Halifax JB 958-W Shot down by night-fighter flown by Lt.Rapp Hool near Sleen	FO G Rawlinson Killed Sgt. WK Warren Killed Sgt. SG Beattie Killed Sgt. E Williams POW Sgt. ES Buck Killed Sgt. J Howarth Killed Sgt. EB Blackarrow Killed
35 Sqdn: Halifax HR 795	Sgt. RJ Ayres Killed Sgt. AH Porter POW Killed in RAF attack 19.4.45 Sgt. LJ Miles Killed Sgt. R Hageman Killed Sgt. FC Cleaver Killed Sgt. L Marsham Killed Sgt. E Carill Killed
51 Sqdn: Halifax HZ 270	PO R Beaston POW WO R Walker POW Sgt. H West POW Sgt. H Court POW Sgt. ED Matthews POW Sgt. AG East POW Flt. Sgt. EH Pertman POW Stalag L6.
51 Sqdn: Halifax NR 789	Sgt. FJ Prothero POW PO ABP Wilson Killed Sgt. JH Mastin Killed Sgt. PJ Smith Killed Sgt. A Aitken Killed Sgt. WF Turner POW Sgt. EJ Cotton Killed
76 Sqdn: Halifax DK 147-A	PO DS Ross Killed Sgt. GJ Beckford POW Stalag L6. Sgt. H Anderson Killed Sgt. WG Styles POW Repatriated Can PO H Langlois POW Inj. Sgt. R Jones POW Inj. FO EF Campbell Killed. Died in hospital of his injuries

SQUADRON AND AIRCRAFT	CREW
77 Sqdn: Halifax HR JD 152	Aust Flt. Sgt. FO Grady Killed Sgt. CG Garrard Killed FO BC McGrath Killed Sgt. WR Beardsmore Killed Sgt. WA Manning Killed Sgt. CB Anderson Killed Sgt. C Clarke Killed
100 Sqdn: Lancaster ED 821 Shot down by night-fighter flown by Oblt. Rudolf Sigmund Witmarsum	NZ FO LA Townrow POW. Died in hospital eleven months after capture Sgt. JP Fitchett Killed Can FO SA Bishop Killed Sgt. E Short died in hospital PO J Bolderson POW Inj. Sgt. PM Cosgrove Killed Aust Sgt. AE Chapman Killed
102 Sqdn: Halifax JD 149-H Shot down by night-fighter near Oosterland	PO JD Jeffrey Killed FO H Entwhistle Killed FO Fewtrell Killed Can/USA Sgt. S Zareikin Killed Sgt. KJ Smith Killed Sgt. JLS Lowings Killed Sgt. T Heslop Killed
106 Sqdn: Lancaster W 4842-H Crash-landed on an island near Lieden	WO EA Robbins POW Sgt. J Seedhouse POW Sgt. LC Carpenter POW Sgt. GE Calvert POW Sgt. HJ Taylor POW Sgt. L Calvert POW Sgt. JN Denton POW
115 Sqdn: Lancaster DS 655 Crashed Gelsenkirchen	NZ FO GW Campbell POW FO GW Cooper Killed NZ FO HD Pye Killed Sgt. GA Parker Killed PO R Ryland Killed PO DS Williams Killed Sgt. EG Baker Killed
156 Sqdn: Lancaster W 4943- Shot down by night-fighter Karroad near Diteloo	Aust Flt. Sgt. DL Wallace Killed Sgt. TH Harvey POW Sgt. RJ Jackson POW Sgt. RJ Twinn Killed Aust Flt. Sgt. D Ross Killed NZ Sgt. HA Lister Killed Sgt. WH Moore POW
158 Sqdn: Halifax HR 775-V Crashed Okenboek	Can Sgt. WH Wyatt Killed Sgt. JL Atha Killed Sgt. RA Tilbury Killed Sgt. G Henderson Killed Can Sgt. RR Mantha Killed Sgt. J Simmons Killed Sgt. WJ Erobeer Killed
166 Sqdn: Wellington HE 752-W Crashed near Hengelo	PO DT Tonkinson Killed Sgt. PG West Killed FO TD Brown Killed PO AD Johnson Killed Sgt. K Raynor Killed Sgt. P Guest Killed

SQUADRON AND AIRCRAFT	CREW
218 Sqdn: Stirling BF 405 Wadden Zea	Flt. Sgt. WD Mills Killed NZ PO WV Fitzgerald Killed NZ Sgt. HHG Hubbard Killed NZ Flt. Sgt. GA Mathias Killed Sgt. S Moore Killed PO JB True Killed Sgt. S Smith Killed
405 Sqdn: Halifax HR 807-G Hit by flak over Essen	Can Sgt. GEJ Lebinhaw Killed PO GS Wilson Killed Can PO LSP Davies Killed Can Sgt. GF Sovereign POW Can Sgt. L Maracle POW Sgt. JY Howston Killed Sgt. J Holmes Killed
408 Sqdn: Halifax DT 674-A Shot down by night-fighter near Essen	Aust Flt. Sgt. KO Grieg POW Can FO CA Vogal POW Can Flt. Sgt. WV Newman POW Can Flt. Sgt. JW Albert POW Can Sgt. J Comeau Killed Can Sgt. J Keys Killed Can Sgt. SJ Blewett POW
428 Sqdn: Wellington HZ 485 Crashed possibly Wanrooi	Can WO1 DH Thompson Killed Can FO AF Beaton Killed Can Sgt. GG Hart Killed Sgt. KG Chilver Killed Can Flt. Sgt. GCP O'Hara Killed
432 Sqdn: Wellington HE 294-P	Can Flt. Sgt. RE Taylor DFM Killed Can PO AR Grant POW Can FO JA Farnham Killed Can PO MR Marshall POW Can WO2 AG Bailey Killed
460 Sqdn: Lancaster ED 804 Shot down by night-fighter near Herveld	PO C Harrison Killed Sgt. WG Schrader POW Aust PO CC Bates POW Sgt. WA Blackwell Killed Sgt. CRS Mono POW Aust Sgt. EJ Kerr Killed Aust Sgt. JA Grant Killed
467 Sqdn: Lancaster ED 504 Crashed Barlo Friedhof	FO JM Desmond Killed Sgt. ES Davis Killed PO G Cribbin Killed PO JN Lockwood Killed Flt. Sgt. GF Paddon Killed PO K Cazaly Killed Aust Flt. Sgt. JR Ryalls Killed
Total 99 Killed, 42 POWs	

29 – 30 May 1943

SQUADRON AND AIRCRAFT	CREW
10 Sqdn: Halifax DT 787 Crashed Dortmund	NZ Flt. Sgt. JE Clarke Killed Sgt. WR Scott Killed Sgt. JH Pickles Killed Sgt. RH Harris Killed Sgt. R Graham POW Sgt. JWS Birrell Killed Flt. Sgt. JA Saunders Killed

SQUADRON AND AIRCRAFT	CREW
12 Sqdn: Lancaster ED 996-J	Flt. Lt. IPC Goudge Killed Sgt. J Gorton POW Sgt. R Richmond POW Sgt. V Wells Killed Sgt. AE Graham Killed Sgt. M Hatch Killed Sgt. J Hardman Killed
35 Sqdn: Halifax HR 833-F Shot down by night-fighter near Antwerp	Can WO JL Lee Killed Sgt. J Jones POW Aust Sgt. HJ Ross Killed Sgt. VS Platt Killed Sgt. FM Trayner Killed PO JL Goodson DFM POW Flt. Lt. WAR Tetley DFC Killed
35 Sqdn: Halifax HR 793-J Shot down by night-fighter	Sqn. Ldr. P Horston Killed Can PO R Wood POW FO RG Houston POW Aust Flt. Sgt. Royall POW Inj. Aust Sgt. AW Cowan POW Sgt. FJ Jarvis Killed Sgt. MT Byrne POW Flt. Sgt. W Roede POW. 2nd Pilot
35 Sqdn: Halifax W 7876-K Shot down by night-fighter	Sgt. AR Sargent POW Sgt. RG Hands POW Sgt. WT Gray Killed Sgt. HBT Knowles POW Sgt. GH Gardiner POW Sgt. CH Gardner Killed Sgt. DR Bown POW
35 Sqdn: Halifax DT 804-C Shot down by night-fighter St. Trond	PO R Hoose Killed Sgt. RW Hodge Killed Sgt. JC Kennedy Killed Sgt. J Davidson POW Sgt. A Tannock Killed Sgt. AM Taylor Killed Sgt. E Bell Killed
44 Sqdn: Lancaster W4838-B Shot down by night-fighter near Peer	Sgt. E Grieson Killed Sgt. C Davies POW Sgt. C Rees POW Sgt. EA Thompson Killed Sgt. J Grant POW Sgt. G Chadfield Killed NZ Sgt. RAF Wood Killed
44 Sqdn: Lancaster EE 123	Can FO PG Holt Killed Sgt. ED Kimpton POW Sgt. D McColl Killed Sgt. W Young Killed Sgt. I Tucker Killed Sgt. RT Stoddard Killed Sgt. H Robinson Killed
75 Sqdn: Stirling EF 398 Shot down by night-fighter flown by Oblt. Maurer near Roermond, Holland	NZ PO RB Vernazoni Killed NZ Sgt. OA Innes Killed NZ PO H Tong Killed NZ CH Riddle Killed Sgt. W Bramwell Killed Sgt. AR Cardor Killed Sgt. J Chandler Killed

SQUADRON AND AIRCRAFT	CREW
75 Sqdn: Stirling EH 881 Crashed Aachen, area of Eilendorf	NZ Sgt. JHR Carey Killed NZ Sgt. JL Roberts POW NZ Sgt. PG Knight POW NZ Flt. Sgt. M Brady POW Sgt. TE Bearer POW Flt. Sgt. WA Owens Killed NZ Flt. Sgt. NA McLeod Killed
75 Sqdn: Stirling BK 776	NZ PP RF Bennett Killed NZ Flt. Sgt. AL Davidson POW NZ Sgt. RF Norman POW NZ Flt. Sgt. FA Baudy Killed NZ Flt. Sgt. SL Cavanagh Killed Sgt. TB Harris POW Inj. Can Sgt. JA Pirie Killed NZ Flt. Sgt. CP Middleton POW
75 Sqdn: Stirling BF 561	NZ Flt. Sgt. SR Thornley Killed NZ Sgt. A McWilliam Killed NZ Sgt. AEA MacPhail Killed Sgt. D Ruocco Killed Sgt. CW Larkin Killed Sgt. JV Dartnall Killed Sgt. FG Hooper Killed
90 Sqdn: Stirling EF 349	PO RWJ Letters Killed Sgt. L King POW NZ FO KT Escourt Killed Sgt. FA Wells Killed Sgt. LW Hughes Killed Sgt. R Raven Killed Sgt. H Maskell Killed
102 Sqdn: Halifax W 7934	Sgt RA Ward Killed PO REC Allen Killed Sgt. J Martland Killed Sgt. RL Hoddle Killed Sgt. PH Sheerman Killed Sgt. P Smith Killed Sgt. J Stewart Killed
106 Sqdn: Lancaster R 5677	Sgt. HRB Wyatt Killed Sgt. RF Coverdale Killed Sgt. EW Cosnett Killed Sgt. NW Moore Killed Can Sgt. LT Delome Killed Sgt. J Leadbeater Killed Sgt. W Chapman Killed
115 Sqdn: Lancaster DS 627 Crashed St. Trond	Sgt. CRR Fleming Killed Sgt. R Adam Killed Can PO CK Coker Killed Sgt. J Currie Killed Sgt. HG Thomas Killed Sgt. KG Berry Killed Sgt. AR Tickner Killed
149 Sqdn: Stirling BF 507	NZ Sgt. AW Flack Killed Sgt. J Shepherd Killed Sgt. FC Deltey Killed Sgt. TB Morris Killed Sgt. H Lloyd Killed Can Flt. Sgt. H Sponsler Killed Can Sgt. RW Stanley Killed

SQUADRON AND AIRCRAFT	CREW
158 Sqdn: Halifax HR 840-R Shot down by night-fighter flown by Oblt. Manfred Muir near Roermond	Sgt. CK Surgery Killed Sgt. C Strand Killed Sgt. KG Cottrell POW Sgt. GT Clyton POW Sgt. ES Costal Killed Sgt. W George Killed Can Flt. Sgt. SJ Manuff Killed
158 Sqdn: Halifax HR 717	Can Flt. Sgt. J Cooper Killed FO WC Luther Killed Sgt. HD Young Killed Sgt. H Simpson Killed FO DR Woodroffe Killed Sgt. F Dykes Killed Can Sgt. WM Ellis Killed
218 Sqdn: Stirling BK 688	Aust Flt. Sgt. WAM Davis Killed Sgt. TW Dixon Killed Sgt. TL Portney Killed Sgt. GAA Grant Killed Sgt. WR Howes Killed Sgt. JA Bramble Killed PO LW Abbis Killed
218 Sqdn: Stirling BF 565	Aust PO SG Allan Killed Sgt. HN Wade Killed PO EG Garai Killed Sgt. WF Henderson Killed Sgt. JL Thomas Killed Sgt. KM Campbell Killed NZ Sgt. DP Stong POW
419 Sqdn: Halifax JB 805	Can Sgt. PS Johnson Killed Sgt. RS Metcalf Killed Can Sgt. STW Reets Killed Flt. Sgt. G Humphreys Killed Sgt. CP Baker Killed Can Sgt. DJ Shtitz Killed Can Flt. Sgt. EL Armstrong Killed
419 Sqdn: Halifax JB 793	Can Sgt. FE Winegarden Killed Can Sgt. RM Mingay POW Can PO FH Hubbs POW Can Sgt. SG Ward POW Sgt. E Hall POW Can Sgt. LR Lamoure Killed Can Sgt. R Rickets Killed
428 Sqdn: Wellington HE 319	Can/USA WO2 FL Shellnult Killed Sgt. DL Smith Killed Can Sgt. JGA Marshall Killed Sgt. JC Langley Killed Can Sgt. McMillan Killed
428 Sqdn: Wellington LN 424 Crash-landed after crew baled out	Can Sgt. JA Fergus POW Can FO GP Fallman POW Can Sgt. JH Edwards POW Flt. Sgt. DL Smith POW Can Sgt. JG Sylvester POW Can Flt. Sgt. J Dwyan POW

SQUADRON AND AIRCRAFT	CREW
429 Sqdn: Wellington HZ 471	Can FO BA Richmond Killed Can Sgt. JS Lewitt POW Can Flt. Sgt. EC Bailey Killed Sgt. EG Coleman POW Can WO2 WS Anglin Killed
431 Sqdn: Wellington HE 203	NZ Flt. Sgt. AH Smith Killed Sgt. JH Bloxwich Killed Sgt. B King Killed Sgt. A Spence Killed Sgt. ML Buxton Killed
432 Sqdn: Wellington LN 435 Crashed Crosswijk	Can Sgt. W Grigg POW Sgt. KM Jordon POW Sgt. JH Barter POW Sgt. L Hardy POW Can Sgt. GW Thompson POW
460 Sqdn: Lancaster W 4985	Sgt. TP Russell Killed Aust Sgt. RW Durn POW Aust Sgt. T Taylor Killed Sgt. PW Findley Killed. Washed up in the Rhine 6.6.43 Sgt. WE Ciggne Killed. Washed up in the Rhine 6.6.43 Sgt. DB Gordon Killed Aust Sgt. GA Kirk POW
460 Sqdn: Lancaster ED 759	Aust Sgt. HE Bull Killed Sgt. FC Sherratt Killed Sgt. DR Munday Killed Sgt. PC Willars Killed Sgt. GC Powis Killed Sgt. RM Anderson Killed Sgt. AWG Meech Killed
466 Sqdn: Wellington HE 212 Crashed Ninsie, Belgium	Sgt. HBR Lloyd Killed Sgt. WR Hendon Killed Sgt. AV Harper Killed Sgt. SC Luke Killed Sgt. WJ Bhumdell Killed
466 Sqdn: Wellington MS 494 Shot down by night-fighter flown by Oblt. Maurer near Roermond	Aust Sgt. LOH Upjohn POW Sgt. J Paterson POW Sgt. RA Napier POW Sgt. WV Garfield POW Flt. Sgt. FAR Hay Killed in combat
Total 158 Killed, 55 POWs	
11–12 June 1943	
12 Sqdn: Lancaster DV 157	NZ Flt. Lt. AW Doel Killed Flt. Sgt. R Durham Killed Flt. Sgt. OK Whyman Killed Sgt. DL Templeman POW Sgt. WF Biggs Killed NZ FO OK Jones Killed Sgt. TR Pagett Killed
12 Sqdn: Lancaster ED 522 Shot down Düsseldorf	Sgt. R Highet Killed Sgt. WA Gillanders Killed Sgt. KJ Tagg Killed Sgt. S Ford Killed Sgt. JE Constable Killed Sgt. LR Evans Killed Sgt. AW Lee Killed

SQUADRON AND AIRCRAFT	CREW
12 Sqdn: Lancaster ED 357 Aircraft located after the war and recovered from the sea. One of the propellers of this aircraft is now a memorial at the new town of Dronten in Holland	Aust Sgt. D Thomson Drowned. Washed up 21.6.43 Sgt. K Bowers Killed in combat Sgt. WM Ward Drowned. Washed up 17.6.43 Sgt. D Campbell Drowned Sgt. J Osbourn Drowned Can Sgt. WT Pingle POW Can Sgt. CW Sparling POW
12 Sqdn: Lancaster W 4791	Flt. Sgt. H Shepherd Killed Sgt. WE Cunliffe Killed Sgt. AA Gill Killed Sgt. L Stephenson Killed Sgt. FN Pink Killed Sgt. KB Davidson RCAF Killed Aust Sgt. WR Berry Killed
12 Sqdn: Lancaster W 4373	Aust Flt. Lt. PR Ford Killed Sgt. JA Osborn Killed Sgt. GW Twitty Killed Sgt. M Harris Killed Sgt. R Avery Killed Sgt. FN Anderson Killed Sgt. RW Stone Killed
15 Sqdn: Stirling BF 571-U Crashed in the sea	Sgt. RE Allen Killed. Washed up 1.7.43 Sgt. CL Aston Survived Sgt. HC Ralph Survived Sgt. WS Champ Killed Sgt. S Wright Killed Can Sgt. LWJ Dawson Killed Sgt. TK Fowler Killed
51 Sqdn: Halifax HR 852	Flt. Sgt. Harvey POW Sgt. GA Galliers POW Sgt. GL Dunn POW Sgt. HL Levere POW Can Sgt. McEnchern POW Sgt. R Limitt POW Can Flt. Sgt. R Deathstone Survived
51 Sqdn: Halifax HR 788 Crashed in the sea	Flt. Sgt. JJ Anderson Killed Sgt. AR Helliwell Killed Sgt. AE Brodie Killed Sgt. D Glassman Killed Sgt. G Luff Killed Sgt. FJ Biddle Killed Sgt. GE Evans Killed. Buried Bergen-op-Zoom
75 Sqdn: Stirling BK 807 Crashed St. Trond	NZ Sqn Ldr. RH Laud Killed Sgt. HS Megnade Killed Sgt. JH Russell Killed Sgt. HS Mulholland Killed Sgt. R Watmough Killed Sgt. AR Waite Killed Sgt. FJ Hawkins Killed
76 Sqdn: Halifax DK 200	Sgt. DS Phillips Killed Sgt. J Hills POW Sgt. GA Bardett POW Sgt. NWS Clark Killed Sgt. GG Bird POW Sgt. E Cadmore Killed Sgt. EWA Brice POW

SQUADRON AND AIRCRAFT	CREW
76 Sqdn: Halifax DK 170 Crashed Woensal, Eindhoven	Sgt. AJN Wilson Killed Sgt. JA Lobban Survived Sgt. J Domnitz Killed Sgt. JJ Lawsey Survived Sgt. CK Burton Killed Sgt. DB Tibble Killed Sgt. KW Lawson Killed
77 Sqdn: Halifax JD 168 Shot down by Hptm. Echart Wilhelm von Bonin. Crashed Oupeye, near Liege, Belgium	Sgt. AG Endicott POW Sgt. RG Goodenough POW Sgt. LS Blanchard POW Sgt. P Wright POW Sgt. J Walsh POW Sgt. DE Burrows POW Sgt. SF Hammond Killed
78 Sqdn: Halifax HR 684	Flt. Sgt. JN Gavagan Killed Flt. Sgt. JL Jeal Killed PO JB Binns Killed Sgt. TA Davies Killed Sgt. AE Hayes Killed Can Sgt. Hollyer Killed
78 Sqdn: Halifax W 7932	Flt. Sgt. F Hemmings Killed Sgt. J Stones Killed PO WCR Foale Killed Sgt. A Shaw Killed Sgt. DJ Muir Killed Sgt. TW Daniel Killed Sgt. D Montgomery Killed
100 Sqdn: Lancaster ED 786	Sgt. Ldr. JR Marcham DFC Survived Wg/Cdr. RA Garrison Killed 2/P PO LJ Collins Killed PO G McKitty Killed Sgt. JH Mitchell Killed Sgt. RE Longster Killed Sgt. WG Watts Killed Sgt. FH Martin Killed
100 Sqdn: Lancaster ED 976	Sgt. AB Magill Killed PO CB Fleming Killed Sgt. WF Bradley Killed Sgt. N Glover Killed Sgt. EN Cummings Killed Sgt. JW Lake RCAF Killed Sgt. LA Stephenson RCAF POW
103 Sqdn: Lancaster ED 914	Sgt. PJ Scholes Survived PO WJH Haydon Killed Sgt. KW Woodcock POW Sgt. R Watkinson Killed Sgt. G Price POW Sgt. A Cook Killed Sgt. Russell Killed
115 Sqdn: Lancaster DS 647 Hit by a night-fighter, Uden	Sqn Ldr. DP Fox DFC Killed Can Flt. Sgt. KL Spring Killed Flt. Sgt. PA Chapman Killed Flt. Sgt. AM Johnson Killed Sgt. PF Nixon Killed Sgt. AD Bulmer Killed Flt. Sgt. AS Spires DFM Killed

SQUADRON AND AIRCRAFT	CREW
158 Sqdn: Halifax HR 719	Sgt. RG Pope Killed Sgt. TF Potter Killed Sgt. RAC Showler Killed Sgt. F Lee Killed Sgt. A Glenn Killed Sgt. GAF Green Killed Sgt. FG Lay-Flurrie Killed
158 Sqdn: Halifax JD 117	Flt. Lt. EAJ Laver Killed PO EJ Plumridge Killed Sgt. HJ Clelland Killed Sgt. FR Johnson Killed PO WS Smith Killed Sgt. FT Adams Killed Flt. Lt. WT Dean Killed
199 Sqdn: Wellington HZ 277	Can Sgt. GR Andrews Killed Sgt. WH Belhouse Killed Sgt. PEKD Merry Killed Sgt. WE Jackson Killed Sgt. LR Barrow Killed
207 Sqdn: Lancaster ED 537	Sgt. JH Elliott Killed Sgt. RAF Stringer Killed PO IC McDonnell Killed Sgt. HJ Leggo Survived Sgt. GJ Morrice Killed Sgt. LEG Bishop RNAF Killed Sgt. DJ Kingsnorth Killed
405 Sqdn: Halifax HR 797 Ditched in the sea 25 miles from the UK having been hit by flak. Picked up by a German flying boat near Amsterdam after 20 minutes in the water	Can PO JC Harty POW Can PO BC Miller POW/Wounded Can PO JE Patterson POW FO TA Fillingham Drowned Can Sgt. WN Fatham POW WO J Somerville POW/Wounded Can PO FE McKay POW/Wounded Can Flt. Sgt. NHA Taylor Killed in combat
408 Sqdn: Halifax JB 972-Q	Can PO AG Grant Killed Can PO RE Carter POW Can FO TB Moor POW Can Flt. Sgt. M Robert POW Sgt. KR Staniford POW Sgt. AE Powell Killed by flak Can Sgt. JMR Lang Killed
419 Sqdn: Halifax JD 142	Can FO WJ Boyce Killed FO DI Black POW/Wounded FO CC Buck POW/Wounded Sgt. DEFC Chambers Killed Sgt. DN Stewart POW Can Sgt. RM Hall POW Can Sgt. JD Gray POW Can WO HA Tripp Killed
426 Sqdn: Wellington HZ 261	Can WO ND Hayes Killed Can PO JL Rawson Killed Can Sgt. DG Richardson Killed Can Sgt. CE Schamehorn Killed Flt Sgt. DA McKenzie Killed

SQUADRON AND AIRCRAFT	CREW
429 Sqdn: Wellington HZ 355	Flt. Sgt. RG Ellison Killed Sgt. WG Bailey Evaded Sgt. HEJ Horton POW Sgt. EG Nicholson POW Can Sgt. WJ Mullaney POW
429 Sqdn: Wellington HE 593 Crashed Woensal, Eindhoven	Can Flt. Sgt. RF Conroy Evaded Can Sgt. GA Keitch Killed Can PO GR Densmore Killed Can Flt. Sgt. GA Nelson Killed Can Sgt. J Burns Killed. Later WO2
429 Sqdn: Wellington HF 542	PO AC Bonner Killed Sgt. MC Jefferies Killed Sgt. H Sweet Killed
467 Sqdn: Lancaster ED 695	Aust FO RS Giddey POW Aust Sgt. SG Keird POW PO PR Collins POW Sgt. WV Morris POW Sgt. RJ Avann POW Can Sgt. AF Birkbeck Killed PO KR Langhorne Killed
467 Sqdn: Lancaster ED 768	Aust Flt. Sgt. JM Parsons Killed Sgt. JP Egan POW Sgt. NJ Validard POW Can Sgt. Selman POW Sgt. B Spencer Killed Sgt. RA Hunt POW Sgt. T Chalmers Killed

Total 153 Killed, 25 POWs

12 – 13 June 1943

9 Sqdn: Lancaster ED 558 Shot down by night-fighter near Arnhem	WO HE Wood Killed PO F Archer POW FO T Mellard POW Flt. Sgt. JL Crawford POW Sgt. LE Clayton POW Sgt. WR Barker POW Can Sgt. HG Watson POW
10 Sqdn: Halifax W 7909 Crashed Lingen, River Emms, Germany	Sgt. QM Innes Killed Sgt. KA Jenkins Killed Sgt. HE Sedgere POW Sgt. FC Mitchell Killed Sgt. W Sharp Killed Sgt. E Smith Killed Sgt. RG Lepetit Killed
49 Sqdn: Lancaster ED 584 Crashed North Sea, near Raalte	Can Sgt. J Hutchinson Killed. Washed up 13.6.43 Sgt. CG Olson Killed Sgt. EWH Johnson Killed Sgt. CW Dudley Killed Sgt. BR Cripps Killed Sgt. EH Pearson Killed NZ Sgt. LE Workman Killed

SQUADRON AND AIRCRAFT	CREW
50 Sqdn: Lancaster ED 472	Flt. Sgt. AJ Weber Killed Can PO FR Fesan Killed NZ FO VW Ferguson Killed Flt. Sgt. F Norman Killed Sgt. NC Carter Killed Sgt. RC Kerley Killed Flt. Sgt. R Goldstraw Killed
50 Sqdn: Lancaster ED 429 Hit by flak Portwaad Bouing Lausen	PO JM McCrossan DFM Killed Sgt. DMCD Buchan Killed Sgt. GL Stewart POW Inj. Repatriated Sept 1944 Sgt. JK Morgan Killed Sgt. JT Wilkinson DFM Killed Sgt. HR Stone Killed Sgt. J Aitken Killed
50 Sqdn: Lancaster ED 828 Crashed Wiersloe	Flt. Lt. PJ Stone Killed PO WJ Glenn DFM POW PO WT Batson DFM POW Flt. Sgt. AJ Mills Killed Sgt. A Hunter Killed FO MDS Hicks Killed Can FO A Smith DFC Killed
51 Sqdn: Halifax DT 568 Crashed Volthe	NZ Flt. Sgt. CA Chambers POW FO A Trott POW. Died 13.6.43 FO E Medgeley Killed Sgt. AW Stevens Killed Sgt. G Wood Killed Sgt. MA Hutchings Killed Sgt. A Roberts Killed
57 Sqdn: Lancaster ED 668	Sgt. KB Dowding Killed Sgt. TMA Burgess Killed Sgt. WG Reman POW Sgt. JL Hyam Killed Sgt. GA Ayres Killed Sgt. SE Tuck Killed Can PO CJ Challenger Killed
76 Sqdn: Halifax DK 177-H Crashed Nieubourg	NZ Flt. Sgt. AAH Pullan Killed PO J Kay Killed Sgt. JG Brown Killed Sgt. LC Gearing Killed Sgt. IB Nicol Killed Sgt. H Baker Killed Sgt. JE Buxton Killed
78 Sqdn: Halifax JD 145	Flt. Sgt. M Baxter Killed West Indies Sgt. WH Jordan Killed Sgt. JN Angus Killed Sgt. CW Payne Killed. Washed up 30.6.43 Sgt. AMC Young Killed Sgt. E Wright Killed Sgt. FG Westall Killed
83 Sqdn: Lancaster ED 603-L Shot down by night-fighter Ijsselmeer near Hindelopen	FO EA Tilbury Killed PO HE Howsam Killed Can Flt. Sgt. AG Fletcher Killed PO AE Moore DFM Killed PO AAB Smart DFM Killed Can FO GR Sugar Killed Sgt. RG Claydon Killed

SQUADRON AND AIRCRAFT	CREW
97 Sqdn: Lancaster ED 816-U Shot down by night-fighter Ijsselmeer	Flt. Sgt. J Thomas POW WO MCI Robertson POW Sgt. E Bloomfield POW Sgt. WE Doyle Killed Sgt. CJ Hanrahan POW Sgt. LT Beard Killed Sgt. R Crawley Killed
100 Sqdn: Lancaster W 4989 Crashed Voolst	WO E Dainty DFM Killed Sgt. RL Howarth Killed Sgt. RB Butler Killed FO G May Killed Sgt. J Kinnear Killed Sgt. AL Payne Killed Sgt. DW Bartholomew Killed
101 Sqdn: Lancaster ED 987	Sgt. RG Claydon Killed FO DC Goodwin Killed NZ Flt Sgt. NH Lavin Killed Sgt. RV Fielding Killed Sgt. AM Law Killed Can Sgt. WD McMurachy Killed Sgt. E Germaine POW
102 Sqdn: Halifax JB 868	PO RR Hale Killed Sgt. AE Muir Killed Sgt. AC Woodley Killed FO ED Wilcock Killed Sgt. WA Habbis POW Sgt. AJ Gibbs Killed Sgt. W Hallows Killed Can Sgt. R Quovillon Killed
103 Sqdn: Lancaster ED 916 Shot down by night-fighter Neuw Baliingge	PO GDJ King POW FO R Hemingway POW Sgt. FN Jay Killed Sgt. GW Backhurst POW Inj. Sgt. ES King POW Inj. Can FO GD Milner Killed Can Flt. Sgt. BM Godden POW
115 Sqdn; Lancaster DS 652 Crashed Wadden Zee	NZ Flt. Sgt. IRV Ruff Killed Sgt. NW Proctor Killed Sgt. JR Glendenning Killed Sgt. PD Deck Killed Sgt. JF Hutchison Killed Sgt. AA Rush Killed. Washed up 23.6.43 Flt. Sgt. F Cuffey Killed. Washed up 26.6.43
158 Sqdn: Halifax HR 740-R Shot down by night-fighter Holland	NZ PO SC Brown Killed WO A Barnard Killed PO JG Fyffe POW WO SC Holroyde Evaded Sgt. LV Martin Killed Sgt. RW Robinson POW Sgt. H Leary POW
158 Sqdn: Halifax HR 724-W Crash-landed Ulft near Aalton, Holland Engine Failure	Sgt. BC Wordsworth POW PO F Oliver Killed Sgt. E Thurlow Killed PO HT Woolridge Killed PO GD King POW Sgt. RV Pallant POW Inj. Sgt. RJ Cock Killed. Died in hospital 13.6.43 Amsterdam

SQUADRON AND AIRCRAFT	CREW
408 Sqdn: Halifax JB 790-V Shot down by night-fighter	Can FO GR Large Killed Can Sgt. AF Raymont POW Can PO FL Milburn Killed Can Sgt. JR Forest POW Can Sgt. N Bainblatt POW Sgt. T Leigh-Ross Killed Can Sgt. DH Hurchinson POW
419 Sqdn: Halifax DT 616	Can Sgt. BD Kirkham POW Can Sgt. HA Taylor Killed Sgt. DB Whittmer POW Flt. Sgt. FJ Callaghan POW Can Sgt. RJ Hamilton POW Can Sgt. JA Mills POW Can Sgt. DL Gray POW
427 Sqdn: Halifax DK 183 Shot down by night-fighter Prins Henrickpolder, Den Hoorn	Can PO AM Fellnor POW Can PO GWR Dalton Killed Can PO WA Thurston POW Can Sgt. BL Tedford Killed Sgt. J Imms POW. Died in hospital Amsterdam. Shot on the ground Sgt. A Dixon Killed Washed up 30.6.43 Can PO GS Hunter Killed
460 Sqdn: Lancaster W 4316	Sgt. RD Vaughan Killed Aust Sgt. CDP Lundue Killed PO CWAY Young Killed Sgt. DA Thomas Killed Sgt. LFC Day Killed Can Sgt. JC Cornish POW Inj Flt. Sgt. A Gordon Killed
460 Sqdn: Lancaster W 4329 Crashed Dortmund	Aust PO CHM Hadley Killed Aust FO UDH Horne Killed Flt. Sgt. JL Stanley Killed Sgt. EH Bond Killed Sgt. EA Baldwin Killed Aust Sgt. NR Simpson Killed Sgt. LN Connor Killed
Total 113 Killed, 47 POWs, 1 Evaded	

14 – 15 June 1943

SQUADRON AND AIRCRAFT	CREW
9 Sqdn: Lancaster LM 329	PO J Evans Killed Sgt. R Borthwick Killed Flt. Sgt. WJ Chapple Killed Sgt. VGL Smith Killed Sgt. AW Wear Killed Sgt. DW Brough Killed Sgt. HI Ashdown Killed Sgt. VJ Tarr Killed
12 Sqdn: Lancaster W 4992 Hit by flak over target	Aust Flt. Sgt. WJ Tucker Killed PO K Truelove POW. Landed in the Rhine Sgt. BO Davies Killed Sgt. R Fletcher Killed Sgt. J Simpson Killed Sgt. J Carter Killed Flt. Sgt. FS McKay Killed

SQUADRON AND AIRCRAFT	CREW
44 Sqdn: Lancaster W 4936 Crashed Holland	Sqn. Ldr. GB Haywood Killed FO R Kirby Killed Sgt. RW Rivers Killed Sgt. RG Foot Killed Sgt. R Boardman Killed Sgt. J Armstrong Killed Sgt. RCH Brand Killed
44 Sqdn: Lancaster W 4949	Sgt. PJ Shearman Killed Sgt. NL Ballamy Killed Sgt. BW Card Killed Flt. Sgt. LS Pugh Killed FO F Richards Killed Sgt. GCA Zedy Killed Sgt. C Akeister Killed
49 Sqdn: Lancaster ED 453	WO N Nixon Killed Sqdn: SD Bird Killed Sgt. RT Moore Killed Sgt. NW Fyfe Killed Sgt. FR Fowler Killed Sgt. RKB Muir Killed Sgt. C Wilde Killed
49 Sqdn: Lancaster ED 434 Attacked by night-fighter flown by Hpt Dieterhans Frank Crashed one mile south-west of Dodewaard	Sgt. R Frost POW Inj. Sgt. NC Hitchcock POW Inj. Sgt. J Coulsey Killed FO AE Whittacker Killed Sgt. V Horsley Killed Sgt. W Chatfield Killed Sgt. PA Toms Killed
49 Sqdn: Lancaster ED 432 Crashed Osterbeek	Sgt. GS Cole Killed Sgt. CAS Barnett Killed Sgt. JF Arnold POW Inj. Sgt. JP Harper Killed Sgt. JW Deacon Killed Sgt. HR Rhodes Killed Sgt. JHD Bryan POW Sgt. H Biggin POW. Extra Nav/BA
50 Sqdn: Lancaster ED 810	FO A Crawford Killed Sgt. AE Davey Killed Sgt. J McHendry Killed Sgt. L Toal Killed Sgt. WG Reed Killed Sgt. CJ Buckle Killed Sgt. KI Bowerman Killed
75 Sqdn: Stirling BK 646-N	FO J Edwards Killed NZ Sgt. EG Dunnett Killed NZ Sgt. BW Rawlinson POW Sgt. JGF Sancoucy Evaded PO RJ Kirby Evaded Sgt. EF Jones POW Sgt. T Maxwell POW
100 Sqdn: Lancaster ED 973	Sgt. R Weddell Killed Sgt. AR Veitch Killed Sgt. GA Mason Killed Sgt. A Boydell Killed Sgt. W Cram Killed Sgt. DGM Ofield Killed Sgt. E Stevenson Killed

SQUADRON AND AIRCRAFT	CREW
103 Sqdn: Lancaster ED 612	Flt. Lt. AM Brown Killed
Crashed München Gladbach	PO F Lewis Killed
	Sgt. J Cliffe Killed
	Sgt. EH Morley Killed
	Sgt. J Greenway Killed
	Sgt. WE Cornell Killed
	Sgt. JH Saville Killed
103 Sqdn: Lancaster ED 396	Sgt. G Whitehead Killed
Crashed Düsseldorf	Sgt. J Renwick Killed
	Flt. Sgt. E Shaw Killed
	Sgt. J Kereven Killed
	FO SH Yates Killed
	Sgt. RJ Bates Killed
	Sgt. DA Ferguson Killed
106 Sqdn: Lancaster ED 649-X	FO HD Oates Killed
Crashed Düsseldorf	PO RH Parr Killed
	Sgt. RA Martin Killed
	Sgt. J Hindley Killed
	PO D Stevens Killed
	Sgt. JV Sweeney Killed
	Can Sgt. RE Bell Killed
106 Sqdn: Lancaster R 5551	Can PO DS Brown Killed
Crashed Arnhem. Shot down by	Sgt. RA Beaton Killed
night-fighter flown by	Sgt. FJ Stoker Killed
Oblt. August Geiger	Sgt. EC McMillan Killed
	Sgt. RS Pegg POW
	Sgt. K Wilcock Killed
	Sgt. AG Ballantyne Killed
	Can PO EG Seall Killed
460 Sqdn: Lancaster LM 324	Sgt. RE Crook Killed
Crashed Amsterdam	Aust Sgt. S Manage Killed
	Sgt. G Grimshaw Killed
	Aust Sgt. J Morrision POW Inj.
	Aust Sgt. CR Buckeridge Killed
	Sgt. GW Fletcher Killed
	Aust Sgt. DR Grant Killed
460 Sqdn: Lancaster DV 160	Aust FO WJ Dennett Killed
	Aust FO A Flashman Killed
	Sgt. EA Bogle Killed
	Sgt. RE Watson Killed
	Sgt. T Williams Killed
	Aust PO W Emery Killed
	Aust Sgt. D Birk Killed
619 Sqdn; Lancaster ED 980	PO K McCulloch Killed
Crashed Brabant	FO H Forshaw Killed
	Sgt. L Timms Killed
	Sgt. RE Tofts Killed
	Sgt. NO Richards Killed
	Can Sgt. RH Van Camp Killed
	Sgt. PJ Ruane Killed

Total 115 Killed, 12 POWs, 2 Evaded

21 – 22 June 1943

7 Sqdn: Stirling R9266-J	Flt. Lt. LD Ince Killed. From Barbados, WI
Tried to force land	PO JW Roch POW
	Flt. Sgt. F Fray POW Stalag 4.
	Sgt. E Davenport POW
	PO AG Collings POW Stalag 3
	Flt. Sgt. Allock POW
	Flt. Lt. HA Winfield POW Stalag 3

SQUADRON AND AIRCRAFT	CREW
7 Sqdn: Stirling EF 366-L	Aust FO RB Meiklejohn Killed NZ PO CGH Redwood Killed Sgt. LE Ellingham POW Sgt. WE Cole POW Sgt. F Hugo POW Sgt. H Kilfoyle POW Flt. Sgt. EA Brown POW
7 Sqdn: Stirling EF 387-D OC 'A' Flight	Sqn. Ldr. CA Hughes POW Stalag 3 Flt. Lt. GB Boreham POW Stalag 3 2nd Pilot Sqn. Ldr. GO Bastian POW Stalag 3 Combat NZ Flt. Sgt. WI Hansen POW Flt. Sgt. ATH Perkins POW Stalag 6 NZ PO TJ Elliott POW Flt. Sgt. CFP Brown POW Flt. Sgt. GT Cox Killed
7 Sqdn: Stirling R 9272-W Shot down by night-fighter flown by Hpt. Mighius near Alphan	Flt. Lt. JS Warr DFC Killed Flt. Lt. FA Tompkins DFC Killed PO JH Ross DFM POW Sgt. DS Donaldson Killed Sgt. AJ Sutton Killed PO MP Ellis POW Sgt. Dukes Killed
15 Sqdn: Stirling BK 815-V	PO EF Curtis Killed Sgt. AF Stephens Killed Can PO RJ Hunter Killed Sgt. RT Davis Killed PO E Billington Killed Sgt. AE Waugh POW Sgt. JP Martin Killed Flt. Sgt. FD McQueen POW
35 Sqdn: Halifax BB 361	Sgt. JW Andrews Killed Sgt. DJ Jones Killed Sgt. RAD Muldon Killed Sgt. RM Scott Killed Sgt. FV Barnard Killed Sgt. NT MacAulay Killed Can Sgt. WD Robertson Killed
35 Sqdn: Halifax HR 685 Shot down by night-fighter over Holland	Flt. Lt. TH Lane POW WO GW Darling POW Flt. Lt. PM Jackson POW Flt. Sgt. REH MacDonald POW Flt. Sgt. FJ Rogers POW Flt. Sgt. PA Balson POW FO DR Alexander DFC POW
35 Sqdn: Halifax HR 799 Hit by flak over Holland	NZ PO WH Hickson Evaded Aust Sgt. SH Kohn Killed. 2nd Pilot Sgt. J Graham Killed Flt. Sgt. AD Hutchinson POW Sgt. PH Croft POW Sgt. J Graham POW Sgt. JF Dowsing POW Flt. Sgt. WGL Brown Killed Sgt. FJ Maltas POW

SQUADRON AND AIRCRAFT	CREW
35 Sqdn: Halifax HR 848 Crashed Eiheneuval near Uden, Holland	Flt. Sgt. R Quigly POW FO ST John Killed Sgt. FJ Williams POW Sgt. JI Barrie Killed Sgt. FR Carpenter POW Sgt. J White Killed FO RB Capon Killed
35 Sqdn: Halifax W 7878	FO MUP Clarke Killed Sgt. FM Mazin Killed Sgt. HR Fink Killed. Washed up Bergen 4.7.43 Sgt. C Harcombe Killed Sgt. BN Dowse Killed Can Sgt. J Richer Killed Sgt. AC MacLeod Killed
44 Sqdn: Lancaster LM 330	Sgt. H Thompson Killed Sgt. SD Mindel Killed Sgt. NN England Killed Sgt. LR McGrath Killed Sgt. L Harrison Killed Sgt. N Metcalfe Killed Sgt. L Welsh 2nd Pilot Killed Sgt. JH Arlow Killed
51 Sqdn: Halifax JD 244 Crashed Belgium	Sgt. F Heathfield POW FO Duthie POW Sgt. W Beresford POW Sgt. D Keane POW Sgt. W Poulton POW Can Sgt. R Masters POW Sgt. R Cooper POW
57 Sqdn; Lancaster W 4377	Sgt. Kitson Killed Sgt. AD Pain Killed Sgt. LJ Ray POW Sgt. G Hull Killed Sgt. M Burston Killed Sgt. G Robinson Killed Sgt. H Alexander Killed
77 Sqdn: Halifax W 1157	Sgt. MJ Fitzgerald Killed Sgt. G Wood Killed WO2 FO Turner Killed Sgt. R Forster Killed FO JM Dalton Killed Sgt. JJ McPherson Killed FO RC Bishop Killed
77 Sqdn: Halifax JD 205-Y Attacked by Night-fighter Crashed Boxdel, Holland	Sgt. J Gardener POW Sgt. F Hawthorne POW Inj. Can Sgt. DA Clarke POW Sgt. S Nicholson POW PO A Hagan Evaded Sgt. RH King Killed Can Sgt. AR Currie Killed
77 Sqdn: Halifax JB 852 Hit by flak Crashed Harskamp	Sgt. G Hirsch Killed Sgt. CW Falckh Killed Sgt. NV Hickering Killed Sgt. J Phillips Killed Sgt. R Kingsland Killed Sgt. WG Garratt Died in a field hospital 11.7.43 Sgt. E Dawson Killed

SQUADRON AND AIRCRAFT	CREW
83 Sqdn: Lancaster EE 121-K Crashed North Sea	PO H Mappin Killed. Washed up 2.7.43 Sgt. AG Boar Killed Sgt. A Crank Killed Sgt. CF Wiggett Killed Sgt. GA Linett Killed. Washed up 24.6.43 Sgt. W Anderson Killed Sgt. F Turner Killed
83 Sqdn: Lancaster ED 997-R Attacked by night-fighter flown by Hpt. Maurer Crashed Uffelt	Flt. Sgt. DW Fletcher Killed Flt. Sgt. L Angell Killed Sgt. V Tanner Killed Sgt. E Lidster Killed Sgt. A McWilliams Killed Sgt. R Metclafe Killed Can Sgt. GC Wiekson Killed
90 Sqdn: Stirling EE 887 Crashed near Workum, Hoogwoud	Aust PO HN Peters Killed Sgt. DJ Daniels Killed Sgt. BA Abraham Killed Sgt. D Gillis Killed Sgt. E Bradshaw Killed Sgt. A Andrews Killed Can Sgt. R Law Killed
100 Sqdn: Lancaster ED 556	Can PO JR Thurlow Killed Sgt. CE Thompson Killed Sgt. A Jarman Killed Sgt. H Pyle Killed Sgt. KE Walters Killed Sgt. S Maisner Killed Sgt. G Norton Killed
101 Sqdn: Lancaster ED 650	Sgt. DH Brook Killed Sgt. G Hopkins Killed Flt. Lt. WJ Sibbard DFC Killed Sgt. R Keightley Killed Sgt. T Latter Killed Sgt. N Ellis Killed Sgt. K Hanson Killed
149 Sqdn: Stirling BK 799-O Shot down by night-fighter near Zandkop Lawrie had only been married seven days. Two ops. to complete his tour. The crew jumped too late	PO J Lawrie Killed FO DH Lynek Killed Sgt. D Fudge Killed Sgt. J Atkinson Killed Sgt. A Coull Killed Sgt. EC Waite Killed Sgt. EG Hird Killed
156 Sqdn: Lancaster ED 885	FO J Marson Killed Sgt. GAP Edwards Killed Sgt. JA Ottey Killed Sgt. EA Bowaman Killed Sgt. FJ Willett Killed Sgt. A Shacklady Killed Sgt. GW Brown Killed
158 Sqdn: Halifax HR 735-N Shot down by night-fighter flown by Hpt. Frank Kaathoven near Breda, Uden area	NZ PO CH Robinson Killed Sgt. G Hull Killed Sgt. HF Barham Killed Sgt. GGB Hayes Killed Sgt. W Dunning Killed Sgt. DG Cuthbert Killed Sgt. GB Maycock Killed Sgt. EH Fisher Killed. 2nd Pilot

SQUADRON AND AIRCRAFT	CREW
166 Sqdn: Wellington HE 924	Sgt. A Burgess Killed Sgt. GR Wright Killed Aust Flt. Sgt. JK Somers Killed Flt. Sgt. WF Payne Killed Sgt. E Jeffs Killed
218 Sqdn: Stirling BK 712	Aust PO W Shillinglaw Killed Flt. Sgt. DJ Ashby-Peckenham Killed Sgt. R Goward Killed Sgt. TR Lunn Killed Sgt. AE Gurney Killed Sgt. ED Hart Killed Danish FO AH Helvadd 2nd Pilot Killed. Attached from 1651HCU
218 Sqdn: Stirling BK 722 Hit by flak Sterkel	Aust PO DR Rich Killed Sgt. F Fawcett POW Sgt. AJ Small POW Sgt. H Hill POW Sgt. Kermode Killed Can Sgt. J McDonald Killed Sgt. S Burrows Killed
300 Sqdn: Wellington HE 327-S	Pol Sgt. M Bronicki Killed Pol Sgt. M Glass Killed. Washed up 8.7.43 Pol Sgt. S Jama Killed Pol Sgt. S Nogacki Killed Pol Sgt. J Lezuch Killed
300 Sqdn: Wellington HE 985-W	Pol Flt. Sgt. M Bialobrowka Killed Pol PO J Blajda Killed Pol Sgt. F Trzcbucholdliski Killed Pol Sgt. T Ciuchinski Killed Pol Sgt. R Jacennik Killed Pol Sgt. S Szpalinsci Killed
305 Sqdn: Wellington HE 347-F Shot down by night-fighter west of Antwerp	Pol Sgt. S Szpalinsci Killed Pol PO J Gasecki Evaded Sgt. R Raczowsic POW Sgt. A Frier POW Sgt. L Makarski Killed
405 Sqdn: Halifax JD 124	Flt. Lt. SL Murrell Killed Can PO FW Hodge Killed Can PO RA Livingstone Killed Can Sgt. AW Nichols BEM Killed Can PO JHJ Lemierig Killed Can Flt. Sgt. ED Rowe Killed Can Sgt. RL Robinson Killed
408 Sqdn: Halifax DT 772-E Shot down by night-fighter Zeist, Holland	Sgt. D Brocke Killed Can Sgt. GE Samuels Killed Sgt. M Shakespeare Killed Can Sgt. CL Sebelius Killed Can Sgt. J MacDonald Killed Can Sgt. WD Welsh Killed
408 Sqdn: Halifax BB 375-T	Can Sgt. C Reichert Killed Can PO JC Russell POW Sgt. J Dockerill Killed Sgt. G McLean Killed PO J Monoham Killed Can PO G Pridham Killed Can Sgt. W Searle Killed

SQUADRON AND AIRCRAFT	CREW
408 Sqdn: Halifax JD 209-B	Can PO JGA Patry Killed Can Flt. Sgt. N Kellner Killed Sgt. GA Freeman POW Can Sgt. JHW Bishop POW Sgt. D Rudge POW Can Sgt. Moorcroft POW
419 Sqdn: Halifax W 1271	NZ PO CR Pearse Killed NZ PO WT Ellis Killed Sgt. WJ Randall Killed Can Sgt. JF Holland Killed Sgt. GJD Thompson Killed Sgt. J Galloway Killed NZ Flt. Sgt. EL Robson Killed
429 Sqdn: Wellington HR 789	Can PO GH Debussac Killed Can PO MB Spence Killed Can Flt. Sgt. GD Coe Killed Can FO WA Follows Killed Can Sgt. D Palmatier Killed
429 Sqdn: Wellington HE 981 Shot down by night-fighter flown by Hpt. Forster Venlo	Can FO LF Lown Killed Can Sgt. A Sieffert Killed Can Sgt. AS Rhodes Killed Can Sgt. J Wood Killed Can WO2 WH Calder Killed
429 Sqdn: Wellington HZ 519	Can Flt. Sgt. E Star Killed Can Sgt. J Kopchuk Can Sgt. CF Orlmiski Killed. Washed up 26.6.43 Sgt. PG O'Reilly Killed. Washed up 22.6.43 Can Sgt. W Parkinson
431 Sqdn: Wellington HF 518	Wg Cdr. J Coverdale Killed PO GCW Parslow Killed FO JBG Bailey Killed Can WO2 HS Fawns Killed PO BS Fudge Killed
460 Sqdn: Lancaster W 4939 Crashed Ijsselmeer	Aust Sgt. AW Teerman Killed Sgt. ALT Hoskins Killed Sgt. J Cassell Killed PO HJ Trafford Killed Sgt. H Thomson POW Sgt. J Hetherington Killed Sgt. BD O'Neil Killed
619 Sqdn: EE 198-H	Sgt. D Jordan Killed FO W Girdwood Killed Sgt. B Howe Killed Sgt. WA Davies Killed Sgt. E Stanley Killed Sgt. WJ Park Killed Sgt. F Burton Killed

Total 221 Killed, 41 POWs, 3 Evaded, 1 Died later

22 – 23 June 1943

9 Sqdn: Lancaster ED 699 Crashed München Gladbach	Sgt. K Dennes Killed Sgt. AG Bryan Killed Sgt. AFS Day Killed Sgt. C Hunt Killed PO RW Winfield Killed Sgt. GF Kilby Killed. Washed up 23.6.43 Sgt. E Gelaghty Killed

SQUADRON AND AIRCRAFT	CREW
10 Sqdn: Halifax BB 324 Shot down by night-fighter over North Sea near Zandvoort	Sgt. RM Pinkerton Killed Sgt. FT Nuttall Killed Sgt. W Warning Killed Sgt. F Holmes Killed Sgt. J Conway Killed Flt. Sgt. TL MacAshill Killed Flt. Sgt. JFK Crowe Killed
15 Sqdn: Stirling EF 348-N Shot down by night-fighter Dutch coast	Flt. Sgt. JW Newport Killed PO D Turner Evaded Sgt. T Mosdale POW Inj. Sgt. A Kellett Evaded Sgt. J Damobuise POW Sgt. D Roberts POW Sgt. W MacAuly Killed
15 Sqdn: Stirling BK 656-A	FO JV Hawkins Killed Flt. Sgt. AW Crozier Killed Sgt. DJ Tickle Killed FO L Gwynne Killed Sgt. GC Hutton Killed Sgt. M Webster Killed Sgt. FH Williams Killed
51 Sqdn: Halifax JD 251 Crashed Cologne	Sgt. RH Elliott Killed Sgt. Bennett Killed Sgt. F Hawes Killed Sgt. J Davidson POW. Repatriated 6.2.45 Arundel Castle Sgt. WR Newton Killed Sgt. S Kennedy Killed Sgt. CJ Matthews Killed
75 Sqdn: Stirling EF 399 Crashed Markelo Wesk Goor, The Netherlands	NZ Flt Sgt. K Burbridge Killed NZ Sgt. W Wilcockson Killed NZ Sgt. DE Martin Killed Sgt. G Lockey Killed NZ Sgt. AJ Mecewin Killed Sgt. G Cameron Killed Sgt. KF Shawk Killed
75 Sqdn: Stirling BK 810 Crashed Ijsselmeer	NZ WO F MacKenzie Killed NZ Sgt. AE West POW Repatriated NZ Sgt. BH Broadmead POW Sgt. RA Triptree POW NZ Sgt. JF Blank Killed NZ Sgt. E McConigal POW Sgt. RG Cyrstal POW
75 Sqdn: Stirling EF 408 Crashed Gelsenkirchen Town	Sgt. BB Wood Killed NZ Sgt. Samson Killed Sgt. EH Reader Killed Sgt. SL Webb Killed NZ Sgt. SR Bissett Killed Sgt. FS Hobbs Killed Sgt. CB Hemmings Killed
75 Sqdn: Stirling EH 889 Crashed Ijsselmeer RD Todd and RE Todd were twins	FO TF McCrorie Killed. Washed up 5.7.43 PO W Stuckley Killed. Washed up 24.7.43 Can Sgt. RD Todd DFM Killed Sgt. E Grainger Killed NZ FO JL Richards Killed Can Sgt. RE Todd DFM Killed Sgt. RA Kennedy Killed

SQUADRON AND AIRCRAFT	CREW
76 Sqdn: Halifax DK 224-Q Crashed four miles south-west of Utrecht Last to reach the target	PO J Carrie POW Sgt. G Thomason POW Sgt. EM McVitie POW Can Sgt. R Hammett POW Sgt. SM Davies POW Sgt. R Huke Killed. Neck broken by parachute Sgt. RW Hibbs POW Gp/Capt DEL Wilson POW. 2nd Pilot. Station Commander, Holme-on-Spalding Moor
77 Sqdn: Halifax JD 213 Crashed Egmont	Aust Flt. Sgt. EA Sims Killed Flt. Sgt. D Kell Killed Sgt. T Ogle Killed Can Sgt. O Thompson Killed Sgt. J Westbain Killed Sgt. TW Luther Killed Sgt. J Fitzsimons Killed
77 Sqdn: Halifax DT 700	Flt. Lt. CC Marshall Killed Sgt. PM Thornycroft Killed Sgt. WF Fades Killed Sgt. W Hughes Killed Sgt. GR Hill Killed Sgt. GK Hazell Killed Sgt. WC Lewis Killed
78 Sqdn: Halifax HB 855 Shot down by night-fighter Dinther	Flt. Lt. LH Knight Killed Sgt. G Duffee Evaded PO H Standfast POW FO RD Caldecourt Killed FO SAC Cutler Killed Sgt. FC Simons Killed Sgt. FJR Bain Killed Sgt. JH Lee POW
78 Sqdn: Halifax W 7390 Crashed on a farm in Renswoude	Flt. Sgt. EA Tipler Killed Sgt. JE Woodward Killed Sgt. W Anderson Killed Sgt. CP Johns Killed Sgt. LD Lingwood Killed Sgt. DE Tuddenham Killed Sgt. TH Bell Killed
83 Sqdn: Lancaster W 4982-O	Sgt. ME Rust Killed Sgt. L Ashworth Killed Sgt. JM Hurson Killed Sgt. EC Stally Killed Sgt. S Williams Killed Sgt. D Chapman POW Sgt. FF Foden Killed
90 Sqdn: Stirling BK 804	Flt. Sgt. JA Robson Killed Sgt. G Kipling Killed Sgt. J Picton Killed Sgt. D Sanders Killed Sgt. CR Kenwick Killed Sgt. R Hammond Killed Sgt. N Graham Killed
90 Sqdn: Stirling BK 665 Crashed Appledoorn	Sgt. DC McNair Killed Sgt. JS Porter Killed Sgt. A Thomson Killed Sgt. FA Hamer POW Sgt. DC Davids POW Sgt. BT Smy POW Sgt. GW Lawson Killed

SQUADRON AND AIRCRAFT	CREW
97 Sqdn: Lancaster ED 928 Shot down by night-fighter Utrecht. A huge fire started several citizens killed	PO GW Armstrong Killed Can WO II JBSPH David Killed Flt. Sgt. JJ Mansfield Killed Sgt. DE Williams Killed FO S Blackhurst Killed Flt. Sgt. AR Laing POW Inj. Sgt. E Bellis POW
101 Sqdn: Lancaster LM 325-U Shot down by night-fighter flown by Oblt. Werner Baake Between Beuningen and Nijmegen	Sgt. RA Waterhouse Killed Sgt. J Osborne Killed FO TB Tomkins Killed Sgt. E Smith Killed Sgt. EA Williams POW Sgt. V Sugden Killed Sgt. RB Cooper Killed
103 Sqdn: Lancaster ED 773-U	Can Flt. Lt. AE Spurr Killed PO FL Griffiths Killed FO DM Grant Killed Sgt. JWM Jones Killed PO WH Wood Killed Sgt. AE Ponsford Killed Can Sgt. WG Moran Killed
156 Sqdn: Lancaster ED 599 Crashed Maarn	Aust Flt. Sgt. J Winterburn Killed PO EG Grove Killed Sgt. W Bembridge Killed Sgt. W Gordon Killed Sgt. EA Duchene Killed Sgt. WP Smith Killed Flt. Lt. J Crawley Killed
158 Sqdn: Halifax JD 259-R	Aust Flt. Sgt. L Cavanagh Killed Sgt. TR Forster Killed Sgt. WR Green Killed Sgt. RJ Sage Killed PO DV Elliot Killed PO RAC Maund Killed Sgt. O Todd Killed
207 Sqdn: Lancaster ED 692-W	FO PG Herrin Killed Can FO WH Flatt Killed Sgt. S Payton Killed Sgt. R Bradshaw Killed Sgt. P Mills Killed PO G Kleinberg Killed Sgt. GAH Male Killed
214 Sqdn: Stirling EH 882	Flt. Lt. J Werner POW Sgt. GR Averson POW Sgt. SG Morrison POW Sgt. GM Phillips Killed Sgt. PE Goldsmid POW Can Sgt. R McNeill Killed Sgt. KS Gillarom POW
218 Sqdn: Stirling BF 572 Crashed Holland	Aust Flt. Sgt. JB Smith Killed Sgt. RH Cramm Killed Sgt. CR Minns Killed Sgt. GE Rose Killed Sgt. WH Davies Killed Flt. Sgt. PW Farr POW Can Flt. Sgt. Glabuik Killed

SQUADRON AND AIRCRAFT	CREW
427 Sqdn: Halifax DK 139 Crashed Warnsveld	Can PO GA Cadmus Killed Can FO GT Vicary Killed Can Sgt. AD Deane Killed Sgt. G Booth Killed FO AJ Manning Killed Can Sgt. CP Bearisto Killed Can PO M Mayer Killed
427 Sqdn: Halifax DK 141	Can Sgt. J Hamilton Killed Can Sgt. J Reansbury Killed Sgt. N Whitting Killed Can Sgt. JA Spencer POW Sgt. GD Sharp Killed Can Sgt. J Dennis Killed Can Sgt. G Tyrone Killed
427 Sqdn: Halifax DK 191	Can FO DM Reid Killed Can PO A Parisean Killed Can PO B Grazie Killed Sgt. D Mann Killed Sgt. P Robinson Killed Can Sgt. H Hexim Killed Can Sgt. NF Notley Killed
427 Sqdn: Halifax DK 225 Crashed on a farm West-Mijzen	Can Flt. Lt. K Webster Killed Sgt. T Mitchell POW. Broke a leg Sgt. AE Humphreys Killed Sgt. C Sampson Killed NZ Sgt. ER Strong Killed Can Flt. Sgt. GL Tucker Killed NZ Flt. Sgt. D Northcoat Killed
429 Sqdn: Wellington HZ 312	Can Wg/Cdr. JL Savard Killed Can FO JS MacIntyre Killed WO J Allen Killed Can WO1 JGA Laberge Killed Can PO R Bonenfant Killed
429 Sqdn: Wellington HF 457 Crashed Haselt	Can PO WA Sneath Killed Can PO RG Clarke POW Can Sgt. J Hindley Killed Can Sgt. J Hills Killed Can PO AB Drummon-Hay POW
431 Sqdn: Wellington HE 394 Crashed München Gladbach	Flt. Lt. DA Hine Killed FO HD Quilter Killed Sgt. RE Mercer Killed Sgt. E Batty Killed Sgt. AE Wilkes Killed
460 Sqdn: Lancaster EE166 Crashed Mulhein area in Heissen Germany	FO LE Harrison Killed Sgt. WH Bartlett Killed Sgt. SK Brown Killed Sgt. JS Calcutta Killed PO RJ Hepperman Killed Sgt. JAC Cotton Killed Aust Sgt. RJ Lockrey Killed
466 Sqdn: Wellington HE 326	PO AL Ford Killed Sgt. CW Hewitt Killed Sgt. RW Fox POW PO RL Amesbury Killed Sgt. AH Richardson Killed

SQUADRON AND AIRCRAFT	CREW
620 Sqdn: Stirling EE 875	Sgt. T Nicholson Killed Sgt. KW Read Killed Sgt. AAT Woodward Killed Sgt. RO Jasper Killed FO WH Boundy Killed Sgt. R Jackson Killed Sgt. HJ Wells Killed
Total 202 Killed, 29 POWs, 3 Evaded	

24 – 25 June 1943

SQUADRON AND AIRCRAFT	CREW
7 Sqdn: Stirling EF 392-N	Aust Sqn. Ldr. JR Savage Killed. OC 'C' Flight WO PH Haines Killed. 2nd Pilot Flt. Sgt. SJ Barnes Killed Sgt. AA Caley Killed FO GH Cox Killed Sgt. GA Errington Killed Sgt. NR Morrison Killed Sgt. DR Spanton Killed
7 Sqdn: Stirling R9281-V Crashed North Sea off Dutch coast	Fiji FO AJ Davis Killed Flt. Sgt. ARJ Hunt Killed. Washed up 30.6.43 Sgt. G Thompson Killed Sgt. R Glover Killed. Washed up 15.7.43 FO JF Hanrahan Killed Sgt. GC Carter Killed. Washed up 11.8.43 Flt. Sgt. F Fazackkerley Killed
7 Sqdn: Lancaster ED 595-Q Shot down by night-fighter flown by Oblt. Rath Rilland. The first Lancaster of 7 Sqdn to be lost near Antwerp	Wg/Cdr. RG Barrell DSO DFC Killed on his 60th operation. One short to complete his second tour. Awarded DSO 11.6.43 PO SG Keatley DFM POW Flt. Lt. HG Hudson DFM Escaped WO EG Pointer DFM Killed WO JA Pieson DFM POW NZ Flt. Lt. F Hilton DFC Killed Flt. Lt. JA Emery POW
50 Sqdn: Lancaster ED 712	Aust Flt. Sgt. JA Brock Killed Sgt. TW Page Killed Sgt. RA Cookson Killed Sgt. B Veall Killed Sgt. TG Williamson Killed Sgt. LL Seal Killed Sgt. W Pearson Killed
51 Sqdn: Halifax JD 250 Crashed in North Sea	FO JN MacKenzie Killed. Washed up 11.8.43 Sgt. RW Stevenson Killed PO A Fitchett Killed. Washed up 15.7.43 Can Sgt. W Blackie Killed FO CA Johnson Killed Can Sgt. W Andrews Killed Sgt. RE Murdoch Killed. Washed up 14.7.43
57 Sqdn: Lancaster ED 781	Sgt. S Fallows Killed Sgt. H Maiman Killed Sgt. WG Day Killed Sgt. JW Sykes Killed Sgt. IH Lamdin POW Sgt. JJM Green Killed Sgt. RB Simpson Killed

SQUADRON AND AIRCRAFT	CREW
75 Sqdn: Stirling EH 902	NZ PO B Bluck Killed NZ Flt. Sgt. J Cooksey Killed Flt. Sgt. M Kendlan Killed Sgt. JW Gillard Killed Sgt. D Armitage Killed Sgt. LR Cant Killed NZ Sgt. GW Strang Killed
76 Sqdn: Halifax DK 166-D Hit by flak	Can Flt. Lt. GH Cheetham Killed PO JD Danks POW Sgt. KR Newton POW Sgt. RH Evans POW Sgt. GI Simpkins Killed Sgt. J Sweeney POW Sgt. S Harper POW
78 Sqdn: Halifax JB 962	NZ Sgt. K Morrison Killed Sgt. P Kennedy Killed Sgt. I McCrae Killed Sgt. T Payne Killed Sgt. W Cox Killed Sgt. W Barry Killed Sgt. E Collingwood Killed
90 Sqdn: Stirling BK 813	Aust Flt. Sgt. WA Teede Killed Sgt. H Levine Killed NZ Flt. Sgt. N Peterson Killed Sgt. EA Stanton POW Sgt. AC Harris Killed Sgt. PJ Taylor Killed NZ Flt. Sgt. G Henderson Killed
90 Sqdn: Stirling BK 628	Sgt. JM Steel Killed Sgt. AN Cooper Killed Sgt. H Taylorson Killed Sgt. CW Dixon Killed Sgt. JC Gardner Killed Sgt. WN Nisbet Killed Sgt. J Yarwood Killed
97 Sqdn: Lancaster LM 327-B	Flt. Lt. JL Moore Killed Can Sqn. Ldr. JP McMillan Killed Flt. Sgt. A Tomlinson Killed Flt. Sgt. RA Kerckhove Killed PO WJ Stephen Killed Sgt. JW Darroch Killed Sgt. LL Davis Killed
101 Sqdn: Lancaster W 4311-O	Sgt. JEW Lane Killed Sgt. TW Connor Killed Sgt. J Barker Killed Sgt. SE Williams Killed Sgt. T Twohy Killed Sgt. N Fotheringham Killed Sgt. CW Ridley Killed
102 Sqdn: Halifax JD 144 Crashed Florennes	Sgt. KRW Shepperd Killed Sgt. AG Tovey Killed Sgt. FA Gettings Killed Sgt. JJ McDonald Killed Sgt. RH Clark Killed Sgt. C Rushton POW Sgt. WR Cole POW

SQUADRON AND AIRCRAFT	CREW
156 Sqdn: Lancaster EE 127	Aust WO L Brown POW Flt. Sgt. A Newell POW Sgt. J Malpas POW Sgt. IH Bradley POW Can Sgt. S Worthington POW Sgt. R Gilbert POW Sgt. C Easton POW
156 Sqdn: Lancaster ED 858-R	PO RJ Hudson Killed Sgt. R Brown Killed Sgt. WS Brooks Killed Sgt. H Jones Killed Sgt. AT Barlow Killed Sgt. K Richards Killed Sgt. KC Adams Killed
166 Sqdn: Wellington HF 594 Crashed Brussels	Can PO RE Currie Killed Sgt. M Cawthra Killed Sgt. GH Williams Killed Flt. Sgt. N Towzel Killed Sgt. F Needham Killed
214 Sqdn: Stirling EE 883 Crashed in North Sea	Sgt. CR Miller Killed Sgt. PD Stratton Killed Sgt. RH Smith Killed Sgt. J Hitchins Killed Sgt. R Akera Killed. Washed up 8.8.43 Sgt. T Jones Killed Sgt. S Seward Killed. Washed up 14.7.43
218 Sqdn: Stirling EH 892	Sqn. Ldr. A Beck Killed PO HB Barrett Killed FO L Flynn Killed Flt. Sgt. SG Garbett Killed NZ PO RV Hopkins Killed Sgt. E Quigley POW FO R Nuttall POW PO RJ Johnson Killed. 2nd Pilot
218 Sqdn: Stirling BF 501	Can Sgt. JW Hoey Killed Flt. Sgt. LA De Botte Killed Sgt. AW Erne Killed Sgt. J Thomson Killed Sgt. RL Ergoose Killed Sgt. DTE Lloyd Killed Flt. Sgt. S Garrod Killed
300 Sqdn: Wellington HF 606-L	Sgt. S Jawoszek Killed Flt. Lt. J Obrycki Killed Sgt. F Skoskiwicz Killed Sgt. E Bartosiak Killed Sgt. F Jalenicz Killed
300 Sqdn: Wellington HZ 376-G Hit by flak near Krefeld	FO W Turecki POW Sgt. A Bielski Killed Sgt. K Zarniewski Killed Sgt. J Bijowski Killed Sgt. R Kosiarski POW
405 Sqdn: Halifax HR 816-C Shot down by night-fighter	Sgt. P Andrews POW Inj. Sgt. G Jones POW Sgt. F Bwker POW Sgt. CW Price POW Sgt. W Kingsley POW Sgt. CG Tisbury POW Can Sgt. JN Kunedsky Killed

SQUADRON AND AIRCRAFT	CREW
419 Sqdn: Halifax JD 258	Sgt. R Whitfield Killed Can PO RJL Fowler Killed FO WA Donnelly Killed Sgt. C Gorton Killed Sgt. B Stephenson Killed Sgt. JE Dean Killed Can Sgt. MP Kimber Killed
419 Sqdn: Halifax JD 214 SOS sent out over target and over Holland	Can Sgt. GV Neale POW Can Sgt. RS Lachlan POW Can Sgt. WN Jaffaray POW Sgt. DJ Griffiths POW Sgt. RA Cleaver POW Can Sgt. DE Kenwell POW Sgt. WR McLeod POW
419 Sqdn: Halifax JD 147	Can Flt. Lt. BN Jost Killed Sgt. EB Pope POW NZ Flt. Sgt. AA Bruce POW Can FO ROE Goodwin Killed Can Sgt. JD Johnson Killed Flt. Sgt. L Barker POW Sgt. RE Austin POW
427 Sqdn: Halifax DK 180-A Crashed Oudorp near Alkmaar	Can FO LW Somers Killed Can FO M Shvemar Killed Can FO VM White POW Sgt. WG Arthur Killed Can Flt. Sgt. JH Walton Killed Sgt. LA Bone POW FC Ashby Killed
432 Sqdn: Wellington HZ 518-A Mercier on his fourth op. The rest on their first op.	Can Sgt. JJC Mercier Killed Can PO JRG Gingras Killed Can Sgt. MR Deverill Killed Can Sgt. M Legace Killed Sgt. MP Tobin Killed
432 Sqdn: Wellington HF 572-J	Sgt. N Goldie Killed Sgt. G Liddle Killed Sgt. FWN Trowbridge Killed Sgt. CK Killick Killed Can Sgt. WA Sparrow Killed
460 Sqdn: Lancaster W4320 Hit by flak over target. Stooke, Crane, Toohig and Conklin captured by the Gestapo in Paris	Aust Sgt. G Stooke POW Aust Sgt. CR Crane POW Aust Sgt. D Toohig POW Sgt. L Broadbent POW Aust Sgt. NF Conklin POW Aust Sgt. FB Shaw POW Aust Sgt. SR Nowlan POW Inj.
620 Sqdn: Stirling BK 800 Shot down by night-fighter near Wuppertal	Sgt. RP Reynolds Killed FO J Needham POW Sgt. J Garbutt Killed Sgt. J Lindley Killed Sgt. JD Cresswell Killed PO R Burke POW Sgt. PJ Court Killed

Total 166 Killed, 55 POWs, 1 Evaded

SQUADRON AND AIRCRAFT	CREW
Crashed in the UK on return	
620 Sqdn: BF 724 Hit by flak. Crashed at Chedburgh Two members of the crew injured	Sgt. P O'Connell
25 – 26 June 1943	
9 Sqdn: Lancaster ED 831 Crashed Ijsselmeer near Andijk	Sqn. Ldr. AM Hobbs DFC Killed Sgt. KG Mott Killed. Washed up 5.7.43 Sgt. EC Bishop Killed Sgt. EW Sanderson Killed Sgt. CP King Killed. Washed up 5.7.43 Sgt. WC Rowlands Killed Flt. Sgt. W Slater Killed FO JH Smas Killed. Washed up 5.7.43
15 Sqdn: Stirling BK 699 Shot down by night-fighter Crashed Wadden Zee	PO MA Chapman Killed PO RJ Pavely DFM Killed Sgt. J Condron Killed Sgt. TE Warbey Killed FO A Woodward Killed Sgt. AK Smith Killed
44 Sqdn: Lancaster R 5740 Crashed North Sea 30 miles north-west of Den Helder	PO DM Sharp Killed Flt. Sgt. T Johnstone Killed Flt. Sgt. RJ Dash Killed Sgt. HC Thompson Killed Sgt. NH Morris Killed Sgt. ELH Griffiths Killed Sgt. KW Langstaffe Killed
51 Sqdn: Halifax HR 731 Crashed Ijsselmeer 14 miles north-east of Hearderujk Part of the aircraft recovered August 1967	Sgt. A Osmond Killed Sgt. GC Mortimer Killed. Washed up 5.7.43 Sgt. J Rorison Killed. Washed up 4.7.43 Sgt. P Blundell Killed. Washed up 5.7.43 Sgt. R Huggan Killed Sgt. TG Barton Killed Sgt. J Emerson Killed
51 Sqdn: JD 261 Crashed Wanrooi	FO DHV Davie Killed Sgt. AH Haws Killed Sgt. AD McFarlane Killed Sgt. J Roberts Killed Sgt. AW Fairmannel Killed Sgt. AM Sanders Killed FO DG Howse Killed
57 Sqdn: Lancaster ED 943	Flt. Lt. DH Reid DFC Killed Sgt. JC Evans Killed Sgt. GS Hodges Killed FO WJ Wheeler Killed Sgt. JW Palmer Killed Sgt. O Taffler Killed PO EH Patrick Killed
75 Sqdn: Stirling BK 768 Crashed Ijsselmeer west of Urk	NZ FO WR Perrott Killed NZ Flt. Sgt. GD Thomson Killed NZ Flt. Sgt. CJ White Killed Sgt. CC Mould Killed Sgt. H Squire Killed Sgt. WM Hilditch Killed Sgt. T Colyer Killed

SQUADRON AND AIRCRAFT	CREW
78 Sqdn: Halifax JB 928 Shot down by night-fighter flown by Major Leuche Bergerwly near Bergen	FO HO Oddie Killed in combat Sgt. AH Whitchurch POW PO P Daulby POW Sgt. AD Gillespie POW Flt. Sgt. AJ Guy POW Sgt. TL Robertson POW Can PO DW Lusty POW
99 Sqdn: Stirling EH 900	Aust FO FC McKenzie Killed FO AVI Cook Killed Sgt. LD Campbell Killed Sgt. E Wilson Killed Sgt. WE Walters Killed Sgt. FW Ealden Killed Sgt. JC Davidson Killed
100 Sqdn: Lancaster ED 988 Crashed near Beemster	Flt. Sgt. LJ Naile Killed Sgt. RW Mepstead Killed FO CP Reynolds Killed Sgt. C Connah Killed Sgt. J Dillon Killed Flt. Sgt. LG Perritt Killed Sgt. L Bennett Killed
101 Sqdn: Lancaster ED 373-K Crashed Ijsselmeer south of Edam	Aust Flt. Sgt. IW Banks Killed Sgt. HJ Tozey Killed Sgt. JHW Snowden Killed Sgt. HV Brandson Killed Sgt. R Pugh Killed Sgt. NS Mould Killed Sgt. J Brook POW
101 Sqdn: Lancaster LM 318	Sgt. G Hay POW Sgt. T MacLeay Killed Sgt. BL Scott Killed Sgt. WA Bush Killed Aust Sgt. HK Smith Killed Aust Sgt. FL Hull Killed Sgt. T Millins Killed
102 Sqdn: Halifax JB 843-F Shot down by night-fighter	Sgt. K Gore Killed Sgt. JH Wright Killed Sgt. FH Mitchell Killed Sgt. TM Sugden Killed Sgt. TE Judd Killed Sgt. DAH Gough Killed Sgt. JB Foskett Killed
103 Sqdn: Lancaster ED 528	Aust Ft. Sgt. AE Egan POW Aust Flt. Sgt. SB Elliott Killed Aust Flt. Sgt. W Miller POW Sgt. J Brown Killed Sgt. JS Johnstone POW Sgt. HA Horrell Killed Sgt. CA Britten Killed
103 Sqdn: Lancaster W 4901 Crashed Niew Kennap	FO AH Langille POW PO EL Grant POW PO CB Reynolds POW PO D Towers POW Sgt. RL Hollywood Killed Sgt. GJ Wallis Killed PO JH Addison POW

SQUADRON AND AIRCRAFT	CREW
106 Sqdn: Lancaster W 4256 Crashed one mile east of Hippolytushoef, Holland	Sgt. SG White Killed FO JED Craigie Killed PO GW Enright Killed Sgt. EC Crook Killed Sgt. ET Harding Killed Flt. Sgt. M Bridgewood Killed Sgt. JF Bates Killed
106 Sqdn: Lancaster W 4367 Crashed Ijsselmeer 13 miles north-west of Hardewijk	PO PJ Page Killed. Washed up 3.7.43 Flt. Sgt. J Hancock Killed. Washed up 3.7.43 Flt. Sgt. J Pass DFM Killed. Washed up 5.7.43 Sgt. EE Tyler Killed Sgt. J MacMillan Killed. Washed up 8.7.43 Flt. Sgt. HE Davies Killed Flt. Sgt. JC Welch Killed
106 Sqdn: Lancaster EE 125	Aust Sqn. Ldr. AM Young Killed Sgt. PE Beris Killed Flt. Sgt. CL Mallet DFM Killed Sgt. JR Hayle Killed Can Sgt. AN Dickson Killed Sgt. GH Peel Killed FO J Bell DFM Killed
106 Sqdn: Lancaster R 5572 Crashed near Baak	Sgt. EW Davidson POW Sgt. JG Williams Killed Sgt. EWH Browne Killed Sgt. S Cowgill Killed Sgt. CH Sinclair Killed FO LF Sparling Killed Can Sgt. JA Francis Killed
115 Sqdn: Lancaster DS 663	Sgt. FA Whitehead Killed Sgt. PE Glover Killed PO F Parry Killed Sgt. EGFB Baker Killed Sgt. WM McGowan Killed Sgt. LF Price Killed Sgt. ER Richardson Killed
115 Sqdn: Lancaster DS 666	Sgt. RF Rashley Killed Sgt. CM Sibbald Killed Sgt. A Corns Killed FO G Davidson Killed Sgt. E Green Killed Sgt. A Worsdale Killed Sgt. E Beeston Killed
166 Sqdn: Wellington HE 346 Crashed Ijsselmeer north-west of Makum	Aust Flt. Sgt. CA Matthews Killed Sgt. A Mortimer Killed Sgt. NR Parry Killed Sgt. JP Priestly Killed Sgt. T Ball Killed
166 Sqdn: Wellington HF 589-W Crashed Hekemdorp	Flt. Sgt. MJ Arthur POW Sgt. J Bailey Killed Sgt. J Orr Killed Sgt. J Gaskin Killed Sgt. LA Butterworth POW
196 Sqdn: Wellington HE 412 Crashed Alphen Aan de Rijn	PO NB Smythe Killed PO GW Pollard Killed Sgt. GWH Beach Killed Sgt. EH Sandell POW Sgt. RA Barlow Killed

SQUADRON AND AIRCRAFT	CREW
214 Sqdn: Stirling BK 767 Crashed Aalken	Sgt. B Church Killed Sgt. EG Taylor POW NZ FO KA Neilson POW Sgt. WH Thompson Killed PO J Tritton Killed Sgt. W Davis Killed Sgt. F Mills Killed
218 Sqdn: Stirling EH 898 Shot down by night-fighter over target area	Sgt. EC Hughes Killed NZ PO AE Boulton POW Sgt. BA Jennings Killed Sgt. D O'Sullivan Killed Sgt. GR Jacques Killed Sgt. E Towe Killed Sgt. HS Pagett Killed
218 Sqdn: Stirling EF 430	Sqn. Ldr. DM Maw POW Sgt. R Baker POW Sgt. KW Durnell POW Sgt. D Holden POW Flt. Sgt. JS Foster POW Sgt. WI Thomas POW Sgt. C Cummins POW
427 Sqdn: Halifax DK 190 Shot down by night-fighter flown by Hptn. Oohtmann Gorssel	Can Flt. Sgt. FJ Higgins DFM Killed Can FO T Matynia Killed Can Flt. Sgt. AK Young Killed Can Sgt. H Stikney Killed Can Sgt. B Kashmar Killed Can Flt. Sgt. HG Fronde Killed Sgt. FS Hunter Killed
427 Sqdn: Halifax DK 135	Can PO GA Gagnon Killed. Drowned Can FO RJ Frost POW Can Sgt. LR Page POW Can Sgt. JR Hooley POW Can Sgt. A McKinnon POW Can Sgt. CR Munson POW Sgt. EA Shannon POW
432 Sqdn: Wellington Shot down by night-fighter flown by Lt. Baaker	Sgt. CK Killick Killed Sgt. G Liddle Killed Sgt. N Goldie Killed Flt. Sgt. WA Sparrow Killed Sgt. FWN Trowbridge Killed
466 Sqdn: Wellington HF 544 Crashed Ijsselmeer near island of Urk	Aust Flt. Sgt. ABR Airy Killed Aust FO WE Riley Killed. Washed up 5.7.43 Sgt. MT Atkinson Killed Sgt. GC Green Killed Sgt. GR Johnson Killed

Total 173 Killed, 35 POWs

9 – 10 July 1943

SQUADRON AND AIRCRAFT	CREW
9 Sqdn: Lancaster ED 480 Hit by flak	Can Sgt. JD Duncan POW Flt. Sgt. HT Brown POW Sgt. S Hughes POW Sgt. GC Blunden POW Sgt. G Bartley POW Sgt. LG Warner POW Sgt. DB McMillan POW

SQUADRON AND AIRCRAFT	CREW
12 Sqdn: Lancaster DV 164	Sgt. LF Jefferies Killed Can Sgt. C Reay Killed Sgt. LR Vincent Killed Sgt. J Irwin Killed PO EB Oldham Killed Aust Sgt. Addusal Killed Sgt. JP Meyer Killed
50 Sqdn: Lancaster ED 617	PO RL Hendry Killed FO K Toner Killed Sgt. A Baldwin Killed Sgt. DD Rhynd Killed Sgt. A McDowal Killed Sgt. PA Chapman Killed Sgt. AS Cousins Killed
61 Sqdn: Lancaster W 4763 Hit by flak	Flt. Sgt. JO Imgram Killed Sgt. JD Skinner POW Sgt. JT Sharp POW Inj. Sgt. JE Wood POW Inj. FO RE Ryder POW Sgt. RJ Westcott POW Inj. Aust Flt. Sgt. JR Patching POW
77 Sqdn: Halifax JD 126-C Crashed Arum Witmarsun	Aust Flt. Sgt. KW Morrision Killed Sgt. EF Fare Killed Sgt. GJ Greening Killed Sgt. W McElroy Killed Sgt. KA Forster Killed Sgt. A Thompson Killed Sgt. H Williams Killed
102 Sqdn: Halifax BB 249-Z Attempted to crash-land	Aust Flt. Sgt. AF Fraser Killed Sgt. T Stockton POW Flt. Sgt. GEJ Mansell Killed Sgt. W Morse Killed Sgt. R Brand POW Sgt. R Glass Killed Sgt. H Edwards POW
158 Sqdn: Halifax HR 933-P	Flt. Lt. JS Bridger POW PO WP Banks POW Inj. Sgt. JG Scudamore POW Inj. Sgt. EW Groom POW Inj. Sgt. BR Elden POW Inj. Sgt. R Lake POW Inj. Sgt. GE Kendrick POW Inj.
408 Sqdn: Halifax JB 922-H Crashed Dusseldorf	Can FO TR Mellish Killed Can Sgt. WH Cleasman POW Can Sgt. AN Pexley POW Sgt. JS Pickering POW PO E Crough Killed Sgt. WG Willis POW Can Sgt. WR Prentice Killed
408 Sqdn: Halifax JD 216-P	Can FO HB Lancaster Killed Can Sgt. JJ Stefanchuk Killed Sgt. JM McDonald Killed Sgt. WR Byans Killed Can Sgt. GV Reid Killed Sgt. JHC McChung Killed Sgt. JW Sturgess Killed Can FO JW Richardson Killed

SQUADRON AND AIRCRAFT	CREW
428 Sqdn: Halifax DK 229-W	Sqn. Ldr. FH Bowden DFC/Bar Killed on his 2nd Tour Sgt. HNF Rowe POW Sgt. AJA Reynolds Evaded Sgt. HC McGeach POW PO RJ Gritten POW Sgt. JWN Hurst POW Can PO BM Fitzgerald POW
Total 45 Killed, 25 POWs, 1 Evaded	

25 – 26 July 1943

SQUADRON AND AIRCRAFT	CREW
10 Sqdn: Halifax JD 207 Shot down by night-fighter Noord-Brabant, Holland 26th op.	Sqn. Ldr. FJ Hartnell-Beavis POW PO W Jones Killed PO DB Ackerley Killed Can FO G Downey Killed Sgt. W Collins Killed Sgt. RA Smith Evaded FO A Downey Killed
15 Sqdn: Stirling BK 805-U	Sgt. WA Towse DFM Killed Sgt. WA Fairweather POW Stalag 4B Sgt. NJ Pawley DFM POW Stalag 4B Sgt. HR Brodie POW Stalag 4B Sgt. D Lewis POW Stalag 4B Sgt. DL Moore POW Stalag 4B Sgt. JA Baldwin POW Stalag 4B
35 Sqdn: Halifax JB 787	FO D Milne POW Sgt. NAJ Pearce Killed Sgt. P Price Killed Sgt. DE Killick Killed Sgt. RE Bates POW Sgt. GM Gaubraith Killed Sgt. SH Piper POW
50 Sqdn: Lancaster ED 753 Shot down by night-fighter flown by Hpt. Dieter Frank Wychen, Uden	Aust PO EA Dennis Killed Sgt. H Rogerson POW Aust PO RE Young POW Inj PO LT Beck Killed Flt. Sgt. GL Hill Killed Flt. Sgt. AG Tanner Killed Sgt. R Toulson Killed. Broke his neck baling out Aust Flt. Sgt. DP Every POW. Passenger
51 Sqdn: Halifax HR 934	FO JS Cole Killed PO JS Smyth Killed Sgt. AJ Edwards Killed Sgt. LA Taylor Killed PO G Parkin Killed PO J Sarginson Killed Sgt. GC Thompson Killed
51 Sqdn: Halifax HR 749	Sgt. EJ Jones Killed Sgt. WC Wallace Killed Sgt. W Reid Killed Sgt. J Crowther Killed Sgt. WAL Huddy Killed Sgt. J Ritchie Killed Aust Flt. Sgt. LB York Killed

SQUADRON AND AIRCRAFT	CREW
61 Sqdn: Lancaster ED 613	FO GF Alderdice Killed Sgt. T Davis Killed Sgt. AV Meads Killed Sgt. PA Gore Killed PO A McIntyre Killed Sgt. JHG Renaud Killed Sgt. GE Clark Killed
75 Sqdn: Stirling EE 892 Ditched north coast or Yarmouth	Sgt. MHC Ashdown Killed Sgt. RK Harold Killed Sgt. EC Denyer Killed Sgt. R Broadly Killed Sgt. RW Threadgold Killed Sgt. A Cleaveland Killed Sgt. HC Dawson Killed
77 Sqdn: Halifax JB 838	NZ FO FD Matherson Killed PO DT Davies Killed Sgt. JR Tullt Killed Sgt. KP Froud Killed Sgt. RA Mitchell Killed Sgt. AJ North Killed Sgt. RV Slater Killed
78 Sqdn: Halifax JD 330	PO G Carrington POW FO F King Killed Sgt. CH Daft Killed Sgt. RT Davies POW Sgt. HW Marshall POW PO AE Gale Killed Sgt. T Morris Killed
90 Sqdn: Stirling EE 904 Crashed in North Sea	Sqn. Ldr. J Dugdale DFC Killed NZ Flt. Sgt. JF Bowman Killed Aust Flt. Sgt. DG Evans Killed. 2nd Pilot PO HA Disbouwe Killed Sgt. NA Young Killed PO PH Conray Killed NZ Flt. Sgt. JH Keeley Killed Sgt. DFA Hobbs Killed
102 Sqdn: Halifax JD 169 Crashed in North Sea	Sgt. JN Whitehouse Killed PO GS Smith Killed Sgt. FC Brown Killed Sgt. DC Moon Killed Sgt. AW Evans Killed Flt. Sgt. H Turner Killed
103 Sqdn: Lancaster ED 884 Crashed Noord-Brabant	Sqn. Ldr. GR Carpenter POW Broken ankle Flt. Sgt. K Archer Killed Sgt. KC Tate Killed Sgt. JH Thorton Killed Sgt. GH Newbolt Killed Sgt. JM Bucklitsch POW Sgt. JL Brazil POW PO JAB Cooper Killed
103 Sqdn: Lancaster JA 855	Can Flt. Lt. HE Ewer Killed Sgt. D Williams Killed Sgt. SH Welch Killed Sgt. JWG Wilson Killed Sgt. S Robson Killed Can Sgt. JR Fitch Killed Flt. Sgt. FE Juggins Killed

SQUADRON AND AIRCRAFT	CREW
156 Sqdn: Lancaster ED 734-H Crashed Noord-Brabant	FO JM Hudson Killed Sgt. AJ Ede Killed Sgt. H Lewis Killed Sgt. J Burroughs Killed Sgt. WE Wakeman Killed Sgt. EFA Ambridge Killed PO K. Weaver POW
158 Sqdn: Halifax JN 884-F Shot down by Hptm. Rudolf Sigmund. Crashed Den Helder	Sgt. KR Larkin Killed Flt. Sgt. PF Watson Killed Sgt. ER Bray Killed Sgt. J Stewart Killed Sgt. RD Raven Killed Sgt. RJ Wyatt Killed Sgt. JL Loudoun POW
214 Sqdn: Stirling BK 686	FO JS Clements Killed PO DM Weddell Killed Flt. Sgt. GB Kielder Killed Sgt. H Owen Killed FO JH Douse Killed. 2nd Pilot Sgt. EN Bird Killed Sgt. SJ Creer Killed Can PO GF McCleary Killed
300 Sqdn: Wellington HZ 486-Z	Sgt. E Garczynski Killed FO E Bember POW Sgt. S Skwarek Killed Sgt. S Gawozyn Killed Flt. Sgt. Z Cipirski POW
405 Sqdn: Halifax HR 864	Can FO ME Tomczak Killed Can FO AD McCracken Killed Can FO AJ Sochowski Killed Can WO2 CJV Kettley Killed Can Flt. Sgt. GJK Smyth Killed Sgt. AJ Wood Killed Sgt. EK White Killed
429 Sqdn: Wellington HE 803 Culumborg Shot down by night-fighter flown by Major Streib	Can FO KM Johnson Killed Sgt. H Clark POW Sgt. E Frost POW Sgt. JMA Lortie POW Flt. Sgt. K Elliott POW
620 Sqdn: Stirling ED 906	Sgt. JRG McDonald Killed Sgt. J Laughlan Killed Sgt. H Hadfield Killed Sgt. GJ Jones Killed Sgt. J Daly POW Sgt. C Mutton POW Sgt. JB Lamont POW
620 Sqdn: Stirling BF 511-H	Sgt. JG Patterson Killed PO WM Goodall POW NZ Sgt. I Walker POW Sgt. G Adams POW Can Sgt. J Froats POW Sgt. S Scott POW Sgt. H Bacon POW

SQUADRON AND AIRCRAFT	CREW
620 Sqdn: Stirling EH 924	Sgt. JD Rathbone Killed Sgt. R Wild Killed FO JF Shepherd Killed Sgt. JF Wells Killed Sgt. A Simons Killed Sgt. JH Wallace Killed Sgt. D Castling POW. Lost a leg
Total 140 Killed, 26 POWs, 1 Evaded	
30 – 31 July 1943	
15 Sqdn: Stirling EF 427-A Hit by flak	PO GG Judd Killed Sgt. D Brown Killed Sgt. WA Wells Killed Sgt. SR Long Killed Sgt. LL Richards POW Sgt. DR Fry POW Inj. Can Sgt. KA Banks POW
15 Sqdn: Stirling EF 428-N	NZ Flt. Lt. JC Dillicar Killed NZ FO BL Jackson Killed NZ Flt. Sgt. IG Ramsay Killed Sgt. AVE Cobby Killed Sgt. GH Beck Killed Sgt. KP Middleton Killed Can Sgt. AJ Gibbas Killed SAAF Lt. AR Ingle DFC Killed. Passenger attached
44 Sqdn: Lancaster JA 895	Wg/Cdr. EAA Williamson Killed Sgt. FT Turner Killed Sgt. RM Jordan Killed Sgt. LS High Killed PO RA Timkins Killed Sgt. GG Jones Killed Sgt. HC McCrae Killed
75 Sqdn: Stirling BF 458	PO AJ Thomas Killed Sgt. HA Steward POW Sgt. RH Baxell POW Sgt. JW Gale Killed NZ PO FW Cupsty Killed Sgt. JH O'Farrell Killed Can Sgt. EE Henry Killed
75 Sqdn: Stirling EE 915	NZ Flt. Sgt. JN Darney Killed NZ Sgt. RJ Stone Killed Sgt. GC Davies Killed PO LCD Robinson POW Sgt. RCG Evans Killed NZ Sgt. TJ Vercoe Killed FO PSA St Ledger Killed
76 Sqdn: Halifax DK 202-Q	Sgt. RA Cole Killed Sgt. RF Russell Killed Sgt. JW Pothercary Killed Sgt. J Lewis Killed Sgt. AB Harper Killed Sgt. JR Williams Killed Can Sgt. D Shaw Killed
78 Sqdn: Halifax JD 329	Sgt. R Shelton Killed Sgt. AH Marshall Killed in combat Sgt. JF Harper Killed PO D Williams Killed FO GI Whitehouse POW Aust Flt. Sgt. GA Rourke Killed Aust Flt. Sgt. KA Skidmore POW

SQUADRON AND AIRCRAFT	CREW
78 Sqdn: Halifax JD 375	Sgt. D Hadwin Killed Sgt. AB Cresswell Killed Sgt. AB Radcliffe Killed Sgt. BJ Bond Killed Sgt. GH Irons Killed Sgt. JC Gibson Killed Sgt. JA Siffield Killed
90 Sqdn: Stirling BK 775	NZ Flt. Sgt. ARG Small Killed NZ Flt. Sgt. AB Wallis Killed Sgt. L Clifton DFM Killed Sgt. WL Gray Killed Flt. Sgt. WA Hebden Killed Sgt. DH Kealey Killed NZ Flt. Sgt. AM Reid Killed
106 Sqdn: Lancaster R 5665 Shot down by night-fighter	PO KM Reid Killed Sgt. J Scott POW Sgt. JFG Renson POW Sgt. V Askey POW Can PO JD Golds POW Inj. Sgt. CM Pearce POW Sgt. J Kirkham POW
218 Sqdn: Stirling BF 519	Sgt. RE Taylor Killed Sgt. J Ferguson Killed Sgt. EA Bartlett Killed Sgt. HM Cornes Killed FO PR Johnson Killed Sgt. EA Stevens Killed Sgt. ECA Barnes Killed
408 Sqdn: Halifax JD 365-J	Sgt. AE Chalk Killed Sgt. RA Dekham POW Sgt. WL Reed Killed Sgt. J Crammond Killed Sgt. RC Davies POW Inj. Can Sgt. RG Edwards Killed Sgt. F Berry Killed
427 Sqdn: Halifax EB 242	Aust Flt. Sgt. SW Westerberg Killed Sgt. RA Marriott POW Sgt. RS Bodycote POW Sgt. LC Goss POW Sgt. RTA Marshall POW Aust Sgt. WR Black POW Aust Sgt. TK Boord POW
620 Sqdn: Stirling EH 896-J	Sgt. P O'Connell POW FO PW Taylor POW Sgt. WJ Shaw POW Sgt. FK Garbuts POW Sgt. R Simms POW Sgt. GJ Higgs POW Sgt. GS Doig POW
620 Sqdn: Stirling EE 905-S Shot down by Ju 88 night-fighter Ten miles south of Brussels	Sgt. FJ Frost POW Sgt. LI Dunbar POW Sgt. WJ Ford Killed Sgt. RB Spencer-Fleet POW Sgt. JL Snelling POW Sgt. JDH Carleton Evaded Sgt. RC Broadbent Killed

Total 72 Killed, 33 POWs, 1 Evaded

Index